VICTIMS IN THE CRIMINAL JUSTICE SYSTEM

CAMBRIDGE STUDIES IN CRIMINOLOGY

VICTIMS IN THE CRIMINAL JUSTICE SYSTEM

Joanna Shapland
Jon Willmore
Peter Duff

Series Editor: A. E. Bottoms

Gower

Published by
Gower Publishing Company Limited,
Gower House,
Croft Road,
Aldershot,
Hants GU11 3HR,
England.

Gower Publishing Company,
Old Post Road,
Brookfield,
Vermont 05036,
U.S.A.

Reprinted 1995

British Library Cataloguing in Publication Data

Shapland, Joanna
   Victims of the criminal justice system.
   (Cambridge studies in criminology; 53)
   1. Victims of crimes—Great Britain
   I. Title   II. Willmore, Jon   III. Duff, Peter
   362.8′8′0941   HV6250.3.G7

   ISBN 0–566–00894–7
   ISBN 0–566–00877–7 Pbk

Typeset in Great Britain by
Guildford Graphics Limited, Plaistow, Nr Billingshurst, W. Sussex.
Printed and bound in Great Britain

Contents

and psychological effects; Knowing the offender; Retaliation; Effects, needs and expressed needs; The provision of help and support to victims; Effects and their remedies

Acknowledgements

The research described in this book would not have been possible without the unstinting help we received from the victims whose experiences we describe. This help often extended over many months or even years, at a time when they had more than the normal pressures upon them. We are very grateful. Equally, we would not have been able to accomplish very much without the great co-operation and welcome extended to us by everyone in the various agencies with whom we worked – the police forces, prosecution solicitors, magistrates' courts, Crown Courts and victim support agencies in the two areas and the Criminal Injuries Compensation Board.

The research was supported by a grant from the Home Office. We would like to thank our steering committee, our colleagues at the Centre for Criminological Research and the members of the Home Office Research and Planning Unit, who have all given us much advice and support. We would also like to express our appreciation to Jennifer Schuster Bruce for acting as secretary to the project and co-ordinating the base office while we were scattered all over the Midlands. Hilary Prior, Nancy Bartrum, Michelle Hicks and Carol McCall have also assisted in the administration of the project and in the typing of the manuscripts.

Parts of the drafts of the book and the reports have been read and most helpfully criticised by, among others, Jon Vagg, Andrew Ashworth, Mike Maguire, Roger Hood, Gerry Chambers, Jan van Dijk and Hazel Genn. Clive Payne, Martin Range and Mrs Hedges of the Social Studies Centre and Paul Griffiths of the Computing Advisory Service spent many hours over a hot computer to find ways in which recalcitrant longitudinal data could be analysed. J. Douglas Allen and Gerry Maher and his colleagues attempted to teach me how the Scottish system of compensation orders works. The views expressed in this book and any mistakes and errors are, however, our own responsibility.

Some of the material in the book has been published in a summary article in the *British Journal of Criminology:* Shapland, J. 1984, 'Victims, the criminal justice system and compensation', *British Journal of Criminology*, vol. 24, pp. 131–49.

Foreword

This volume marks, in two ways, a new beginning for the *Cambridge Studies in Criminology*. First, after nurturing the series since its inception as the 'English Studies in Criminal Science' in 1940, Emeritus Professor Sir Leon Radzinowicz has decided that the time has come to lay down his distinguished editorial pen. After forty-five years and over fifty volumes, the *Cambridge Studies* owes him an immense debt of gratitude. Second, the series has a new publisher in the Gower Publishing Company, already a leading name in social science publishing, with whom the Institute of Criminology and the *Cambridge Studies* look forward to a long and happy collaboration.

It is particularly apposite that the first volume to be published by the series in its new style should be on the subject of Victims in the Criminal Justice System. This is a topic which has been for far too long neglected by criminologists, and by those responsible for criminal policy. There are now welcome signs that this neglect is coming to an end, and there can be no doubt that this very important volume by Dr. Joanna Shapland, Jon Willmore and Peter Duff will help to awaken interest in many aspects of the subject.

It gives me especial pleasure that the first volume in the series to be published under my editorship should be based upon research conducted at the Oxford University Centre for Criminological Research. This emphasises that the *Cambridge Studies in Criminology*, although based here in Cambridge, is not intended to be restricted to Cambridge authors, but exists to promote the publication of important criminological writing from whatever source.

A. E. Bottoms
Wolfson Professor of Criminology,
University of Cambridge
Series Editor, Cambridge Studies in Criminology

1 Introduction

The victim of crime has been the 'forgotten man' of the criminal justice system. This lack of knowledge about victims is astonishing, given that the criminal justice system as we know it today would collapse if their co-operation was not forthcoming. The victims' experiences with the professionals of the system – police, lawyers, court officials and those running compensation agencies – are rarely considered, but will affect their attitudes to that system. If victims come to regard their treatment as too stressful, demeaning, unfair, distorting of reality, too remote or too little concerned with their own rights, feelings and interests or if decisions are made which are felt to be unsatisfactory, it is possible that this 'secondary victimisation' by the system may lead to disenchantment, disinterest and future non-co-operation, not only by the victim, but also by his friends and relatives.

The growth of the victim movement

Although we know very little about what victims think, interest in and concern about their plight has recently grown very rapidly. The first expression of this movement was in the setting up of state compensation schemes to compensate victims of violent crime. A scheme was set up in New Zealand in 1963, followed by the Criminal Injuries Compensation Board, which covers England, Scotland and Wales, in 1964. State compensation schemes are now almost worldwide.

The provision of other forms of aid to victims, such as emotional support and help in dealing with the criminal justice system, is even more recent. Mutual help societies, limited to particular occupations or interest groups, have of course existed from time to time to provide help with the criminal justice and prosecutorial functions of the victim. In the last century, for example, Associations for the Prosecution of Felons (Shubert 1981) encouraged and financially assisted their members to bring prosecutions. Such institutions, however, fulfilled a specific need and were confined to particular groups. Projects to assist all victims first appeared in the United States in the early 1970s (McDonald 1976) and tended to be associated with the desires of those working in the criminal justice system to give more information to victims about their case and to help them to attend court more punctually. In Great Britain, the movement for victim aid has taken a different form, less connected with the criminal justice system. Victim support schemes, by which volunteers give practical and emotional support to recent victims, started in Britain in the early 1970s and expanded rapidly. It is only in the last few years that trends in the two countries are merging. New victim aid centres in the United States are starting to provide support for victims of all crimes from the time of the offence, while some victim support schemes in Great Britain are beginning to move into longer-term work with victims, including aid with applications for compensation and support for court appearances.

In Britain, there is still only limited interest in the experiences of the victim in the criminal justice system in general. However, compensation by offenders to victims as part of the sentence passed by the court has been a feature of the criminal justice system since the expansion of the powers of the courts in the 1972 Criminal Justice Act for England and Wales. Compensation orders were subsequently elevated to the status of a full sentence in the 1980 Criminal Justice (Scotland) Act and the 1982 Criminal Justice Act (for England and Wales).

Mediation and reparation work started with some pioneering experiments in the United States and Canada in the mid-1970s. The impetus behind the work was to find a forum other than that of the criminal justice system, one that would be more meaningful to both victim and offender and less bureaucratic. The consequent 'voluntary' nature of participation in these schemes and intrinsic tensions between victim and offender have caused some problems, but there is now interest in extending the experiment to Great Britain (Parliamentary All-Party Penal Affairs Group 1984).

The four strands of the 'victim movement' – victim aid and assistance, victim experiences with the criminal justice system, State compensation and reparation by offenders – have been brought together in the current deliberations by official bodies, such as the United Nations and the Council of Europe. The Council of Europe backed up its 1978 Resolution on State compensation for victims of violent crime with a Convention in 1983, which seeks to establish minimum standards for such compensation throughout member States. The other three areas of concern will be covered in the near future.

However, despite 'strong evidence that concern with the victim has become a powerful motif in contemporary western societal responses to crime' (Bottoms 1983), little thought has been given to the experiences, thoughts or feelings of actual victims. The whole edifice of the 'victim movement' has largely been built according to other people's ideas of what victims want or should want. Even many researchers have taken what van Dijk (1983a) has called the 'victimagogic' path and advocated greater support for victims, without any particular consideration of their own wishes. This is both rather premature and potentially dangerous. If provisions set up nominally in the name of victim support prove neither to aid victims nor to produce the services victims actually want, then they run the risk of alienating both victims and also the general public. Victims form a substantial part of that general public (Hough and Mayhew 1983; Chambers and Tombs 1984) and public sentiment seems strongly behind a greater place for and concern with victims.

Victim attitudes and experiences

The few studies that have looked at victim experiences in the criminal justice system have found disturbing results. Knudten *et al.* (1977), in their report to the United States Department of Justice, stated: 'Often forgotten in the criminal justice system and concerned for their manipulation by others, victims and witnesses frequently express negative attitudes to the existing criminal justice system.' More recently, Elias (1983) has shown that claimants to the State compensation bodies of New York and New Jersey became disillusioned with both those bodies and the whole system.

In Britain, Sparks *et al.* (1977) found that those who had been victims in the last year were more likely than non-victims to think that the police did only a fair or a poor job. Vennard (1976), in her small-scale study of victims whose offenders were convicted in the magistrates' courts, concluded: 'Many of the people in our study were victims who reported crimes but were left with unpleasant memories of a frustrating and unhelpful experience with the law. They may in future turn to the law only as a very last resort.' Yet Chambers and Millar (1983) found that their Scottish rape victims, while being very dissatisfied with questioning by the police and the lack of information and follow-up given to victims, would still probably report a similar offence to the police. Maguire's (1982) burglary victims included a majority who were satisfied with the police, but also a significant minority who felt that the police had shown no interest or sympathy at the time of the offence and had not subsequently informed them of the progress of the case. The British Crime Survey – the first national victimisation study (Hough and Mayhew 1983) – discovered that around four out of five victims were satisfied with the contact they had had with the police but only half the victims felt that if caught their offender should be brought before the courts. The major reason for dissatisfaction was police inaction, rather than slow response, unacceptable attitudes or poor follow-up.

The picture is obviously not a simple one. Victims do seem to be dissatisfied with the operation of various parts of the criminal justice system, but their reasons vary, not surprisingly, according to the agency being considered. The likelihood of that dissatisfaction affecting present or future co-operation with the system is also not clear. Though it appears that there are some quite surprisingly similar findings from different countries and as regards different offences, the particular kind and seriousness of victimisation may induce different reactions.

The present study

The aim of our study is to attempt to remedy this lack of knowledge by providing a victim's eye view of his or her experiences, attitudes and difficulties as the case passes through the whole of the criminal justice system, including applications for compensation to the various compensation agencies. It is not a victimisation study but a study of victims in the criminal justice system. It is a longitudinal study, that is, a sample of victims were followed from initial reporting of the case to its outcome, whatever that might be, and on to include any award of compensation. This involved re-interviewing them several times over a period of up to three years, as well as interviewing police officers, prosecution solicitors, justices' clerks, other court staff and compensation agency personnel and analysing police and compensation agency files of the cases and newspaper reports.

Most studies of victims have employed the method of asking victims to look back on their experiences after the outcome of the case. This has two major disadvantages: first, memory loss over what may be many months or even years. Secondly, if victims' attitudes change as they pass through the different stages of the system, this change will not be apparent. Later experiences may override and alter victims' perceptions of the earlier parts of the system. The longitudinal method adopted in our study, though very much more difficult to carry out, proved invaluable in detecting changes in attitudes and in enabling a full picture to be obtained at each stage of the process.

Victims and offences

In a longitudinal study, the only control possible over the outcome of the cases to be studied and the resulting analysis of the parts of the criminal justice system which will be involved lies in the original selection of the sample of victims to be included in the study. After that, one can only follow the cases as they progress through the system and document the fate of these cases and the experiences of the victims. As this was the first such study to be attempted, it was thought essential to concentrate on the experiences of those brought most immediately to mind by the word 'victim', those for whom the measures for aid and compensation described above have been set up – that is, adult (18 years or over) personal victims of crimes. Other groups, such as child victims or organisational victims, may have slightly different problems and experiences, and this points to the need for further research.

The choice of offence is also important. We chose to focus on those who had experienced offences of violence, rather than property offences, because they offered us:

(1) A directly identifiable personal victim who suffers obvious harm and whose evidence is usually necessary for the detection of offenders and the prosecution of cases;

(2) The only category of victims who are eligible for State compensation, which has been one of the major aims of the victim movement;

(3) A high proportion of cases in which the offender is detected fairly rapidly, so that the victim's reactions can be assessed as soon after the offence as possible;

(4) A series of offences graded in seriousness, a considerable proportion of which are liable to be tried at the Crown Court, so that the experiences of victims with all parts of the court system can be ascertained;

(5) A considerable proportion of cases in which the offender is likely to be known to the victim or in which the victim-offender relationship may pose questions about the victim's participation in the incident. This would enable the study to examine the problems the victim may face in dealing with the offender and in establishing his credibility with the police; and, lastly,

(6) Offences which incorporate different elements such as physical assault, sexual assault or the loss of property (robbery). The inclusion of sexual assault victims is particularly important, since the problems of rape victims have been instrumental in focusing attention on the experiences of victims with the criminal justice system. It has been suggested that the problems facing rape victims are qualitatively different from those of other victims. By including offences of violence which vary both in seriousness and in the presence or absence of a sexual element, it was hoped to throw light on this question.

So far, the word 'victim' has not been treated as problematic. Obviously, the ascription of the label 'victim' to one or another person involved in a criminal act is an important step and one which is very significant to the person so labelled. The label 'offender' is equally important. The problem of ascription is particularly acute in the case of offences of violence, where close victim-offender relationships are fairly common and where both parties may have 'contributed' to the act (see Miers 1978). It is, however, necessary to find a word by which to refer to the person included in the original sample and we shall use 'victim' for this purpose, even though some of the victims in the sample were eventually prosecuted (and convicted) as offenders. Again for ease of terminology, we shall use the male pronoun to refer to either male or female persons.

The sample was taken at the point at which the offence had been reported to the police and recorded by them as a crime. The victim was then the person recorded as the injured or aggrieved party on the original police crime report form, whether or not he in fact defined himself as a victim and whether or not he had reported the offence to the police or was ultimately seen as a victim by the police or the courts. The study starts, therefore, when the offence has been reported to the police and recorded by them as a crime. It cannot provide any information on the experiences of those whose offences are not reported to the police or not recorded by them as crimes (for a discussion of these stages, see Bottomley and Coleman 1981).

It was also thought vital to look at the experiences of victims in more than one geographical area, so that the influence of different police force practices could be studied and a number of courts with different problems of access and facilities included. The areas chosen needed to be of sufficient size (over 100 000 population) to provide enough of the rarer offences within the time span of the research. Each also had to have its own magistrates' court, which would commit cases to a local Crown Court. The towns or cities in the South Midlands region which best fitted this description were Coventry (part of the West Midlands police force area) and Northampton (part of the Northamptonshire police force area).

The actual offences used in the study (as classified on the initial police crime report) were as follows:

(1) *Physical assaults*
   (a) Assault occasioning actual bodily harm, contrary to s.47 of the Offences against the Person Act 1861. Triable either at the magistrates' court or at the Crown Court.
   (b) Unlawful wounding or assault inflicting grievous bodily harm, contrary to s.20 of the Offences against the Person Act 1861. Triable either at the magistrates' court or at the Crown Court.
   (c) Wounding or causing grievous bodily harm with intent to do grievous bodily harm, contrary to s.18 of the Offences against the Person Act 1861. Triable only at the Crown Court.
(2) *Offences involving both physical violence and property loss* – robbery (including attempted robbery and assault with intent to rob), contrary to s.8 of the Theft Act 1968. Triable only at the Crown Court.
(3) *Sexual assaults*
   (a) Indecent assault on a woman, contrary to s.14(1) of the Sexual Offences Act 1956. Triable either at the magistrates' court or at the Crown Court.
   (b) Rape (including attempted rape), contrary to s.1(1) of the Sexual Offences Act 1956. Triable only at the Crown Court.

It can be seen that the sexual assault offences included were against women only, whereas physical assault or robbery victims might be of either sex. The only types of robbery used in the study were those involving an obvious individual victim who was threatened or assaulted, even though the money or property taken might not be owned by that individual. Examples are so-called 'mugging' robberies and robberies of small shopkeepers or sub-postmasters. Robberies in which a number of victims were threatened or assaulted, as in a bank raid, were not included.

not consider wider victims

Study methods

The fieldwork part of the study began in January 1979 in Coventry and in April 1979 in Northampton. New cases were taken in both places up to July 1980. The fieldwork did not finish until July 1982.

Victims were interviewed at different stages of the process: first, as soon as possible after the recording of the offence by the police; secondly, after committal proceedings (if the case was committed from the magistrates' court to the Crown Court); thirdly, after the outcome of the case; and fourthly, after the result of any application or award of compensation (for those victims involved in compensation proceedings). The outcome of the case might be that no offender was caught and the case was filed by the police, that the decision was made not to prosecute the offender, that the offender was cautioned or that he was convicted or acquitted at the magistrates' court, juvenile court or Crown Court. If, after the final interview, either an offender was caught or the offender appealed against conviction or sentence, an additional interview was carried out.

Victims were always contacted first by letter. If there was no reply after a second letter, at least three visits were made before a victim was classed as uncontactable. If a refusal was received at any stage, however, no subsequent approach was made. The number of victims interviewed for each type of offence in each town is given in Table 1.1. The total number of victims taking part in the first interview was 276, 188 from Coventry and 88 from Northampton. (The two victims from Birmingham, interviewed in an attempt to increase the number of rape victims in the study, have been dropped from this analysis, though they are included in previous reports of the study. Their feelings and experiences were no different from those of victims in Northampton and Coventry, but it is felt that their inclusion would be an unnecessary complication.)

The success rate for first interviews was 60 per cent, with 20 per cent refusing, 6 per cent having moved and left no forwarding address, 12 per cent being uncontactable and 3 per cent having withdrawn their complaint before a letter could be sent to them (once a letter had been sent out, the victim was included in the study no matter what the outcome of the case might be). There was no significant difference between those agreeing to be interviewed and those for whom no

Table 1.1   The sample of victims receiving a first interview

	Coventry	Northampton	Total
Physical assaults:			
– assault occasioning actual bodily harm (civilians)	45	29	74
– assault occasioning actual bodily harm (police)	15	10	25
– wounding or assault inflicting grievous bodily harm	35	28	63
– wounding or assault with intent to inflict grievous bodily harm	30	6	36
Total	125	73	198
Robberies	35	5	40
Sexual assaults:			
– indecent assault	24	8	32
– rape or attempted rape	4	2	6
Total	28	10	38
Overall total	188	88	276

interview was obtained on sex, age, social class (according to the Registrar-General's classification of occupations), whether there was a named offender known to the police or type or seriousness of offence. These were the only items of information available from the police file. In addition, the impression of the researchers was that there appeared to be no other factor which differentiated those who agreed from those who did not receive a first interview – the sample of those who agreed included many who might be expected to refuse, such as victims of domestic incidents or crimes committed at work, victims with previous experience of the police as offenders and so on. The success rate for first interviews is comparable to the results of other studies in this field, such as the 41 per cent in Sparks *et al.*'s (1979) study of people known to have reported offences to the police and the 62 per cent in Maguire's (1982) study of burglary victims.

Separate committal interviews were done with 53 victims and, in addition, the committal proceedings were discussed with another 10 victims where the short interval of time between committal and either first or final interview made it impossible to attempt a separate committal interview. The success rate for committal interviews was 95 per cent.

Final interviews were obtained with 216 victims (78 per cent of the original sample). Given the long period of time between first interview and outcome in many cases, response rates for the final interview are high and show the willingness of victims to co-operate with the study. Victims who had applied to the Criminal Injuries Compensation Board and those who were the beneficiaries of compensation orders from the courts were approached again two to three years after the offence. Forty victims were re-interviewed at this stage.

Although the study concentrated on the views of victims, these need to be set in the context of the procedures that make up the investigation and prosecution of offences and the awarding of compensation. Accordingly, interviews were also conducted with police officers, prosecution solicitors, justices' clerks and those involved in the administration and enforcement of compensation orders in both Northampton and Coventry, with the chief clerk (main administrative officer) of one of the Crown Courts and with the administrative officers of the Criminal Injuries Compensation Board (CICB). The police file of each case was seen by the researchers and a summary of its contents made. The CICB file for those victims who had made applications for compensation was analysed. So far as possible, all court appearances of the victims' cases at both the magistrates' court and the Crown Court were attended by at least one researcher. If it was not possible to attend a particular appearance (on occasions there were more appearances on one day than researchers), the result of the appearance and as much other detail as possible were obtained from the magistrates' clerks or the Crown Court administrative staff. Attending appearances, though very time-consuming, is the only way to follow the progress of the case through the courts and to be able to understand and amplify the victim's experiences in court. Finally, the main local newspapers for both towns were read throughout the period of the study and cuttings taken of all crime reporting.

Who were the victims?

Before considering the victims' experiences as they pass through the criminal justice system, it will be helpful to look briefly at the offences and the victims in the study and to see whether there are any differences between victims from Coventry and Northampton. Comparisons will also be made with the results of victimisation studies.

1. The offences: time and place

The majority of physical assaults and robberies occurred on weekend evenings, though this was more marked in Coventry than in Northampton. Sexual assaults, however, showed a significantly different pattern, with a much more even spread over the days of the week and the time of day.

Physical assaults were most likely to occur in the street (43 per cent) or at work (27 per cent), with the more serious assaults taking place in the street or in pubs and clubs. Robberies were almost all committed in the street, as were indecent assaults and rapes (as opposed to at home, at work, in a pub or club or in another public building, such as a shop, bus station or cinema). Victimisation studies in several countries (Hough and Mayhew 1983; Chambers and Tombs 1984; LEAA 1977) have also found that the majority of crimes against the person occur in the street or at work with a small percentage at home. This has been related to the lifestyle of the victim; people who go out more or who have particular types of occupation are more likely to be victimised. In our study, we found that all but two of those assaulted at work had occupations that were likely to put them more at risk because they had to oversee premises or vehicles and remove people causing trouble (licensees, betting office managers, security guards, bus drivers, taxi drivers etc.).

2. The victims: personal details and knowledge of the offender
The assault and robbery cases contained a large proportion of men (75 per cent), a finding which is replicated in victimisation studies. The sexual assault victims were, by definition, all women. In both Northampton and Coventry and over all types of offence, younger victims were much more prevalent than older victims. Indeed, the 18 to 22 age group contained 32 per cent of our victims. Most of our sample were single (except for indecent assault victims, who were predominantly married), which reflects their relative youth.

Victims were no more likely to be unemployed than the rest of the population in those areas at that time. In fact, the distribution of socio-economic status was very similar to that of the general population, though the somewhat higher percentage of victims in class II of the Registrar-General's classification reflects the relatively high number of assaults at work. There were very few non-white victims in Northampton, but 19 of Asian origin and seven of West Indian origin from Coventry. The majority of the victims of Asian origin had only fair or poor English and did find some difficulties in communicating with the police and the courts (and, occasionally, with the researchers, though other members of the family would act as interpreters).

3. Victims' knowledge of offenders
Of the 276 victims in the sample, 169 (61 per cent) were assaulted by offenders entirely unknown to them. There appeared to be three main

categories of offence types. The first comprised the less serious physical assaults, in which approximately half the offenders were unknown to victims. The second group included the most serious physical assaults, robberies and indecent assaults, for which the number of stranger-to-stranger offences was much higher. Thirdly, there were the rape victims, of whom five out of six knew at least one offender.

The offender might be known to the victim as a relative or friend (47 victims), at work (28 victims) or through the neighbourhood where both parties lived (30 victims). The sample does, therefore, include a number of victims of so-called 'domestic' assaults, where the victim (usually female) is assaulted by her spouse, ex-spouse or boyfriend and these victims, as will be seen later, did experience some particular problems with the criminal justice system and with retaliation by the offender.

4. Victims' previous experience with the criminal justice system
About a third of the victims had some previous experience of the criminal justice system as a victim of a similar offence which had been reported to the police. Another third, however, had no previous experience at all of reported victimisation. A number of the victims of domestic violence had been assaulted in the same way previously, but had not reported it to the police.

Another way of acquiring knowledge of the criminal justice system is by making a statement to the police or by having been to court. A remarkably high percentage of victims in both towns (46 per cent) had made a prosecution witness statement to the police, either as a victim or as a witness of a previous offence or traffic accident. Again, however, there was around a third of victims who had had no experience of making a statement before and, equally, a third who had had no experience of being in any form of courtroom for any reason (including the civil courts). The present offence was to bring these latter into contact with completely unfamiliar procedures and settings.

A number of victims said that they had previously appeared in court as a defendant (72 at the magistrates' court, 11 at the Crown Court and 19 at the juvenile court). This might be for any offence, including motoring offences. It has been suggested that those who become victims of crime, particularly violent crime, do so because they frequent pubs and clubs in which violence takes place. Sparks *et al.* (1977) found an association between reported victimisation and being a violent offender. The Scottish part of the British Crime Survey (Chambers and Tombs 1984) discovered that 40 per cent of respondents who admitted having committed an assault during the survey period had themselves been the victim of an assault during the same period. Of the physical assault victims in our study, a total of 85 said that they had appeared in court at some time as a defendant. Eleven of these had been accused of a violent offence, 30 said that they had never been in court for an offence of violence and the offences for the remaining 44 were unknown. Therefore, something between 6 and 28 per cent of our sample of physical assault victims had appeared in court accused of a violent offence.

As a result of the offence which brought them into our study, eight victims were themselves brought to court as offenders. All were physical assault victims and were charged with offences of assault or breach of the peace. Perhaps surprisingly, four thought it was right that they should be charged and prosecuted. The other four took the completely opposite view and were very indignant that they, the victims, should themselves be brought to court. All eight were convicted, with one given a prison sentence, one a suspended sentence, two being fined and four being bound over to keep the peace.

5. The victims: summary

The stereotyped picture of a victim of crime is the little old lady. However, the victim of assault or robbery in our study was more likely to be a young, single, skilled man and the victim of a sexual assault a young woman. The offence will have happened on the street, or in a pub or club, on one evening at the weekend. According to victimisation studies, the picture of the typical victim in our study is the correct one.

However, there are other, numerically smaller sub-groups of victims who may well have slightly different problems. These include those who are assaulted at work (often directly as a result of their employment), those who are assaulted at home (often by members of the family or friends) and those who do not speak English as their native language. We shall attempt to bear all these groups in mind as we consider the experiences of victims of violent crime in the criminal justice system and their attitudes to it.

The plan of the book

The book sets out to present the experiences of the victims in terms of the stages of the criminal justice system they encounter. This does not mean that these stages will occur over the same length of time for every victim – some cases take only one or two weeks while others are still continuing over a year after the offence. Neither are the stages necessarily chronologically distinct – police investigation of the case may continue after the offender has appeared at court –even up to the date of the final appearance. Some victims may apply to the CICB immediately after the offence, while others may only learn of its existence after the court outcome of the case or decide to wait until then before making an application. However, victims did separate their experiences according to the agency with which they were interacting, and that order has been reproduced here.

The initial police investigation of the case, including the decision to report, calling the police, their initial response and the victim's first impressions of the police, is described in Chapter 2. Chapter 3 looks at the investigation of the case by the police, the gathering of evidence and the decision to prosecute. Chapter 4 concentrates on the courts. The charges laid against the offender and the convictions and sentences obtained are described. This is related to the victims' knowledge of the progress of the case, their reaction to what the courts did and their experience of attending court and giving evidence. The changing attitudes of victims to the criminal justice system as the case passes through investigation and prosecution to the outcome are the focus of Chapter 5. Victims' satisfaction with the police and the courts is examined and their future co-operation with the system explored.

The second section of the book starts with an examination in Chapter 6 of the effects over time of the offence on victims and their consequent need for various forms of aid and compensation. The current possibilities for compensation available to victims and their knowledge about these is considered in Chapter 7, whereas Chapters 8 and 9 look at their experiences with compensation orders from the courts and the CICB, respectively. In Chapter 10 the whole position of the victim in the criminal justice system is analysed. Suggestions are made as to the form which a more victim-oriented criminal justice system might take and its implications explored.

2 Entering the criminal justice system

The victim's first contact with the criminal justice system is with the police. Very often the police will remain the closest agency to the victim throughout the investigation of the case and the prosecution of the offender. For those victims whose assailants are not caught and for many whose assailants plead guilty, it is the police, rather than the courts, who will, in practice, structure their experiences with the criminal justice system and delineate their role.

The reaction of the police is, therefore, very important for the victim. The reverse, however, is also true, as we shall see, since victims play a major role in the reporting and investigation of cases, and in the detection of offenders. Police and victims are mutually dependent.

For the victim, however, another facet comes into play when the offence becomes known to the police. Once an offence is recorded as a crime, it acquires an official identity. The victim will become caught up in the various stages of a process which may involve many different agencies. He may drop out of that process, but, after the police are involved, the offence will have become recorded as a 'crime' and the victim as a 'complainant'. The offence will be processed according to agency rules and practices.

Reporting to the police

The decision to report

All the offences in this study were (at least at some stage) recorded by the police as crimes. However, not all the offences were reported by victims themselves and not all the victims were willing to be classified as victims or willing for the police to be involved. There are two possible processes operating here, often simultaneously: first, self-definition as a victim and, secondly, the decision to involve the police, rather than forgetting about the offence or dealing with it in some other way. They may well be interactive: a feeling that involving the police (and prosecution of the offence) would be too severe a response, would be congruent with self-definition as a victim not of a crime but of a nuisance and with definition of the offence as trivial. This is not a minor effect: the British Crime Survey (Hough and Mayhew 1983) found that only half the victims identified (of all types of offence) felt that, if caught, the offender should be prosecuted. It also showed that four out of ten offences involving violence were not reported to the police. A major reason was that the offence was seen as too trivial. The reasons for and against reporting to the police have been found to be very similar in different victimisation studies (for example, those from Britain by Durant *et al.* 1972; Sparks *et al.* 1977; Hough and Mayhew 1983; Chambers and Tombs 1984; the United States National Crime Surveys by the US Department of Justice; the Dutch surveys by, for example, van Dijk and Vianen 1978).

Another way of defining one's role in the offence can also lead to non-involvement of the police and not considering oneself as a victim. This happens when the offence is seen as a 'normal' occurrence, as part of everyday life, for instance, in a 'fair fight' between acquaintances in (or just outside) a pub or club or as part of a continuing quarrel. In such cases the labels 'victim' and 'offender' became hard to apply and involvement of the police may be thought of as inappropriate. This is another major category of reasons for not reporting to the police in victimisation surveys.

The majority of victims in our study (80 per cent), however, both thought themselves to be victims of an offence and thought the offence should be reported to the police, whether or not they themselves had actually reported it. They found it very difficult to express concrete reasons why they felt like this. For most, it was a natural response, rather than the outcome of a long period of rational thought or argument. Where someone else had reported the offence, or the police had appeared of their own accord on the scene, the victims were, to some extent, judging the result of action taken by others – a situation in which, again, few concrete reasons could be given. The major factors involved in the decision to report the offence are given in Table 2.1.

Table 2.1 Why offences were reported to the police

	No. of victims
It's natural, right – it's all you can do	22
It could have happened to someone more vulnerable	17
I don't think the offender should get away with it	14
I needed help – it was serious	12
I was lucky it wasn't worse	11
(Police officer victims) – I have to report it	9
Fear of repetition of offence to victim	9
(The offender) used a weapon – it wasn't a fair fight	7
These kinds of things shouldn't happen	7
I was so furious	6
Offender using foul language, insulting neighbours or attacking others as well	6

The idea of a 'fair fight' did occur among those victims who believed the offence should be reported to the police – but here, the 'rules' for the fight had been broken. A 'fair fight' seemed to require the use of fists only by participants, some sort of decision by both parties that such a fight would occur and the pitting of only one fighter against one other. If these rules were broken, the police were called:

If it had been in a fight, I wouldn't have bothered with the police but he just attacked me.

I'd thought of getting my mates and going after them but my mates are greasers and use knives and I thought I'd leave it rather than get labelled like them. I'd be a hooligan then – same as them (the offenders) or I could take them to court and get them in a different way to a smack in the gob.

⌐ or some of the women attacked by their husbands or boyfriends (the so-called 'domestic assaults'), similar kinds of rules pertained. Women might have endured a long series of assaults without taking any official action, but then the assaults took on a different character – the man had attacked the children as well, or used a weapon on the woman. Then the police were brought in and prosecution supported.

Violent social interaction is a form of ordinary social interaction and so here, too, there are rules. The involvement of the police and self-definition as a victim can depend more crucially on those rules breaking down than upon any legal or even majority opinion of what is a violent offence and who is a victim.

Those victims in our study who were initially doubtful about reporting (11 per cent) and those who never felt that the police should have been involved (9 per cent) included proportionately more sexual assault victims than physical assault or robbery victims. The reasons for not reporting given by physical assault and robbery victims included both that they did not feel they were victims and that they did not wish the police involved. They were, in general, the obverse of reasons given by those who wished the offence reported. Some felt the offence was not worth bothering about – it was not serious enough. Some were victims whose previous experiences of the police had not lived up to their expectations – they (the police) had done 'nothing'. In other cases, it was the existing relationship between victim and offender that made the victim draw back from involving the police. This might be either from fear of retaliation or from care for the offender. Finally, there were those for whom the offence was too trivial to bother about – a few said that they did not really think they were a victim. Reasons for subsequently deciding to report were either that it could happen to someone else or the victim discovered that the offence was more serious than he had originally thought.

Sexual assault victims, however, gave rather different reasons.

Twenty-six per cent of the indecent assault and rape victims were initially doubtful and 5 per cent never wanted the police involved. Their initial reasons for not reporting included that they had read that the police would question this type of victim in such a way as to make the victim feel degraded and accuse her of egging the man on; because the victim felt 'dirty'; because the police would come in a marked car and the neighbours would be nosy; and because of fear of reprisals from the offender. All finally decided to report it because the offender could do it again to someone more vulnerable – a young girl or a pensioner. The attitude of the first group is perhaps best summed up by one of the rape victims.

I thought I hadn't got a case – I'd read they don't class it as rape because there wasn't much violence – no marks on you and you didn't attack the rapist – I thought they're not going to believe me. I know it's not a lie but if someone had said I was making it up it would have been awful.

It appears that the publicity being given to the treatment of rape cases by the police and courts at the time may also have made indecent assault victims chary of contacting the police.

These reasons for not reporting – whether the victim subsequently changed his mind or not – are similar to those found in other studies. It is noticeable that the reasons given by sexual assault victims appear to be different in kind from those of physical assault or robbery victims. Sexual assault victims seemed to feel ashamed and even guilty about the offence and were afraid of what the police or courts would say or do. Physical assault and robbery victims might feel the offence was not serious because their rules for (violent) social interaction had not been broken – fights were commonplace in their social milieu (even though several of these cases involved very serious injury). Alternatively, they were scared of the offender (not the criminal justice system).

Contacting the police

Willingly or unwillingly, all the offences and the victims in the study did come to the attention of the police. How did this happen? Who reported the offences and were there any difficulties experienced in contacting the police?

Victims and other civilian witnesses or bystanders were vital in the reporting of offences. In only 3 to 4 per cent of offences (depending on the town) did the police appear spontaneously on the scene. Between 35 and 41 per cent of cases were reported by the victim himself and another 50 per cent, a remarkably high percentage, by other civilians. Some previous studies (for example, Steer 1980) have distinguished between offences reported by someone acting on the victims' instructions and those by 'genuine' bystanders, but this distinction is very hard to make in offences of violence where the assault may produce a severely injured, often unconscious victim, and where the process of self-definition and deciding to report is still going on. It is best, perhaps, merely to report that both victims and other civilians are necessary to the reporting of offences and that, where crimes of violence are involved, reporting by others may be either beneficial to the victim (because he is himself incapable at that moment) or lead to later complications (because he did not wish the police involved).

Who are these 'other people' who play such a large part in reporting offences? A considerable proportion of them (28 per cent) were people in charge of or working at the place where the offence occurred, such as licensees of pubs, managers of shops, security guards at bus stations or shopping centres, etc. Some were neighbours of the victim (21 per cent), though often the victim might not know this neighbour very well. Some were friends of the victim (14 per cent) or work colleagues (9 per cent). The last was particularly prevalent in work assaults on bus drivers and taxi drivers. However, a considerable number (23 per cent) had no relationship with the victim or with the place in which the offence happened – but were just passing through: the 'Good Samaritan'.

Other studies have shown the importance of victims and witnesses in reporting the offence to the police rather than the police discovering it themselves, whether the offence be violence, burglary or sexual assault (for example, McCabe and Sutcliffe 1978; Steer 1980; Mawby 1979; Bottomley and Coleman 1980; Chambers and Millar 1983). Maguire (1982), for example, found that the vast majority of offences in his study of burglaries of dwellings was brought to the attention of the police by the victim. Steer (1980) reports that 50 per cent of his sample of violent offences were reported by the victim or someone acting on his behalf. Indeed, the Royal Commission on Criminal Procedure states: 'the overwhelming majority (of offences) . . . is not discovered by the police, but by the public.'

Previous studies have tended to produce larger percentages than the present study for offences reported by the victim himself and lower percentages for those reported by others. Some of this discrepancy is due to the serious injuries and consequent temporary incapacity inflicted upon the victims of violent crime in the present study and the fact that many of these offences occur in public places. Another reason is that most studies (apart from those of Maguire and Chambers and Millar) have relied on police data as to who reported the offence, rather than on asking victims. In the present study, substantial discrepancies were found between victim and police accounts of who reported the offence. For example, the victim only agreed with the police that the victim had reported the offence himself in 57 per cent of cases recorded as reported by the victim. Police and victim also might be in disagreement about cases recorded as 'police found' or as 'reported by other'. This is not surprising, as the policeman filling out the crime complaint form is often not the same person who took a 999 call or a telephone call to the local police station. He could not necessarily be expected to have accurate data.

These discrepancies do imply, however, that previous studies may, through relying on police data, have underestimated the contribution of other people, particularly uninvolved bystanders or neighbours. Bottomley and Coleman (1980) have suggested:

> It may be that certain forms of police-community campaigns or related research projects could have a significant effect upon the role of such members of the public in taking more positive steps to combat an apparent reluctance to get involved.

If the findings in the present study are correct, it does not appear that this is needed.

Delays in reporting

It has been suggested, primarily in American studies (for example, Caplan 1976), that victims wait for so long before reporting offences to the police that a prompt police response is unnecessary. Conversely, particularly with offences of violence where the perpetrator is in immediate contact with the victim, if it is found the delay between an offence of violence and reporting it is short, then a prompt response by the police may well result in the apprehension of the suspect or the prevention of further injury.

For certain types of offence, notably violence by one family member against another or rape, it has also been thought that the police will be more suspicious of the case if a long delay has occurred between the offence and reporting. Indeed, many of the police officers interviewed in both Coventry and Northampton felt that calls might be treated differently according to how long ago the offence occurred: 'We would look into it as to why he'd not complained earlier.'

The only way of measuring the delay between the offence and reporting is to rely on victims' estimates. This has considerable problems due to faulty memory and the inability of people to measure accurately intervals of time, particularly when they are in a stressed or injured condition (Schneider *et al.* 1978). The longitudinal method used in the present study, however, has to some extent lessened the problem of memory loss.

In our study, 71 per cent of cases were reported to the police within 15 minutes of occurrence, 58 per cent within 5 minutes. In these cases a prompt response by the police may have meant that they could have apprehended the offender in the neighbourhood of the offence. In all except seven cases of delays of up to 15 minutes, the delay was caused by the victim or a witness attempting to obtain assistance to contact the police – for example, the victim trying to attract someone's attention or getting a friend or neighbour to run to phone the police or run to the police station. Where delays were between 5 and 15 minutes, the victim had often been knocked unconscious for a short time.

For the longer delays of over 15 minutes, the action taken by victims covered a much wider range of behaviour. This included going home and discussing with friends or family whether to report the offence; going about their normal activities until meeting someone who persuaded them to report it; or seeking medical attention first. Interestingly, a few indecent assault victims looked for the offender themselves first and only reported the offence to the police when this search drew no results. It appears that the actions of relatives and friends of the victim are important, not only in reporting an offence to the police, but also in persuading the victim to report the offence and, in a small number of cases, in chasing the offender rather than immediately reporting the offence.

It is worth exploring here whether different kinds of victims showed different patterns of delays. Those assaulted at work, particularly bus drivers and taxis drivers, did tend to report the offence first to their controller, usually by radio (when it was working). The controller then immediately contacted the police but usually also sent out other work colleagues to help the victim. These often arrived before the police did and were able to search the area and comfort the victim. However, other kinds of victims, in these towns at that time, showed no greater hesitation in contacting the police then anyone else. There were, for example, 38 offences committed by a member of the victim's family or a friend known very well or well by the victim (35 physical assaults and three rapes). There was no significant difference between family/friend assaults and other offences in the length of delay before reporting to the police. There was also no significant difference in delay time for assaults committed against minority groups.

Given that the majority of offences in the present study was reported to the police within 15 minutes of their occurrence, it would appear that there is a need for a prompt police response to such incidents. Unless the policeman answering the telephone call has ascertained that the offence was committed some time ago, there is also no necessary reason to assume that victims of assaults committed by family or friends have delayed any longer than other victims in contacting the police.

How the police were contacted

Victims or other civilians can contact the police by a variety of means – by dialling 999, by ringing the local police station, by going in person to the police station or by stopping a passing policeman or police car in the street. In addition, taxi drivers and bus drivers may be able to reach the police by passing a message through their radio controller. Table 2.2 shows how the police were contacted, according to the victim's account. The police data could, unfortunately, not be used, given the discrepancies cited above. There was a remarkably similar use of the different possibilities in the two towns. The number of people using the 999 service seems low, since it is precisely this category of offences for which the 999 system was designed (offences requiring immediate assistance for the victim, with the possibility of apprehending an offender). Neither was there any increased tendency for victims or others to use the 999 system for the physical assaults classified as causing more

Table 2.2 How the police were contacted (percentages)

	Physical assaults	Sexual assaults	Robberies	Total
Coventry				
*999 call	22	25	26	23
Telephone to local police station	18	50	9	21
≠Telephone call	21	14	23	20
In person to police station	17	0	17	14
Stopped passing policeman or police car	14	11	17	14
Police/taxi/bus radio	4	0	3	3
Unknown	5	0	6	4
Northampton				
*999 call	22	10	40	22
Telephone to local police station	16	50	20	21
≠Telephone call	22	20	20	22
In person to police station	14	10	20	14
Stopped passing policeman or police car	8	10	0	8
Police/taxi/bus radio	5	0	0	5
Unknown	12	0	0	10

*999 calls included both those asking for the police and those asking for the ambulance.

≠Police contacted by telephone either using 999 or ringing the local police station (victim unclear as to which).

Note that the numbers of sexual assaults and robberies in Northampton were very small.

serious injury (grievious bodily harm or wounding as opposed to actual bodily harm).

This unwillingness to use the 999 system has been documented before, though never with such serious and recently occurring offences. McCabe and Sutcliffe (1978), using police data, found that, in Oxford, the proportion of 999 calls was very similar to calls to the local police station for crime as a whole and also for their categories of 'domestic', 'assault', 'robbery' and 'rape/indecent assault' taken together. In Salford, however, 999 calls far outstripped calls to the local police station. Ekblom and Heal (1982), in a study of the total telephone input to the police in Hull, found that, although more urgent calls tended to come through the 999 system, there could be no expectation that this would occur in any given case. There was a very broad overlap in the use made by the public of the two methods.

Problems in contacting the police can be divided into two groups – problems to do with communicating satisfactorily with the police and problems in persuading the police to take action about the offence. Problems in communicating with the police (9 per cent of cases) seemed to be concentrated on the 999 system, particularly in Coventry. Seventeen people (27 per cent of those known to have used the 999 system) had difficulties with it. In 12 cases, no police car arrived for what the person thought a considerable time (up to 15 minutes) so he either dialled 999 again or rang the local police station.

Others found difficulty in communicating with the police controller who receives 999 calls. This was exacerbated in Coventry by the siting of the controller in Birmingham and the consequent lack of local knowledge. People ringing 999 from Coventry, often in a disturbed condition, had no idea they were not speaking to someone in Coventry. The results could sometimes be farcial, were they not potentially so serious. One example was:

Victim:	I've had an attempted mugging at A Park.
Controller	I don't know where that is.
Victim:	It's B area, C Road.
Controller:	Where's B?
Victim:	Coventry.
Controller:	Oh, *Coventry*, right we'll send someone around.
Victim's comments:	'I *shouldn't* have rung 999. When the policeman came he said ring the local police station – they'll be quicker. I think it's all wrong to take it away from one city and put it in another.'

Another and more serious example was that of a woman shopkeeper, assaulted and robbed in her shop. During the attack she phoned 999 and gave the number, name of the road and area of Coventry the shop was in. She assumed the police would know where it was. At this point, the attacker hit her over the head and she dropped the phone. Ten minutes later her nephew came back to the shop and stopped the attack. He picked up the telephone and discovered the police were still on the other end, wondering what was happening. He asked if they were coming and they said they did not know where the area was because they did not know Coventry. He told them and they then dispatched a car (which did arrive quickly).

A third case involved a ticket inspector, who was attempting to report an attack in the station car park, having to give the complete postal address of the railway station before the police could understand where it was.

It does appear that, in both Coventry and Northampton, the 999 system was producing considerable problems for a small, but certainly not negligible, proportion of victims. In both places there were times when it seemed that the call 'got lost' between the controller and the car responding from the local division. This might, of course, have been due to some extent to the incoherence of victims or others, but the offences in the present study are precisely the ones for which the 999 system was set up and, therefore, those with which it might be expected to deal. It is noteworthy that calls to the local police station did not appear to produce such problems, although it is always possible that victims dialling 999 had a greater expectation of fast police action than those dialling the local station. In Coventry, also, the use of a centralised force control system produced additional problems for victims who did not realise that they were speaking to someone in a totally different city. There are good reasons for centralisation of control rooms (for example, being able to mobilise a large response force in a major emergency) but it is essential that controllers understand the expectations of callers and the pressures under which they are operating. As Manning (1981) has pointed out, there is a considerable gap in communication between caller and controller, who appear to have different priorities and to exist in different conceptual universes. Members of the public will only use the 999 system occasionally. They cannot be trained to understand the way of thinking of the controller. The adaptation needs to be the other way round.

In contrast, very few victims fell into the second category of problems – that of persuading the police to take some initial action about the case (usually sending a policeman or police car to the victim's house or place from which the offence was reported). These problems were diverse in their details, but all concerned instances in which the victim wished the police to take action and the police hesitated. That action was taken in these cases seemed to be due to the persistence of the victims and their provision of all possible information to the police. What might seem important to the police (for example, that the case was potentially a robbery rather than an assault) was not necessarily so to the victims. These disputes between police and victim, although occurring only in a small minority of cases, were very distressing to the victims concerned.

It may perhaps seem surprising that these disagreements were so few and so diverse. There has been considerable publicity about victim-police disagreements both in 'domestic' assault cases and sexual assault cases, both of which were represented in the sample. The reason is almost certainly that this is not the stage of process where such conflicts emerge. The police do tend to respond to almost all calls by a visit to the complainant, whether immediately or at a later time (Ekblom and Heal 1982; Shapland 1983). Where this does not occur, it is extremely unlikely that the offence will become the subject of a crime report (the criterion for inclusion in the present study). Such offences either never appear as crimes at all (whether or not a visit is made) or disagreements arise later, during the investigation of the case.

Response time – the response by the police to telephone calls

We saw earlier that the majority of the offences were reported to the police within 5 minutes of the offence taking place, with over 62 per cent being reported within 15 minutes. A fast response time by the police would, therefore, enable them to ensure immediate aid to the victim and to have a good chance of apprehending the offender near the scene of the offence. What were the response times to telephone calls?

Table 2.3 shows the response times for Coventry and Northampton from the first telephone call, according to victim estimates. These estimates of response times are, of course, even more likely to be faulty than estimates of delays before reporting. An American study (Schneider et al. 1978) found that 'survey respondents consistently over-estimated the amount of time before the police arrived, or the police under-estimated it'. Similar processes occurred in the present study, as is

Table 2.3   Response times by the police to telephone calls

Time	% of cases	% of victims given that response satisfied	% of victims given that response neutral	% of victims given that response dissatisfied
Up to 5 minutes	38	31	66	3
6–10 minutes	21	8	84	8
11–15 minutes	11	5	58	37
16–20 minutes	8	0	53	47
21–30 minutes	7	8	59	33
Over 30 minutes	5	0	22	78
Unknown	8	–	–	–
Other response (appointment, refusal etc.)	2	–	–	–

shown by some of the comments from victims who said the police arrived within five minutes: 'It was very fast but it seemed like ages' or 'It was very short but it seemed like eternity.'

Nevertheless, the figures for the two towns are again very similar. In a majority of cases the police arrived within 10 minutes. Given the comments made earlier about the difficulties in communications with the police, it is interesting that, according to victims' estimates, there was no significant difference in response time according to whether the 999 system was used or whether people telephoned the local police station. There was some evidence in one town that cases reported to the police over 15 minutes after their occurrence were associated with a slower response from the police but this was a minor effect. It seems that all these violent offences were being responded to by the police without any particular offence grading or differential response. It also appears that using the 999 system did not guarantee any faster response. In neither town were the police prepared to give an estimate of the average response time at which they were aiming, but senior officers expected the response time for first priority calls to be within 10 minutes to any place in the area. However, though this did not appear to be occurring with our sample, not all offences of violence (for example, assaults between family or friends) would necessarily be given first priority by all officers.

Satisfaction, pleasure and on occasions, surprise, was expressed by victims for whom the police arrived within 5 minutes and a few victims for whom the police arrived within 10 minutes (see Table 2.3: victims were asked if they were satisfied, neutral or dissatisfied at the speed of response). On the other hand, victim dissatisfaction grew rapidly where the police took much longer than 15 minutes. Although people's expectations obviously vary, it would appear that victims of these offences of violence expected the police to arrive in about 5 to 10 minutes. This compares with expectations of around 30 minutes in burglary cases (Maguire 1984) where the offender is often long gone. The speed of reporting and the expected speed of police response for offences of violence underlines the automatic and emergency nature of the decision to report and suggests victim expectations of immediate aid and rescue by the police.

Meeting the police

When the victim first meets the police, he becomes caught up in the police process of investigating the offence and catching and prosecuting the offender. Once he has decided to press charges, much of the power to direct the way the case proceeds passes to the police. At the same time, the victim requires an emergency response by the police to provide aid and assistance. We shall discuss the whole investigation process and its outcome in Chapter 3, but shall concentrate here on the first meeting with the police as a result of the decision to involve the police and the victim's consequent experiences with the introduction of an investigating and prosecutorial system, as well as any provision of aid and support.

The nature of the first meeting with the police will obviously vary for victims in different circumstances and with different degrees of injury. The police response, the police officers interviewed agreed, has a set routine which should be performed when first arriving on the scene of an offence. Police officers are concerned to discover what has happened and what the victim's complaint is, to attend to the victim's immediate physical needs, to acquire a description of the scene of the offence if they are at that place and to ascertain what further action is needed and set it in motion. They may, in addition, do many other things if circumstances allow, such as apprehend the offender if present, search for him, ask the victim or witnesses to point him out, take a statement from the victim at the time or ask the victim to go to the police station, call an ambulance or take the victim to hospital in a police car, and so on.

Victims experienced a wide range of different police procedures in the initial contact. The length of time that contact took was correspondingly varied – from less than 10 minutes for some victims, involving the standard procedure only, to over 12 hours for one rape victim. There are considerable differences between offences in the length of this initial meeting. Those non-sexual offences where the victim is not badly injured (assault occasioning actual bodily harm, robbery) tended either to have short initial contacts where only the standard procedure was performed by the police (statements being left until the next day) or several further investigatory procedures were followed during the initial contact, prolonging its duration. Where the victim was more seriously injured, only a short initial contact was done before the victim was taken to hospital. In a few cases the police stayed at the hospital and then took the victim to the police station afterwards. Sexual assault cases had longer contact times than non-sexual assault cases – no sexual assault case had a contact time of less than 10 minutes. Rape cases were the longest of all – the contact times ranging from 3¾ hours to over 12 hours.

Pressing charges

When a victim decides to report an offence to the police, he is not necessarily deciding that he wishes to press charges against the offender. The police may have been called in as an emergency measure to stop a fight or as an incidental part of obtaining medical assistance for the victim. If the victim has not himself reported the offence, he may well not have made any decision up to the time the police arrive. It is during the initial meeting with the police, particularly if the police at that time ask the victim to make a statement, that the victim may first have to decide whether to press charges against the offender. In the present study, we found that the police were keen for the victim to make the decision immediately they arrived. This, they felt, was particularly important in cases of assault by family or friends (the so-called 'domestic' cases):

We take a statement immediately in domestics because otherwise they turn round and say they don't want to proceed.

If you're going to act, you must have backing immediately to substantiate the arrest.

You have to find out whether he's prepared to go to court – often where they know the person they're not. You explain it to them when they make a statement.

Almost all the victims (except those who were badly injured) were asked by the police whether they would press charges. In many cases this was done at the initial contact. For most victims, this caused no problems but some victims were undecided. The police then used a variety of methods to persuade the victims – saying that the assault could happen again, that it could happen to a person less able to cope, that the next offence could be more serious or, on occasions, that the offender had done it before and was dangerous. These are very similar arguments to those used by relatives or friends of the victim in the cases where the victim was initially doubtful about reporting the offence. There were very few cases at this stage in which the police did not wish to take action. Such reluctance was much more likely to occur either at the time of first calling the police or much later when the investigation was complete.

Victims did not always realise, however, that agreeing to press charges and make a statement was a fairly irrevocable step and that trying to drop the charges later could be a difficult process. Though a statement by the victim that he will press charges is not a legal requirement for prosecution, it can be used subsequently to persuade the victim to carry on supporting a prosecution (see Chapters 3 and 5). A shocked or injured victim may not be able to comprehend the nature of this step, nor to be able to think clearly about his future role in the process, at the time of the initial contact.

Victim attitudes to the first meeting with the police

The great majority of victims in both towns were satisfied or very satisfied with the police at the time of the initial meeting. Thirty-five per cent of victims in Coventry and 42 per cent of victims in Northampton were very satisfied (on a five-point scale ranging from very satisfied to very unsatisfied). Forty-one per cent of Coventry victims and 35 per cent of Northampton victims were satisfied. The kinds of things that impressed them most were the same for victims of different kinds of offences and victims in both towns. These were the manner of the police, the speed at which the police came and whether the police were seen to do what the victim expected they would do.

Those few victims who were unhappy about this first meeting with the police cited a negative attitude by the police as the main reason why they were so dissatisfied (10 per cent of Coventry victims and 5 per cent of Northampton victims were dissatisfied; 2 per cent of Coventry victims and 3 per cent of Northampton victims were very dissatisfied). A positive, helpful and understanding manner on the part of the police produced comments such as:

She was marvellous, she listened to everything.

They did their best, they were very kind.

She (WPC) didn't seem to have an attitude – she kept an open mind but she had to – I could have been making it up – she just did her job – she was very nice – she looked after me.

Most (84 per cent) of the sexual assault victims were at least satisfied with the police at this stage. Some expressed surprise that they were treated so well:

You know how they say victims get questioned but she wasn't like that – she was sympathetic – not very old.

I'd heard so much about what would happen – it would be an ordeal but it was their job – they did it well. It was good to question me otherwise I would have forgotten it. I had to go to too many offices – they should have one place where you can sit down and stay in – it didn't really upset me but I felt silly walking around wearing a sheet. I accepted the length of time – it was necessary – it was important – they were treating it seriously.

Those that did experience an uncaring, routine or even hostile attitude on the part of the police commented:

His attitude was terrible initially – perhaps because I live in X, perhaps he always uses this style here. I felt like a criminal, a slut, I wished I hadn't called them.

I was crying but no sympathy – just pen and paper – just as if it were happening every day to them – just one of a crowd but you think you're the only one.

The police weren't interested – what choice have you got if the law doesn't protect you?

These victims often rated the policemen and women they encountered as being unhelpful. Unhelpfulness meant that the police were officious, accused the victim, could have done more, were not concerned or did not believe the victim. A nice distinction was made by one victim: 'they weren't unhelpful but more helpful towards themselves and not very helpful towards me.'

The attitude of the police was, then, the prime determinant of victims' feelings of satisfaction or dissatisfaction. Other elements did, however, play some part. Satisfaction was expressed where the police met or exceeded victims' expectations as to speed of arrival. Failure to appear promptly, however, was not regarded as seriously. Victims also had certain expectations as to what the police should do when they arrived. Again, satisfaction was expressed when these expectations were exceeded:

He did everything he could possibly do.

He was very good – he explained things.

Where victims' expectations were not fulfilled (such as when the police did not chase after a just-escaped offender), some niggling worry or doubt was felt, which, when the matter caused great subsequent inconvenience, could affect overall judgements of satisfaction. Two major problems for a few victims were the lack of transport provided to injured victims (one victim had to walk 40 minutes home in his socks on wet pavements because he had no money for a taxi) and the problem of using marked police cars in sexual assault cases where victims worried about the reaction of neighbours.

Some victims (22 per cent) reported some inconvenience associated with this initial police contact. The situations which caused inconvenience were the same as those which prompted dissatisfaction: transport difficulties in getting home, to hospital or the police station; having the statement taken while the victim was still dazed, confused or in pain; being worried about children or spouse; getting home very late; and the neighbours seeing marked police cars (in sexual assault cases).

With more thought, more care or more concern for the victim, almost all these reasons for dissatisfaction or inconvenience could have been avoided. It should be possible to provide transport for victims to their homes or the police station late at night after the buses have stopped. Statements rarely need to be taken when victims are dazed or in pain – indeed most of the police officers interviewed said it was a bad thing to do. A statement taken under such conditions is unlikely to be a complete or accurate account of what happened. In general, however, victims tended to view most inconvenience as not very severe compared to the necessity to help the police to catch the offender and prosecute the case.

Measures of satisfaction are intrinsically problematic, as Ekblom and Heal (1982) have pointed out. Evaluations of police performance are crucially shaped by people's prior attitudes and expectations. It is also difficult to know what assumptions respondents to questionnaires or interviews are building into their replies: are they speaking about the tangible results of police action, the realisation that the police have done their best or the belief that the action taken would achieve results eventually?

One cannot, therefore, conclude that victims were unconcerned with what actions the police took or expect that, if police action were to change in the future, then victims will continue to express satisfaction. One can say that, at present, most victims are content with what the police actually do at this first meeting. They are not so happy, however, about the attitude of some policemen. This is not merely a problem of 'attitudes'; it can be seen as a symptom of a much deeper problem – a misunderstanding on the part of the police as to victims' expectations of the police role. Victims expect support and reassurance from the police both at this initial meeting and subsequently. Fifty-two per cent of victims who suggested particular support agencies plumped for the police:

There should be more help and co-operation, listening and interest from the coppers in areas like this, there's nothing you can do about it, you just have to live with it. Say I was living in . . . where the snobs are, I'd get a lot more help from the police.

If the police sort of worked more with the victims than they do I think crime would cease a lot. Now people probably think 'what difference does it make?', I think more people would probably co-operate.

The worries of victims about the attitude of the police, about lack of transport and about lack of consideration during interviews tend to show a common denominator: that the police do not necessarily value the victim as an important part of the criminal justice system and that they do not necessarily see their role as offering emotional support to victims. Because the victim is not sufficiently valued and appreciated (even for his part in reporting, detecting and prosecuting), it is not seen as vital to respond to his needs, as opposed to, for example, those of pursuing the offender or preparing a prosecution case swiftly. Police officers interviewed varied considerably in their views on whether they should play a role in providing victim support.

We don't do enough for victims. There's too much social security for offenders, nothing for victims.

No, (no support needed) it's just one of those things.

As a police officer, if it's a victim in the area you've worked in, it could help to reassure them if you made yourself known.

Other studies, on victims of different offences and from different countries, have found remarkably similar results: that victims are generally well satisfied with the police at the initial encounter and that any dissatisfaction is related primarily to an uncaring, routine or hostile attitude on the part of the police, to police refusal to take action and to general unthoughtfulness or disregard of obvious victim needs (see, for example, the studies on burglary victims in England by Maguire (1982), Burns-Howell *et al.* (1982) and Howley (1982); those on sexual assault victims in Scotland by Chambers and Millar (1983) and in the United States by Holmstrom and Burgess (1978) and Kelly (1982); and general surveys on all offences such as the British Crime Survey (Hough and Mayhew 1983) and Ekblom and Heal (1982)). Howley (1982) found that police priorities were different and inimical to victim priorities: the police have become 'preoccupied with technical efficiency, whereas victims look to the police for support and reassurance'. As we follow the victims further into the criminal justice system, we must temper this view of general satisfaction and goodwill with a strong suspicion of differences in perceptions and priorities between police and victims.

3 Investigating the offence

Once an offence has been reported to the police, the focus for determining subsequent action moves from the victim to the police. The police will be concerned with catching the offender and also with gathering evidence so that he can be prosecuted. The victim will be involved in or concerned with many of these activities and decisions, but it is the police who will usually set the timetable and control what is happening. In this chapter, we shall consider how important victims are to the detection and investigation of offences, which procedures they become involved with and their feelings about the way in which the police investigate their cases.

Gathering the evidence

In offences of violence, the victim will often be a major prosecution witness. The evidence that he can provide will include not only his statement of what happened, but also evidence of the injuries he sustained (in words and in photographs), identification evidence as to the offender, samples for forensic analysis and evidence as to the place of the offence. There are many police procedures that the victim may experience and, obviously, the requirements in each case vary. It is only possible here to give an idea of how likely it was for victims to undergo particular procedures and then to describe their experiences with and their reactions to the most common and the most problematic of these.

The percentages of victims experiencing particular types of procedure are shown in Table 3.1. Of all types of contact with the police, the most common was for the purpose of making a statement about the offence. Checking up about details in that statement, eliciting further information or persuading the victim to take a particular view on prosecution, together with victim attempts to contact the police themselves to provide information, was the next most common category of contact. The more specialised investigation or evidentiary aids such as identification procedures, forensic tests or taking photographs of the victim's injuries happened to only a minority of victims, often a very small minority. Table 3.1 only represents what the victim knows about the police investigation and those parts of it in which he participates. It does not provide a full picture of police use of investigative techniques. Nor does it cover the subsequent experiences of those victims from whom it was not possible to obtain a second or third interview. However, most

Table 3.1 Evidence procedures experienced by victims (percentages of victims)

	Coventry	Northampton
Statement	91	97
Further statement(s)	15	20
Photograph of victim	12	42
Identification evidence:		
ID parade	0	5
Street ID	4	1
Informal ID	7	8
Identikit	2	3
Looking at photographs	13	5
Search of area	12	7
Scene of crime officer	0	2
Fingerprints	1	0
Clothing	2	8
Other police procedures	7	9
Other investigative contacts	55	53
Making appointments	47	30
Reporting retaliation	5	7

collection of evidence by the police was completed before the first study interview with the victim (see below). The table does show that victims often only experience a very limited range of police procedures and that subsequent judgements of satisfaction with the police investigation are likely to be made on the basis of having had a statement taken, plus some additional discussion about the offences (together with a knowledge of the overall result of the case), without having experienced any more 'sophisticated' procedures.

Most victim contacts with the police were concentrated in the first few days after the offence. Ninety-six per cent of victims had some contact with the police in the first 24 hours after the offence, 43 per cent in the second 24 hours and 54 per cent in the rest of the first week. By the second week, the figure dropped to 38 per cent and, after the eighth week, to around 14 per cent of victims whose cases were still outstanding. The time that victims spent in helping the police to investigate and prosecute offences (often many hours) occurred during the period when victims were injured, shocked and very often exhausted. They willingly, however, gave up their time and their earnings and incurred transport and other costs in order to help the police. We would not expect any person injured in any other way to do the same.

After this initial period of regular police contact, the frequency of contact appeared to drop off very sharply. From then until the end of the case (and over 50 per cent of cases lasted longer than 20 weeks), there was minimal contact and hence minimal support, help and information.

Making a statement

For most victims, the first statement was taken very soon after the offence had occurred (within the first 24 hours for 59 per cent of victims and within the second 24 hours for another 16 per cent). Police officers interviewed did stress the desirability of an early statement, though different views were expressed about its necessity in all cases. Some felt it important, particularly in so-called 'domestic' cases, to justify any action the police might have taken, such as arresting the offender, and also lest the victim might later change his mind. On the other hand, the first statement should provide a full and coherent narrative for evidential purposes, and taking a statement when the victim is shocked, injured or very upset does not make this very likely.

Most of those who did make statements in the first 24 hours after the offence did not mind this, considering that the time and inconvenience required was justified. A small minority, however, were very unhappy that their statement was taken when they were shocked or in pain and knew that they had not done it well. Indeed, in several of these cases, a subsequent statement had to be taken to cover points that had been omitted. There is no legal requirement for a statement to be taken before a complaint of crime can be recorded and investigated and it would appear that statements could be left to the next day without detriment to the police case. Indeed, as one police officer said:

If they're so confused and upset we take it a bit later, when they've got it clear in their mind. For example, if they're raped or knocked about, a confused statement would be ammunition for the enemy.

Where and when a statement is taken seems to depend in some cases more on traditional police practice and on convenience for the investigating officer than on convenience for the victim. For example, relatively few were taken at the victim's home and victims often did not appreciate that this was possible.

In general, victims were satisfied with the way in which their statement was actually taken (30 per cent were very satisfied and 42 per cent satisfied, compared with 4 per cent who were unsatisfied and 2 per cent who were very unsatisfied). The major determinants of satisfaction were a positive attitude on the part of the police (concerned, helpful, chatty, sociable), that the police put down everything the victim said ('like a tape-recording') and that the police did not pressurise the victim ('let me take my time', 'didn't press me to say anything I shouldn't').

Problems appeared where the police officer was seen as unfriendly (especially in sexual assault cases) or where the victim felt the police were attempting to make him say something which he did not want to say. Given the recent police policy that statements from sexual assault victims should be taken by women officers, sexual assault victims were asked whether they preferred a woman or a man. It seemed that, as with physical assault or robbery victims, the attitude of the officer was judged more important than his sex or rank. Twenty-seven of the 35 sexual assault victims who made statements had at least one woman officer present during their first statement, but only nine of these said they preferred this. Where the woman police officer was unfriendly or cold (thought by the victims to be due to inexperience), the victims would have preferred a (more friendly) man. One rape victim who had both a male and a female police officer present said:

It was quite good except the WPC being there – she just sat there watching me – she never took her hat or gloves off – she looked as though she didn't believe me.

After the abolition of policewomen's departments, the number of trained and experienced women police officers to deal with sexual assault cases has fallen. It is possible now for a woman police constable to have to take a statement from a rape victim with only the few days' training provided at initial training courses. This can cause difficulties, both for the rape victim and for the evidentiary value of the statement. Some forces, recognising this lack of experienced officers, have begun running voluntary courses on sexual assault cases for women police officers. Other studies (for example, Chambers and Millar 1983) have shown the concern and dissatisfaction expressed by sexual assault victims over hostile or inexpert questioning, particularly by CID officers. The development of these courses can only be of benefit to future victims.

Victims had certain expectations about the way statements should be worded and what they should contain. For example, they felt that the statement should cover the whole incident, including any trouble leading up to it, whereas the police tended to compartmentalise in time the commission of the offence so that the statement was restricted to the illegal act. In a few cases, victims felt that the police had already decided what should be in the statement and they were just being asked to sign it. This tended to occur with second statements where the victim had decided not to press charges:

That's why I don't want to go to court. I ended up contradicting myself, he was putting words into my mouth. He wasn't nasty, just doing his job I suppose.

The general impression, however, was that victims were quite satisfied with and even pleasantly surprised by the way in which their statements were taken.

Identification evidence

There are several different procedures used by the police to identify an unknown suspect or provide evidence of the identity of an arrested suspect. Where no suspect is known by name, the victim may be asked to look at photographs of possible suspects to see if he can pick someone out. If the victim feels that he could describe the person well, an identikit picture may be made. Alternatively, a street identification may be requested (see details below). The best identification evidence for an arrested suspect, if the suspect and victim agree to participate in the procedure, is an identification parade, the details of which are strictly controlled and laid down in Home Office Circular 109/78. Finally, there are informal identification procedures, covering a range of situations. If the offender is still at the scene of the crime when the police arrive, the victim may be asked to identify him to the police. The victim may also be asked to identify a suspect held at the police station. A total of 62 victims (22 per cent) participated in one or more of these identification procedures.

Experiences, problems and inconvenience for victims varied according to the procedures used and the arrangements customary in the police forces. So, for example, photographs of suspects in the West Midlands force are held centrally in Birmingham. Coventry victims had to go to Birmingham to view the pictures. Although it was the practice of the police to provide transport, the time involved for both victims and police was considerable. Coventry police officers themselves felt that this location for photographs produced tremendous problems for them to persuade victims to view photographs, although they appreciated that the larger number of photographs available at Birmingham might increase the accuracy of any identification. In Northampton, officers would show victims an album with about a dozen photographs in it selected from their stock. This caused no inconvenience. The utility of this procedure when used as a routine measure to find the offender, rather than as confirmation of the identity of an already suspected offender, seems small – only 20 per cent of victims made any identification and there was considerable criticism of the quality of photographs (particularly that many were under- or over-exposed). Identikits or photofits, though rarely used, were found difficult but interesting by victims.

Street identifications, identification parades and the various informal identification procedures may all involve the victim coming face-to-face with the attacker and so produced a considerable degree of anxiety. Identification parades have the most evidentiary value, but their formality and the requirement to pick out the offender during the parade while he is staring at the victim made them the most frightening of all these procedures for victims. In fact both the victims who actually took part in such a parade failed to pick out the offender, though they said they knew he was there, because they were so scared about possible retaliation. Street identification involves the victim being taken by the police to a place where they know the suspect is likely to pass by, such as the factory gate at the end of his shift, or a street on his way to work. The victim is then asked to point out the offender. The procedure is controlled, with instructions being laid down in force orders, and can be used in evidence. In our study, it was used primarily with indecent assault victims and all of these said they were nervous about meeting the offender again: 'I was in a state, very frightened at seeing him again – the whole thing was an ordeal picking him out of a crowd.'

In informal identification procedures, the victim was confronted with just one suspect, at the scene of the crime, at the police station, at hospital or in pubs or clubs to which the victim was taken by the police. No informal identification caused any inconvenience and in most cases victims were not frightened, possibly because there was no period of time for anticipating any consequences before the identification took place.

This informal form of identification appeared to be the least stressful for victims, although it cannot be used where identification is likely to be a major issue at court, for example, where there is no corroborating evidence. The problem with identification evidence is that the necessity to have rigorous and formal conditions for the protection of the suspect increases the amount of stress caused to the victim. For certain types of offence, particularly sexual assaults, the conditions necessary for the more valuable types of identification, such as identification parades, may make the victim so stressed that he or she is unable to face picking out the offender.

Photographs and forensic evidence

Sixty victims had photographs of their injuries taken by the police, to provide additional evidence of the extent of the injury for the court. Principal evidence of injury is given in the doctor's statement made as the result of the victim's visit to the casualty department of the hospital or to his GP (as described in Chapter 6) or in the victim's own statement. There was a difference in policy between the two forces about when photographs should be taken. Northampton police would photograph any injuries that would show up on black-and-white photographs (bruises are notoriously difficult to photograph in black-and-white). West Midlands officers were far more selective, reserving this for those serious assaults (such as rapes) which showed obvious injuries. Colour photography was, however, about to be introduced to help with the bruise problem.

In both forces, there was a suspicion that too little consideration was being given to the time and place at which photographs were being taken and to the convenience of the victim. Although there is no evidential necessity for photographs to be taken at the police station early in the morning the day after the offence, this was commonly done because it was more convenient for the photographer. However, with more liaison, it would be possible to see victims later in the day, so that they would be better rested. Victims assaulted at night and then required to go to the police station early in the morning for photographs did find this particularly inconvenient, the more so if the photographer himself was unable to keep the appointment. Mostly, though, victims considered it worthwhile: 'it's a good thing – it shows it happened', although a few felt that being photographed at the police station made them feel 'a bit like a criminal'.

Forensic procedures usually involved the victim giving the clothing he had been wearing at the time of the offence to the police for forensic tests. If the offender was caught, the clothing would not normally be returned to the victim until after the end of any court case. This caused several victims considerable inconvenience and anxiety, particularly if it involved an essential or expensive item, such as the victim's only winter coat, which might be kept for nine months or a year. It was not made clear to victims by the police when, or even if, their property would be returned and several victims contacted the police on many occasions to try to discover when they could have their property back. This issue of retention of property has emerged in several studies of victim experiences with the police, particularly in the United States and Canada (see, for example, Canadian Federal Provincial Task Force 1983). The numbers of victims involved in such procedures in our study may be low, but they confirm what Greenwood (1980) has found in the United States – that forensic evidence is rarely gathered and badly used. It also exemplifies a rather thoughtless attitude on the part of the police towards victims.

Discussing the evidence
Apart from the specific procedures we have just discussed, most victims saw the police on one or more other occasions, to discuss the victim's evidence, take statements from other members of the victim's family, explore discrepancies between the victim's statement and those of other witnesses or persuade the victim to press charges. There were 285 of these contacts involving 152 victims, but 42 of them (involving 27 victims) were occasions on which the victim contacted the police himself to provide further information, such as the names and addresses of witnesses, or to tell the police that he had moved. Most contacts initiated by the police were received with pleasure by the victim, who appreciated the police's continued interest in the case. This picture of

continuing contact between police and victim, together with the more active role played by some victims in providing evidence themselves, indicates that the role of the victim does not stop with reporting or detection but continues during the whole of the investigation of the case. This will normally, for offences of violence, take several weeks and may continue for months.

Situations which caused adverse reactions in victims were when the police and the victim differed over whether charges should be pressed (see below) or where the police did not keep an appointment they had made. This latter situation occurred in 33 cases, involving 28 victims (10 per cent of the sample). It could cause considerable inconvenience to victims including missing time from work and waiting in all day for the police. Of course, the police also experienced the same problem with some victims and, given the nature of police work, it will not always be possible to keep every appointment. However, there was again a suspicion that the police did not always appreciate either the value of the victim's contribution towards the investigation of the offence or the inconvenience they caused.

The police and the press

Studies of press reporting of crimes of violence have shown that they are much more likely to be reported than other offences (for example, Ditton and Duffy 1982) but have not looked specifically at the role of the victim. An exception is Mawby and Brown's study of several national newspapers and one local newspaper. They questioned the view that the press over-represents crime against the elderly:

On the contrary, female, young and rather high status victims were most likely to make the news, and a particularly sympathetic picture of the victim was *not* common, except for the very young victim.

Press reporting can be both a boon and an additional cost to victims. It can provide them with information they may not receive from other sources, but it can also expose them to possible retaliation and inform people whom they would rather did not know about the offence. This equivocal role can reflect on those that provide the press with information, especially the police. During the study, the main local newspapers in Coventry and Northampton were monitored for reports of cases in the sample and victims were asked for their views on the local paper and on the reporting of their case.

A high proportion of victims saw the local paper in both towns. Over 60 per cent read it every day and only about 7 per cent said that they never saw a copy. Reactions to the quality of reporting were very mixed (see Table 3.2), but the proportion of victims who were pleased is high enough to suggest that local newspapers were both an important source

Table 3.2   *General views of Northampton (N) and Coventry (C) victims about their local newspapers (percentages)*

	Good N C	Neutral N C	Poor N C	Mixed N C	Don't know N C
General reporting	29 33	27 29	29 24	6 9	8 5
General accuracy	25 26	8 27	40 32	6 4	21 12
Crime reporting	23 39	15 13	50 29	0 7	13 11

of information and a source that many had confidence in. The suggestions in some studies (such as Glasgow Media Group 1976) that local radio or television have supplanted newspapers as a trustworthy source of information did not seem to apply to these towns at the time of this study.

Newspaper reports of offences in the study were classified as incident reports, inquiry reports or court reports. Incident reports normally appeared on the day following the offence and gave brief details of its circumstances and the victim and a description of the offender (if any). Forty-three per cent of the Coventry cases and 12 per cent of the Northampton cases were reported in this way, with robberies and sexual assaults the most likely to attract publicity. Incident reports were usually neutral in tone towards the victim, treating him rather impersonally with a brief description including name, address, sex, age, occupation and injury. However, a small number of reports were given much more dramatic treatment. These included rape cases (often reported on the front page) and cases involving a small number of elderly victims. Enquiry reports would be issued after incident reports in a small number of cases and described the investigation of the offence. They would often contain an appeal by the police for witnesses. They might refer to the victim's progress in hospital or to the presence of a suspect 'helping the police with their inquiries'.

Victims whose cases were reported as an incident were almost certain to have seen the report, to have been shown it or to have heard about it. Several victims had kept the cutting and showed it to the researcher. Three-quarters of the enquiry reports printed had also been noticed by victims. Victims were much more likely to be upset than to be pleased by the report of their case, though displeasure was more prevalent in Coventry than in Northampton. Overall, 50 victims were actively displeased for some reason, whereas only 10 were pleased. Their feelings can best be indicated by quotes:

It was completely different from what happened.

All my friends saw it. They said, 'it's a shame, you shouldn't go out on your own' and so on. I didn't like it being in really. The people that did it will have a laugh.

It said that it was gang warfare. It was completely inaccurate though. I felt very bad about it.

It said 'man attacked with iron bar'. I wondered where they got it from. It said I was carrying a substantial amount of money. The address was there, I thought, they'll look at that, I'll have the vandals down here, breaking in.

I didn't like the way they reported the incident the day after the offence, they gave our names and the street where I live. I didn't want him (the offender) knowing where I live.

Two aspects of victims' reactions stand out as being of particular concern. First, victims were frequently affected by newspaper reports because of the reactions of relations, friends, neighbours or workmates. Secondly, victims were often very uneasy that they had been, or might be, identified from the report. Even where a victim's name and address was not given, some felt that the site of the offence and details such as sex and age would allow people in the neighbourhood to identify them.

Much of this information was given to the press by the police. They are the 'gatekeepers' (Chibnall 1977) for this aspect of news reporting. In both towns, the police spoke to a reporter every day. As one officer remarked, the stories that were given to the press were 'the ones that are of interest to the public, or might do us good . . . where property is stolen (we) might get it back, or descriptions (of offenders)'.

We asked police officers what the policy was on releasing victims' names and addresses. In Coventry, there was general agreement that victims were usually asked whether they had any objection to press publicity and that names and addresses were never published in sexual assault cases. In Northampton, there was some diversity of opinion among officers as to whether they thought victims were consulted. A number of officers in both Coventry and Northampton expressed sympathy for those who received unwelcome publicity in the press. The press itself was largely held responsible for this, and a few officers said that, on occasions, neighbours and hospitals rather than the police were a source of information for the press.

Victims, however, told a different story. Only one victim in Northampton (out of 11) and 11 victims in Coventry (out of 81) said that they had been consulted by the police prior to the report appearing. Many victims said they wished they had been asked. In many of the incident and inquiry reports in both towns, victims could be identified. In Coventry, for example, 29 per cent of such reports gave the name and full address of victims and 25 per cent partial information. All sexual assault victims were, however, not identified (even though there is statutory protection under the Sexual Offences (Amendment) Act 1976 only for rape victims).

It seemed to be a police decision in both towns as to whether the press was given sufficient information for a report to appear and a matter of police discretion as to the amount of information provided on the victim. Despite a policy that victims should be consulted in at least one of the towns, they were not being consulted. The result was a considerable degree of dissatisfaction, directed towards both the press and the police.

Catching the offender

Offences of violence generally show high detection rates, particularly for physical assaults, and this study indicates no exception. Table 3.3 shows the detection rates (rates of detecting at least one offender for the offence) for both Northampton and Coventry. The level of detection is very similar to the findings of Bottomley and Coleman (1980) that 79 per cent of their sample of offences of violence in a medium-sized city in the North of England were cleared up and to the national *Criminal Statistics* (1979). However, over all types of offence, Northampton shows a higher level of detection than Coventry. In order to discover why this might be, we need to look at how the offenders were caught.

Table 3.3   Percentages of cases in which the offender was caught

	Physical assaults	Sexual assaults	Robberies	Total
Coventry	71	43	37	61
Northampton	92	50	60	85

By examining both the police file of each case and the victim's account, the ways in which cases were detected were identified. These could be:

(1) As a result of definite information from the victim (offender caught by the victim and handed over to the police or where the name or address of the offender was given by the victim to the police);
(2) As a result of definite information from a witness (offender caught by the witness or where the name or address of the offender was given by the witness to the police);
(3) As a result of a description of the offender being given to the police by the victim;
(4) As a result of the offender giving himself up to the police; or
(5) As a result of police action (or some other means).

It was unfortunately not possible to discover from the information in the police file what action it was that resulted in catching the offender.

In most cases, of course, the police have several different leads to the identity of the offender and these may all have to be followed up in order to amass sufficient evidence for prosecution. At present, however, we are interested in specifying which piece of information from which source resulted in the identification of the person who was eventually to be designated by the police as the offender. This is shown in Table 3.4.

Table 3.4 *How the offenders were caught* (percentages of cleared-up cases)

	Coventry	Northampton
Definite victim information	55	61
Definite witness information	8	13
Victim description	9	9
Offender action	2	3
Police action	25	15

For these offences, the victim plays the dominant role in detection. In over half the cases, the offender was caught as a result of definite information given by the victim or through being detained by the victim himself. In another 9 per cent, it was the description of the offender given by the victim which provided the major clue. In only 15 to 25 per cent (depending on the town) was detection the result of a police initiative. The higher detection rate in Northampton than in Coventry was largely the product of the greater help that Northampton victims could provide to the police.

This major role of the victim in detection is not, however, to deny a role to the police. Without a quick response by the police where victims or witnesses have detained the offender or fast action where a name or description has been supplied, offenders would not be caught. The police may not be the major detection agency in these offences, but they are responsible for gathering evidence such that the offender, once caught, can be prosecuted.

In offences of violence, victim and offender must physically be present at the same point in space and time. The importance of the victim in detection is, therefore, perhaps not surprising. A recent plethora of studies on police effectiveness has, however, confirmed the small role that 'traditional' police investigation work plays (Bottomley and Coleman 1980; Greenwood 1980; Mawby 1979; Steer 1980). Even in Maguire's (1982) study of domestic burglary, information given to the police by a victim or witness was the most important aid to detection of the offender, despite the prevalence of cases in which the trail was cold (in 70 per cent of cases, the victim had been out of the house or asleep in bed for over six hours and had no precise idea of the time at which the burglary had taken place). For most offences, victim and police are mutually interdependent.

When the offender is not caught

Despite the efforts of victims, witnesses and police, a number of offenders will not be caught. This happened for 40 per cent of the Coventry victims and 15 per cent of the Northampton victims in our study. At their final interview with the researchers, victims were asked about the progress of the case, and, if necessary, told the outcome. When the offender is not caught within a certain period of time (which varies according to the type of case and the police force), then the case is filed. No more work will be done on it by the police unless further information comes to light.

The reaction of victims to this outcome was, in general, fairly low-key and matter-of-fact. The majority felt that the police had done all they could have been expected to do. Often victims blamed themselves for the failure, feeling that they had not been able to provide a sufficiently detailed description of the offender:

They don't catch him because I can't give them any information – they had little chance.

I don't expect anything – they haven't got much to go on because I couldn't identify him.

These feelings mirror the expectations of the same victims at the beginning of the case. Fifty-five per cent never had any belief that the offender would be caught. A few of these, however, ascribed this to their belief that the police were never interested in the offence:

The police aren't interested – they don't believe me – I wish I hadn't reported it.

The police are doing nothing – they should have let me know what was happening and taken me to Birmingham to see photos as they promised.

By the final interview, some of these views had solidified:

The police have put the case in their back drawer or trash can. If I weren't living on this estate the police would be different.

I don't think they were ever interested in it.

This perceived lack of interest was tied up with victims' annoyance at not being informed of the result (or lack of result) by the police and a suspicion, fuelled by the disbelieving or unhelpful attitude of some police, that the whole thing was being seen as unimportant. Lack of information, or of contact, can itself be seen as lack of interest. The complaint was not that the police had not performed their duties properly (only two victims had any points on this). There was in fact no particular relationship between expectation of catching the offender and final satisfaction or dissatisfaction at the offender not being caught.

The problem was lack of information and a feeling that the police did not care, two views which tended mutually to reinforce each other. Victims wanted to know that the offender had not been caught and they expected the police to tell them. Those that were clearly told the result of the case were very pleased that this had been done:

It's a courtesy. I was very pleased – otherwise you don't know.

I was very pleased that they were being straight – telling me there was nothing they could do.

I was quite surprised and pleased I had heard something – I didn't think I would – they said they'd made as many investigations as they could – there was nothing more they could do – the case was closed.

The police themselves supported the idea of telling the victim the outcome of the case. Indeed, it was force policy in the West Midlands (though not in Northamptonshire) that officers should notify victims of the result of the case, whatever that might be. The officer in the case was required to write in the file of the case that the complainant had been seen and notified of the result. In our study, that remark was present in the police files for all but three of the cases in which no offender was caught.

The Coventry victims, however, had a rather different impression. The majority had no recollection of being informed at all. Some police officers did feel embarrassed at having to go and confess to victims what they saw as their 'failure'. They obviously did not appreciate the realistic expectations of victims and their wishes to be informed of the result. Victims also wanted to be told it 'straight', that is that no more action would be taken by the police unless new information was forthcoming. Those who were confused by the police 'information' were considerably more dissatisfied.

We are left with a picture of realistic victim expectations of technical success on the part of the police, but, unfortunately, unrealistic expectations as to information about the outcome of the case. This is congruent with the results of some other studies (for example, those of Maguire 1982 and Sparks *et al.* 1977). It is also consistent with Howley's (1982) findings on the stress placed by police officers on technical efficiency in their dealings with victims, compared to their relative lack of appreciation of the emotional and reassurance needs of victims. Police and victims do not appear to have the same priorities, though victims would dread to interfere in what the police would define as the performance of their duties, in order to press their own needs.

The decision to prosecute

The police have the ultimate power to decide whether to prosecute in any case. When there was disagreement between victim and police about prosecution, this caused the most concern and anxiety, on both sides. Such a conflict could arise where the victim does not wish to press charges, where the police feel that there is insufficient evidence of a crime or where the police consider that no purpose would be served by prosecuting a particular offender. The police indicate these categories by choosing one of a number of categories suggested by the Home Office, such as 'No crime' (subsequent discovery that no crime had in fact been committed), 'Detected – complainant declined to prosecute' (victim refuses to give evidence), 'Detected – insufficient evidence to prosecute' or 'Detected – other reasons' (including public policy). In our study the position was made complicated by the fact that several of these categories could be said to apply to some cases and that, in others, disputes between victim and police arose at different stages of the case and were resolved, only to crop up again. It was very difficult in practice to ascertain why cases were assigned to the category in which they were finally classified, a problem which has bedevilled other research on police use of crime recording forms (see Bottomley and Coleman 1980). However, using both victim accounts and police files, it was possible to distinguish between cases in which the victim was unwilling to prosecute and those in which the hesitation stemmed from the police.

Victim unwillingness to prosecute

At some stage of the case, 17 per cent of victims showed some unwillingness to help to prosecute the offender or to press charges. The majority of these cases did end up at court, either because the victim was finally persuaded to prosecute or because the police went ahead anyway. The few instances in which the police decided to prosecute, as a matter of policy and against the expressed wishes of victims, caused the greatest distress. All these victims felt that it should be the victim, rather than the police, who should have the final word on prosecution:

> It's not my case – it's now theirs. I think in this sort of case the police ought to see the person concerned a few days later – see if they feel the same. Now once you've made a statement you can't get out of it. I feel I've been pushed into this thing I didn't know would happen.

This victim is expressing the central dilemma of a criminal justice system with a centralised power of prosecution – that of the ownership of the case (see Christie 1977). The police need to have the power to initiate and continue prosecutions, so that victims and witnesses are not terrified into dropping cases. Yet, if we move from an ideology of automatic prosecution given sufficient evidence, to one of discretionary prosecution, then overriding the wishes of the victim can be seen as more dubious, unless everyone is agreed on the circumstances in which this discretion will be used. A criminal justice system, in its modern incarnations, implies some supra-individual power of decision-making over whether a case is continued and prosecution takes place and also over the verdict. There is little dispute that some check on individual proclivities to prosecute is necessary to make sure that minimum standards of evidence are fulfilled in each case. There is more concern about whether particular classes of offender should not be prosecuted (because they are young, or old, or in some way ill). Here at least, however, it might be possible to lay down guidelines, which could then be discussed until they command both respect and adherence (see van Dijk 1983b, for a practical example of this in the Dutch context). To adopt discretionary prosecution, against victim wishes, in vaguer areas of public opinion, such as domestic assaults and sexual assaults, begins to raise questions about who should make such policy. Should Parliament or even the Home Office (by issuing a circular) feel a wish to produce detailed guidance, then it could be taken as representing the policy of a criminal justice system. The victim, as well, has an obvious stake in such matters – it was, after all, an assault against him. The present position, however, is extremely messy and may be difficult to justify, especially if victims do not realise how potentially irrevocable reporting an offence and making a statement are.

This problem is not, however, confined to the police. It can be followed back into the nature of the substantive criminal law. The law tends to make the conception of the offence primary and not to consider the roles of victims or offenders in behaviour which typically surrounds that offence. So, the criminal law overrides the ability of the victim to consent to being a victim (in the rare cases where this might occur, such as in a 'fair fight' or in some domestic situations). It prescribes that it is not possible for anyone to consent to such conduct. At the same time, some societal (but not necessarily victim-preferred) exceptions are made, so that particular types of people may be allowed to commit such offences (common examples being assaults during medical treatment and sporting activities, or rape and indecent assault by husbands). So, the criminal law can itself override the wishes of the individual in the interests of society, either by making him a victim when he does not consider himself to be one, or by denying that he is a victim when he may feel he is one. We shall return to the underpinning of the criminal process by ideas stemming from the criminal law later (see Chapter 5). Conflicts between victim and police over prosecution, however, are but an example of conflicts between the victim and the ideology behind the current criminal law and criminal justice system.

In practice, of course, these conflicts are rare, since, even if the police have the power to continue prosecution with an unwilling victim, they will find great difficulty in so doing. A hostile witness, even if dragged to court and made to give evidence, has many ways of obstructing the prosecution case, especially if done in conjunction with the offender. The police stereotype (and that of others as well) is that it is domestic assault victims who are most likely to play this role. In our study, 40 per cent of the victims who were at some stage against the idea of prosecution had been assaulted by a relative or friend. They formed, however, only half of the domestic assault victims. The other half never wavered in their desire to see the offender prosecuted.

Police unwillingness to prosecute
The police showed some unwillingness to proceed to prosecution in 6 per cent of the cases in our study. In another 2 per cent, the offender was cautioned. Again, police doubts about the efficacy of prosecution were not necessarily shared by the victim:

They said that was the end of it. I thought that was terrible – he could do it the next time. They should have taken him to court.

There's not much joy if the police don't take action. Is this justice? What a waste of time but I suppose there's nothing the police could do.

More annoying than the decision not to proceed, however, was not being told about it. Where the police do decide not to prosecute, or to caution, it would seem advisable to notify the victim of the decision, if not also to explain it to him. If we are to see a greater use of discretion by prosecutors, whether this be as a result of a move towards diversion of juveniles or because of the opportunities afforded for national policy by an independent prosecution system, then it would seem essential that such moves should be accompanied by a definite policy of informing victims, of consulting with them and of explaining to them the possibilities for action.

Informing the victim
We have seen that many victims are actively involved in helping the police to detect the offender and to gather evidence towards prosecuting the offender, taking part in many procedures to do this. There have been hints, at several parts of the process, that victim satisfaction is linked to the amount of information they receive as to the progress of the case. As far as catching the offender and investigating the offence are concerned, we can consider the amount of information victims have by looking at the contacts between the police and victims which provide such information, separating out occasions when the police volunteered information from those where the victim contacted the police to ask for information.

Of a total of 327 contacts in which information was obtained by the victim, 35 per cent involved the victim himself contacting the police. Victims appeared to be almost as active in requesting information as the police were in providing it. This tends to suggest that victims feel that insufficient information is provided as a matter of course. When they were interviewed by the researchers well into the progress of the investigation, their state of knowledge about the case was both scanty and rather patchy. If an offender had been caught, the vast majority of victims knew about it (93 per cent). Where the victim is not present when the offender is caught, the police in both towns appear to be very active in letting him know soon afterwards. As we have seen, however, victims are not necessarily informed if the police have not caught the offender, but are filing the case.

If the offender was caught, victims often knew few other details. Fifty-seven per cent knew whether the offender was on bail or in custody, but only 40 per cent had learnt it from the police. Most of the rest had read it in the local newspaper. Only 42 per cent knew of any charge brought against the offender. Thirty-five per cent had received this information from the police. Even victims who were police officers found difficulty in following what was happening to the offender. The researchers had the same problem. The reason for all this is that, after the investigation is complete, the police file is passed to a prosecutions department to await court appearances. The officer in the case, who is the person in contact with the victim, will no longer have ready access to the file and so will not be able to provide current information. There was no one police officer who would have up-to-date knowledge of the entire case and of the victim and witnesses. As well as this structural problem in obtaining information, police officers varied considerably with regard to the kind of information they considered victims should have. There appeared to be no consistent supervisory practice on this. Where, however, senior officers encouraged the provision of information to victims, it was more likely to happen. Victim experiences in the two towns mirrored these divides.

Victims wanted to know all sorts of details: whether the offender was caught, obviously, but also what the charges were, whether the offender was on bail, what would happen next, what the victim would be required to do and whether he would be informed when this might occur. Victims felt aggrieved if they were not told and could not easily find out:

They didn't tell me what they were doing.

I went to the police station and spoke to a guy on the desk. I asked about the case – he said they'd write to me – then he wandered off and said it was still proceeding. I was annoyed. I felt I was getting nowhere.

One of the worst things is you've made a statement so that something should be done about that offence but if they don't take any action or give a verbal warning they don't tell you they're doing it – they don't give you the satisfaction of knowing that something however small has been done – they have the attitude that it's too much bother. (In fact the offender in this case had been caught and his case was going through the courts.)

A few victims wanted to see a copy of their statement. This was always denied, despite instructions to the the contrary in a Home Office Circular (82/1969), which states '. . . notwithstanding that criminal proceedings may be pending or contemplated, the chief officer should normally provide a person, *on request,* with a copy of his statement to the police. It is recognised that on occasions a chief officer may think it necessary to exercise his discretion to refuse to supply a copy of a witness' statement. Circumstances giving cause for refusal are where the chief officer has reason to suppose that the statement is sought for some sinister or improper purpose which might prejudice the course of justice – for example, to enable the witness to lie consistently or where others are bringing pressure on the witness to obtain a copy of his statement with a view to persuading him to go back on it.' The practice in the areas in which our study was being done, however, was a blanket refusal.

We have seen, throughout the recording, detection and investigation of the case, that the victim is vital to the police. Yet the police do not seem to be concerned to fulfill the victim's needs to be informed, occasionally consulted and treated with dignity and respect. The victim does not seem to be seen as a very important participant in the criminal justice system. We have two contradictory facets of the role of the victim – his practical importance and, in contrast, an apparent ignorance of and an ignoring of his attitudes and his experience by those involved in recording and investigating offences – the police. It is this paradox which we need to remember as we follow the victim into the courts.

4 At court

Once the decision is made to prosecute an offender, control of the case passes from the police to the courts. Its progress is affected by many factors: for example, the legal requirements for the place of trial; the defendant's plea and his decision whether to elect trial at the Crown Court; the views of the police and the magistrates as to how serious the offence was and where it should be tried; and, to some extent, the willingness of the victim to give evidence. Victims' experiences with the courts were correspondingly varied. They were only required to attend and participate if they were to give evidence because the offender had pleaded not guilty or there was a request for a 'full' committal from the magistrates' court to the Crown Court, including the hearing of prosecution witnesses. Only a few victims did give evidence (46 cases or 17 per cent of the victims). However, all those whose assailants were prosecuted (163 victims or 59 per cent of the total sample) did have some interest in the progress of their case through the courts, if only because they did not necessarily know until shortly before the trial whether they would have to give evidence.

Throughout the process, three aspects are of particular interest: what happened to the cases, whether (and how) the victims came to learn about it and what they thought about it. We shall follow the cases and the victims through the court process in terms of these three questions, looking at whether the offender was on bail or in custody; what the charges were and how they changed; committals to the Crown Court; the experience of being a witness; the length of time the whole process took; the outcomes and sentences; press reporting of court cases; and victims' satisfaction with the court process.

Bail or custody?

Whether an offender is allowed bail by the courts or whether he is remanded in custody is of great interest to victims. In fact, only a minority of offenders were remanded in custody at any stage during the progress of the case through the courts. For 75 per cent of victims, therefore, the offender was on bail throughout the proceedings. Bail may be either unconditional or conditional, in which case one of the conditions may be that the offender should not contact the victim. This was imposed in only 12 cases. The large majority of victims (85 per cent) were not given any specific protection by the courts throughout the whole course of the proceedings.

In the last chapter we saw that victims' knowledge of the police action in their case rarely extended beyond an awareness that the offender had been caught. They often did not know initially whether he was on bail or what the charges were. This lack of information continued with regard to court appearances before the trial and the resulting decisions on bail and on charges. There were 146 cases in which there was at least one court appearance prior to the trial. Thirty-six per cent of these victims had not heard of any pretrial appearances. Eighteen per cent had heard of less than half. Only 22 per cent of victims knew of all the pretrial appearances in their case. The major source of this information was the police, though they tended to tell the victims only about bail decisions. The local newspaper gave the fullest coverage of appearances – letting the victim know the charges, whether bail had been granted and, often, the next court date.

Victims felt this lack of information keenly:

I'd have liked the police to tell me – you should be kept informed.

I think it's pretty disgusting really I've never heard anything. I'd have expected to have known what was happening.

No-one's bothered to come and tell me what's happening. Waiting is torment. They should make it easier on the victim – the longer it is the more frightened I get – you need to know where he is – if he's on bail you might meet him. Right now I'm in the dark, then I'll be thrown into court – I don't know what'll happen.

A particular worry of victims was that they did not know whether the offender was in custody or on bail. Not knowing the whereabouts of the offender, they were constantly afraid that they would meet him unexpectedly in the street. However, where victims knew the offender was on bail, this fact did not worry them unduly, even though they might not agree with the decision. It would appear that it was anxiety born of ignorance that produced concern. Fear of the unknown was more frightening than knowledge of the feared reality.

Charges and dropping charges
By the time of the trial, the initial offence recorded by the police was often not the only one the defendant had to face in court. Defendants were sometimes charged with other offences committed during the same incident (such as criminal damage, theft or possession of an offensive weapon). Offences committed at entirely separate times might be added to the final list facing the defendant. Combine this with the possibility of several offenders assaulting or robbing one victim and the fact that a few victims were themselves tried for offences arising out of the original incident and the picture becomes very complicated. But since our data includes the charges and results of every court appearance of the cases in the study, we can chart the progress of the court cases and assess the

reactions of victims to the pattern of charges with which the defendant was finally confronted.

Perhaps the simplest way of analysing the progress of the cases is to consider how the most serious charge relating to the attack on the victim in each case fared from initial recording by the police through the stage of charging the offender to the final court appearance. Other charges arising out of the same incident and charges arising out of separate incidents may then be added until a picture emerges of the charges faced by the defendant at trial.

Between initial recording of the crime by the police and charging an offender, few changes in offence occurred. In 85 per cent of cases, the offender was charged with the same offence as was recorded initially by the police. By the time of the final court appearance, however, the defendant was required to answer to the same charge as that originally recorded in only 71 per cent of cases that led to court appearances. If one considers the most serious charge put to the defendant at any stage, whether by the police or by the court, there were 37 cases (23 per cent of those coming to court) in which the charge the defendant had to answer at the final court appearance was apparently a less serious one. In addition, in nine cases (6 per cent), the offender did not face any prosecution relating to the offence against the victim at the final court appearance. These two categories form a surprisingly high proportion of cases in the study (28 per cent of those that went to court) and it is interesting to find the points at which these developments were occurring.

The most substantial cause of the reduction in charge was that the prosecution offered no evidence against the defendant on the original charge at the final court appearance. The defendant then pleaded guilty to a 'lower' charge (29 cases). This occurred entirely with physical assault charges and was enabled by the way in which such charges are framed in the provisions of the Offences Against the Person Act 1861 (the statute still applicable).

Physical assault offences can be seen as forming a 'scale' of offences, ranging from common assault (an offence at common law) through assault occasioning actual bodily harm (s. 47), wounding or assault inflicting grievous bodily harm (s. 20), to wounding or causing grievous bodily harm with intent to do grievous bodily harm (s. 18). The notion of a scale of seriousness is not a perfect one, as, although grievous bodily harm generally involves a more serious injury than actual bodily harm, the dividing line is unclear. A wound can, in fact, be a trivial injury, though a s. 18 charge could be founded on it. The maximum sentences do not give much guidance here either, as the maxima for both s. 47 and s. 20 are the same (five years imprisonment), although the maximum for s. 18 is considerably more (life imprisonment). Unfortunately, we do not have much research evidence on the views of prosecutors or sentencers about this, although in our study, it was clear that both police and prosecuting solicitors regarded these offences as forming such a scale. Equally, no 'objective' view of the victims' injuries can be given here, as it is extremely difficult to compare injuries of different kinds (for example, a broken arm against a stab wound) or to relate the physical injuries inflicted to any standard speed of recovery or effects on victims (see Chapter 6). Despite all the problems, however, it was the impression of both researchers and prosecutors that such dropping of charges would lead to a lesser punishment for the offender.

It is clearly difficult to say whether the reduction in the cases we observed was prompted primarily by evidential considerations, by questions of the potential cost of a trial, by an inappropriate initial level of charging or for any other reason. Discussions between prosecution, defence and, on occasions, the judge, before the final court appearance might have proved illuminating on this point, but were not open to the researchers. In some instances, however, the nature of the discussion between the prosecution and the judge in open court allowed the researchers to infer that the primary motive was to save court time and public money by avoiding a not guilty plea. Indeed, in two separate s. 18 cases, the judge trying the case on the first appearance at the Crown Court refused to accept that the prosecution should offer no evidence on this charge (as he is entitled to do, see *R. v. Broad* 1978), and said that the case should be relisted for trial on the s. 18 charge. When the two cases came up again, they were heard before a different judge, who agreed to accept no evidence on the s. 18 charges and proceed on the basis of a guilty plea to a s. 20 charge. Twenty-four of the 29 cases in which the defendant pleaded guilty to a lesser charge appeared to involve this 'dropping charge' phenomenon. Twenty of these were at the Crown Court and seemed to be at the instigation of prosecuting counsel. The other reasons for charges being reduced or dropped involved much smaller numbers of cases and were the result of decisions by the police or the Director of Public Prosecutions that there was insufficient evidence to proceed on the offence as originally charged or recorded. In this situation, the charge might be reduced or dropped at any stage of the proceedings. The major factor where charges were reduced appeared, therefore, to be a decision by the prosecution at the Crown Court that it would be more beneficial to proceed with a guilty plea on a lesser charge rather than face a full-blown trial.

As well as changes in the original charge against the defendant, other, sometimes unrelated, charges might be added at court or before. The presence of these other charges may affect the outcome of the case (in potentially altering the total range and weight of evidence presented to the court if there is a not guilty plea) and will certainly affect the overall sentence, if not the sentence on the most serious charge relating to the victim in our study. In only a minority of cases did the offence against the victim in our study form the only charge against the defendant by the time of the final court appearance (42 per cent of cases coming to court). In 18 per cent there were also other charges relating to the same victim (criminal damage, burglary, arson etc.) and in 27 per cent other charges arising out of the same incident (public order offences, assaults or property losses involving other victims). In 22 per cent, charges relating to entirely different incidents were added at some stage before the final appearance (on the principle that all outstanding charges against a defendant should be dealt with on the same occasion). These ranged over the entire spectrum of the law, from robbery to parking offences. It is not a simple task to relate outcome and sentence to the charges affecting only the victims in our study, nor for the researcher (or the victim) to react to those sentences.

The reactions of victims to the more serious charges being dropped varied considerably:

They dropped the s. 20 because he was prepared to plead guilty to the s. 47. They dropped the offensive weapon too – it was wrong.

They dropped the s. 18 to s. 20 – there was not a lot else they could have done – it sounds fair enough.

Similarly, views varied when no evidence was offered at all on any charge relating to the victim or when that offence was merely taken into consideration. Victims were agreed in all these instances, however, that they should have been informed of the decision not to prosecute on that charge and, preferably, consulted. Unlike the cases in which no prosecution was attempted at all, these victims did not want to take over the power to decide on prosecution and did not seek a veto on withdrawing charges. They merely wanted to be informed and to be considered:

I don't mind but I should have been told.

I assumed that he was being tried for the offence against me. I really think he should have been prosecuted – the police seem to ignore you. I'm not saying that what he did to me was worse than the others but they should have told me – they seem to ignore you.

Well, I can understand it – they let them go so they'll plead guilty to the others – it saves a lot of time and paperwork if they don't have to have a trial.

Whether or not it is felt that victims should play a more active decision-making role in the system, it would appear that the victim should at least be notified of the decision not to prosecute on some or all charges. This would be a job for the prosecution, as only they have any contact with a victim not required as a witness. The question of consultation over prosecution would also bring in those prosecuting on behalf of the police (prosecuting solicitors and counsel). Their relations with the victim seem to be even more problematic, as we shall see later.

Pretrial appearances, committals and witness orders

The length of time that cases took to come to trial varied considerably (see Table 4.1). Delays were longer when there was a not guilty plea and where the case was heard at the Crown Court. For one case in which the plea was not guilty, for example, the delay was nearly 18 months. Some cases involved up to 16 court appearances (though these might be the result of the offender being in custody and having to be produced every week). Where there were long delays, particularly for not guilty trials at the magistrates' courts and Crown Courts, victims were faced with waiting a long time to give evidence. This was the subject of much worried comment. They felt that they would not be able to remember the details of the offence and would perform badly.

We saw above that victims generally had little idea of the progress of the case through the various pretrial appearances (only 22 per cent

Table 4.1   Delays within the court process from first appearance to outcome

	Coventry		Northampton	
	Mean (days)	Number of cases	Mean (days)	Number of cases
Magistrates' court guilty plea	37	37	57	24
Magistrates' court not guilty plea*	129	6	134	14
Juvenile court guilty plea	19	6	54	2
Juvenile court not guilty plea	–	2	–	0
Crown Court guilty plea	134	26	161	19
Crown Court not guilty plea	196	14	172	9
Committal for sentence to Crown Court	205	2	108	1

*The two cases discharged after full committal proceedings are included.

knowing of any pretrial appearance), though they were keen to have such information. Most did not actually wish to attend these appearances. A few, however, did, and were particularly concerned that the police did not tell them the date of the next appearance. The one or two victims that rang the magistrates' court to find out did not fare much better:

> The magistrates' court told me to ring the Crown Court. I rang them but they didn't know anything about it and gave me a number in Birmingham – but that's engaged when I've rung – I'm very confused.
> (The case was in fact still proceeding through the magistrates' court.)

This lack of knowledge about where exactly a court case is in the system is not a problem for victims alone. It bedevils many other courtroom participants as well (including researchers). Unless the previous court appearance has been attended and a note taken of the next date, it is very difficult to find out such information. There is no one who has overall knowledge of the progress of all cases. As we described before, the police officer in the case passes the file on to a prosecutions department. Police and prosecution are then reliant upon their own notes about the case or upon information from court clerks, if the case is suddenly relisted (because of illness, requested adjournments by other parties, lack of court time or judges etc.). Cases are, however, passed from one court to another (committed from the magistrates' court to the Crown Court or transferred from one Crown Court to another). Although all the court clerks and administrative staff tried very hard to assist callers, they can have very little idea about cases that had been transferred. There are also certain gaps built into the system (such as the time between being committed by the magistrates' court and the file arriving at the relevant Crown Court) and, at the time of the study, nothing could be found out about cases in this state. Furthermore, cases are filed and referred to by the name of the defendant, with consequent difficulty in matching victim to defendant. There are in existence computerised systems which track cases through the courts (such as the American PROMIS system), but these had not been adopted by the courts at the time of our study. Without such a system, it is difficult for anyone, especially victims, who do not have a good knowledge of court procedure, to follow a particular case.

Magistrates' courts are required subsequent to committal to send to each prosecution witness (including the victim) a witness order. Since all but three cases in our sample were committed to the Crown Court without prosecution witnesses giving evidence, this was often the only official communication between initial investigation by the police and finding out about the outcome of the case. It, therefore, assumed considerable importance.

There are two forms of witness order – one that says the victim will have to give evidence at the Crown Court (the absolute order) and one that says he may have to (the conditional order). The latter is used where the defendant has indicated that he is likely to plead guilty (so that witnesses will not be required). He can, however, change his mind, and then another (absolute) order will be sent. The wording of the order will vary slightly from court to court, but its main contents are fixed. A sample of a witness order is shown below:

To: . . . .
You are hereby ordered (if notice is later given to that effect*) to attend and give evidence at the trial of : . . . . before the Crown Court to be held at . . . ., or at such other Court, place or time as you may be directed.
Dated:
                    Clerk to the Justices
NOTE: Under section 3(1) Criminal Procedure (Attendance of Witnesses) Act 1965, a person who disobeys a witness order without just excuse may render himself liable to a term of imprisonment not exceeding three months and a fine.
*deleted in the case of an absolute order

There are two points to note about this: first, no date or place is given for the witness to attend court. The only date on the document is the date it is sent out. Secondly, the wording of the order is very stern, and is backed up by a threat of imprisonment. It requires the witness to do something, but does not tell him when or where he is required to do it, or who will inform him.

Perhaps predictably, nearly a third of the victims who received an order failed to understand what it meant and, given the sternness of the wording, were extremely worried about what they had to do. Their main problem concerned the lack of a date for their appearance, but the presence of a date long gone:

It came on April 16th but said I was to go to court on March 19th. I was completely confused.

It had no dates or anything. I wasn't too pleased – I didn't know if they'd let me know or if I should phone them.

Another problem was that those who had received conditional witness orders were not at all sure whether they did or did not have to go to court:

I don't know when I have to go and whether I have to do anything. I felt frightened when I received a letter with magistrates' court on it – I thought, what have I done?

This is exacerbated if witnesses are not subsequently told if they do not have to go to court. Some victims, who never heard anything further, were still keeping their best clothes ready for a summons to court two or three months after the case had in fact ended with a guilty plea by the defendant. This anxiety is a real cost of participating in the criminal justice system – or even, some might say, further victimisation by that system. It is certainly unnecessary. Victims are usually almost completely uninformed about the progress of their case prior to the trial. The only information they may receive from official sources – the witness order – was itself found to be uninformative, even confusing, and added to victims' worry. Again, this is unnecessary. As some magistrates' courts have done subsequent to this study, it is possible to add a few explanatory notes to the end of the order, telling the victim or witness that this is merely a formal notification and that they will be informed if and when they have to give evidence. A telephone number for queries can be added.

It is not that victims are apathetic about the progress of their case – they very much wish to know what is going on – and some would like to attend the court appearances, even though they will incur costs and not be entitled to expenses if they do. Some try, often unsuccessfully, to find out what is happening through official or unofficial means. Most feel either that the police or courts are too busy to be bothered by them or that it is not their place to find out; it is up to the system to inform them. This is not a criticism of any individual participant in the system. It seems rather that, because victims have no official, documentary role to play between reporting an offence and acting as a witness in a trial (except rarely at committal), they are forgotten in the business of processing the defendant as quickly as possible through the courts to the trial.

Attending court

For those victims who do attend court, the experience is not confined to answering questions in the witness box or listening to what is being said. There are the contacts they may have with the police and the courts when being warned to come to court. There is the experience of waiting outside the courtroom and any contact they may have there with police officers, prosecution solicitor or counsel or, of course, the offender. Even after giving evidence, there is the problem of obtaining witness expenses and whether these meet the costs of victims in attending court.

Warning witnesses

Every person who will be required to give evidence at court has to be notified (or 'warned') of the time and place that he will have to attend. The systems for warning witnesses for the magistrates' court and the Crown Court are very different. At the magistrates' courts and the juvenile courts in the study, a date for the trial was fixed at a previous court appearance, usually many weeks ahead. The police had a considerable amount of time to tell witnesses about the trial (either personally or by letter). Usually a form was also sent on which the victim could indicate whether he would lose earnings by attending the trial and which his employer would sign to verify this. All the victims in our study who received letters warning them to attend the magistrates' court said that they had had ample notice and found the letters easily understandable. Letters were as satisfactory as personal visits.

At the Crown Court, the position was very different. All the Crown Courts at which cases in our study were tried (Birmingham, Warwick, Coventry and Northampton) are administered under the same system and are part of the same circuit. To notify witnesses, the Crown Court administrators used to issue a 'warned list' of cases that were liable to be tried in a certain week three weeks beforehand. The police officer in the case was then supposed to contact all witnesses in his case to ascertain whether they would be available. The resulting viable cases were then put on a 'fixed list' issued 10 days before the relevant week. Police officers were then supposed to go back to all these witnesses and tell them the expected date of the trial. Unless the case was likely to be very long and so was fixed well in advance (which occurred in only three cases in our study), witnesses could receive only about eight days notice of the trial. Given that cases might still be put off at any time up to the morning of the trial because previous cases had lasted longer than expected or new cases had been brought in, victims might only know definitely the night before.

Thirty-one victims with whom final interviews were conducted attended the Crown Court. They received a total of 66 visits or phone calls from the police, representing a considerable amount of police time. Thirteen victims were warned for more than one date because their case was put off. This caused considerable dissatisfaction, since victims had made arrangements to take time off work which they then had to cancel. They had also worked themselves up to attend court:

After two dates, I was beginning to take what was said with a pinch of salt – they're just messing everyone around – I told them that if they put it off again I would refuse to go to court the next time.

The length of notice that victims received varied from six days to being told on the morning of the case. This caused considerable aggravation to victims, some of whom had no chance to tell their employers that they would not be coming in to work the next day, to find someone to look after their children, or, if they were themselves employers, to find staff to fill in for them. One victim's wife was telephoned by the police on the morning of the case. She rang the victim at work:

I dashed home, changed my clothes and drove straight to Warwick. It was a champion bit of inefficiency – it was clear chance that my wife knew where I was working that day. When I got there I rushed straight into the witness box – they were waiting for me.

For another victim, that chance did not occur. His wife did not know where he was working so he missed his case:

It was an amazing way to organise it – I wondered if it affected the outcome of the case. I was very annoyed.
(The outcome was that no evidence was offered on that charge, the offender pleading guilty to other, unrelated matters. The absence of the chief prosecution witness did appear to the researchers to be the main factor contributing to this decision.)

Although it is the Crown Court which organises which cases should be heard when, it is the police officer in the case who bears the burden of the disgruntlement felt by victims and witnesses. Police officers interviewed felt this keenly:

The Crown Court warning system is a pain. They expect us to get in touch with witnesses on four or five occasions and witnesses get fed up.

Complainants get sick to death of it – they get two days' notice and then they move the venue – the complainant gets fed up with you.

We upset a lot of witnesses on this – after a while they say they're not interested then we have to say you've got to go.

There is no doubt that this system of warning witnesses for the Crown Court causes a considerable amount of inconvenience and distress to victims, as well as using a large amount of police manpower in what is often a thankless task. The problem is common to all prosecution witnesses. The prosecution (the police in this instance) are expected to be able to produce their witnesses on whatever date the case is finally listed for trial. The victim is not considered to have any special interest in the proceedings, compared to any other prosecution witness. The court adminstrator's task is a difficult balancing act, juggling available court time, judges, prosecution and defence counsels' prior commitments and witness availability. The priorities seemed to be in that order, with the necessity to utilise to the full courts and judges the major object. The Crown Court have already tried hard (for example, by the introduction of the warned list system) to minimise the number of cases put off at the last moment and hence to reduce the inconvenience caused to witnesses, the defendant and counsel. If the considerable problems still being caused to witnesses, and particularly victims, are to be lessened, then it is probably necessary to reconsider who should be seen as most important and whose convenience is most to be considered. Should lists be organised for those whose profession it is to attend court, or for those on whose evidence the courts rely?

Waiting at court

None of the courts which our victims attended were designed with the needs of victims and witnesses uppermost in mind. There was usually only one general waiting area for everyone – defendants, defence witnesses, prosecution witnesses, victims, lawyers and any of the general public that wished to attend the court hearings. In some, particularly some of the Crown Courts, these areas were large and it was possible for victims to wait at some distance from the defendants in their case. In others, everyone waiting was squashed together standing up in small corridors. Seating was usually limited and consisted of wooden benches. These were often no facilities for obtaining a hot drink, let alone a snack, and certainly no facilities for children. In these surroundings, victims might have to wait hours to be called and, in the Crown Court, days.

The court staff themselves had some appreciation of the problems that faced victims and witnesses. There were some plans to rebuild or redesign some of the worst courts in our study, but these have been subject to spending cuts:

It's very poor – only a few benches. We want witness waiting rooms and a room for nappy changing and tea facilities. (Northampton magistrates' court)

You would be perfectly justified in saying conditions are appalling. In the new courts, when they're built, things will be better – more space, individual rooms for privacy, seats, first aid and refreshments. (Coventry magistrates' court)

Victims themselves complained primarily about their forced proximity to defendants and the fear and distress this caused:

I waited in the same place as him – no-one cared.

The defendants sat in the same place – it was ridiculous.

We were sitting with the defendants next to us, they were talking about the case – they would have liked to talk to us.

Indeed, on two occasions, attempted intimidation of the victim took place:

The defendants were trying to influence me – everyone's mixed up there – it didn't make any difference to what I said – but there was no supervision of them – they're violent.

A defence witness came down and said the other victim had come – he wanted a fight.

The major impression of victims was that of a cold, cheerless wait with nowhere to have a cup of tea and no possibility of going out to find one. Those victims who had been called to court to give evidence were usually confused and worried about what they had to do. Such surroundings are not conducive to any witness giving a clear and accurate account of what happened months before.

For victims who had decided to come to a pretrial appearance (and managed to find out where and when it was) and for those victims whose assailants pleaded guilty at the trial, the experience at court was even worse. The victim had no accepted role. Because he was not essential to the proceedings, no place was provided for him:

> I sat at the back of a small court – it was very unsatisfactory, very uncomfortable – full of lawyers with their briefcases all standing up. I didn't feel welcome. They say you can go in but when you get there there's not enough room. It was worth going – but for the waiting and the discomfort.

> The police should have told me when the appearance was. They treat me just as a witness but I'm more than that. I went – I waited in the corridor – it was very unsatisfactory – terrible – nowhere to sit. It was worth going to court – at least I knew what they said. But it's not very nice sitting in the corridor staring at (the offender) and they don't really let you know when it's going into court.

In this atmosphere, about half the victims who were going to give evidence were allowed to read their statements before the case started. They were, however, rarely allowed more than about 10 minutes to read what was often five or six pages and the conditions were hardly ideal. As we mentioned in Chapter 3, victims were not allowed to see their statement before the morning of the court hearing. The distressed and confused state in which some flipped through their statement at court did not allow them to remind themselves of the details of an event that occurred a long time previously and on which they were about to be subjected to possibly searching cross-examination.

This type of account of magistrates' and Crown Courts has been documented before in studies of defendants' experiences (for example by Carlen 1976; Shapland 1981). Defendants, however, usually have a defence solicitor or defence counsel to explain to them what is happening, when the case will come on and what they will have to do in court. Even more important, somone checks that they are there and the case is announced in their name. Victims have no one specifically acting for them. Police officers, prosecution solicitors and prosecution counsel are at court to represent the State, not the victim. Any explanation they may give the victim about what may happen in court is not a mandatory duty but a kindness, and did not often occur. Victims were not looked out for and not told when the case was coming on, unless they were specifically required to give evidence. The experience of victims waiting outside the courtroom was one of feeling superfluous and ignored.

In the witness box

Most commentators have stressed the passive nature of the victim in the witness box, replying only to questions put to him, unable to affect the way the case is handled by the professional participants and vilified by the defence with no right of redress (for example, Holmstrom and Burgess 1978). McBarnet (1976), however, has argued that the victim, particularly the victim who is not willing to see the offender prosecuted, may be an active partner in the trial, himself posing problems for the prosecution and the court. Several of the victims in our study gave evidence at court. A final interview was conducted with 19 who had given evidence at the Crown Court, 15 who had given evidence at a magistrates' court trial, three who were called as witnesses at full committal proceedings at the magistrates' court and two who gave evidence at the juvenile court.

The constraints documented by Holmstrom and Burgess in their study of rape victims applied to many victims in our study, notably in the ways in which victims felt their answers were cut short by lawyers, they were not able to say exactly what they meant and they could not say what they felt was relevant in a question-and-answer framework. There was also attempted vilification by the defence in trying to cast doubt on the victim's role in the offence. Not all victims, however, felt that they had been vanquished by these techniques: 'It's how you answer – you have to be honest but not give them a loophole.' Although 12 victims felt that it was difficult to say what they wanted to say, many found a way to get it across, even though this was not the way in which they would normally speak:

Keep it short – don't give or take anything.

You keep your cool and you're all right.

You are restricted – there's pressure on you to conform to a certain format.

As McBarnet found, this pressure was seen to come from the prosecution as well as the defence, although most found the defence slightly more difficult:

I had problems with all of them.

Both were against me.

You're in a verbal straightjacket but the prosecution was a bit more sympathetic.

Such problems were not restricted to the rape and indecent assault victims in the study. Physical assault victims noticed them as well. The perceived severity of questioning seemed to depend more on the individual circumstances of the case and on the victim's personality and expectations than on the nature of the offence, although the sample is too small to provide conclusive evidence.

Where the defence were trying to trip the witness up, again many victims considered that they had dealt with it reasonably well:

The defence was trying to prove exactly the opposite – he was trying to blame me. I think I dealt with them OK.

The defence had everything back to front. I had to correct him – he said thank you. He'd got it all wrong – I said I think you'd better bring your papers over here – he did!

Most victims expected the defence to put forward some (false) story and did not blame them for saying what the victims considered completely wrong or for trying to make the victim out to be a liar:

Obviously he was trying to get me to say something wrong.

He did what he was paid to do – get his client off – but he didn't make a good job of it.

It was a cock and bull story – but what I expected.

On the other hand, victims were not so satisfied overall with the prosecutor. Some commented on his apparent disinterest in the case. Others complained that he did not seem well-prepared, did not emphasise the right points or did not protest when the defence was casting doubt on the victim's story.

The judge or magistrates were in general considered to be good. One of the victims in a rape trial went further: 'He was a scream – he made me laugh – he was very nice.' Of the 33 victims that felt able to give a rating on the judge (the others not being present at the summing-up), 72 per cent were very satisfied or satisfied. Even where the victim was displeased with the way the prosecution or defence had conducted the case or where the result was an acquittal, the judge or magistrate often did not come in for criticism.

The present study, from the victim's viewpoint, suggests that most victims do experience problems in adjusting their normal manner of speech to the demands of giving evidence, but that they take active steps to get over these difficulties and in general feel they have succeeded. This was as true of the few victims that came to court determined that the defendant should be acquitted (and were treated as hostile witnesses) as of the majority who wanted the defendant convicted. So, the victim does feel manipulated by prosecution and defence, who use the structure of formal questioning to present their own view of the offence. However, the victim's problems are not all the result of courtroom tactics. They can also be seen as difficulties facing all lay participants in the courtroom, exacerbated by the nature of the 'ideal victim' portrayed in the substantive and procedural criminal law.

The evidential question-and-answer format compels the witness to follow the sequential description of the event used by the questioner (in the legal sphere, usually a chronological one). Even prompts to witnesses to get them to expand on an answer will often adopt this chronology ('And what happened next?'). Other ways of associating material, such as by logical connections or by cause and effect, may not be allowed. Similarly, witnesses may be confined to short answers ('Just answer yes or no'). They will not be allowed to turn the question back onto the questioner ('But what would you have done?'). Attempts may be made to rouse them, but expressions of anger are discouraged both by the judge and by the surroundings. They will not be sure whether to attempt the rather antiquated and artificial manner of address used by the judge and counsel ('Your Honour'). In general, witnesses, whether for the prosecution or for the defence, will not be able to tell their own story in the way they would tell it in their everyday lives. Courtroom discourse is a specialised art. It is not surprising that the victims in our study were actively aware that they were changing the way in which they spoke.

The problem of a specialised discourse is one common to all witnesses. The victim, however, may also be affected by the image of the 'ideal victim' embodied in the criminal law. The word 'victim' itself is in fact rarely mentioned in English criminal law, either in the common law or in statute. Despite the necessity in all personal property or violent offences of specifying the existence of a 'person' against whom these offences are directed, that 'person' remains shadowy and indistinct and is not accorded a status other than that of a witness. However, the criminal law does address some attributes that these 'persons' are expected to have in its ideas, for example, about provocation.

It is not possible here to describe the intricate operation of the idea of provocation in all the places that it occurs in the criminal law. We shall merely indicate its general nature to illustrate the image of the 'ideal' victim which appears to be present. Provocation by the victim is seen as mitigating (or, sometimes, as in the case of murder, entirely negating) the offence. The 'ideal' victim should, therefore, be passive. He should be inert, playing no part in any action prior to or during the commission of the offence. This aspect is reinforced by the tendency of the criminal justice process to consider discrete episodes – to pull out a segment of time and to look only at the action occurring within it. The criminal law is much more time-circumscribed in its concerns than are everyday ideas of causation. Particularly in adversarial systems, such as the English one, there is little allowance in the 'ideal' case for presentation of prior relationships or contacts between victim and offender in evidence. The 'ideal' or 'innocent' victim is passive, impinged upon, has only interacted with the offender during the short period of time encompassing the commission of the offence and has not taken any action during that time (Jaywardene and Jaywardene 1982). Where these conditions are not fulfilled (or where it is not possible by emphasising particular aspects of the case to present the victim in this way), there appears to be a tendency in practice to switch to an idea of the provocative victim – the victim as sharing blame for the offence. The 'ideal' victim and offender are white and black, not different shades of grey.

Unfortunately, the everyday conduct and behaviour which is examined in a criminal trial does not conform to these expectations of the victim and the offender. The incident may be difficult to disentangle, the case may have a long history and the victim may have played an active part. This is particularly likely in offences of violence, including sexual assaults. Here, such a pattern is statistically normal. A case similar to the image of the criminal law would be abnormal. There is an intrinsic tension in the operation of the criminal law between its image of the 'ideal' victim and the nature of the cases examined. The difficulties faced in trying offences of violence may stem from the particular image of the victim adopted in the criminal law. There is a tendency to make the conception of the offence primary and not to consider the roles of victims or offenders in behaviour which typically surrounds the offence.

This portrayal of the victim as a shadowy, passive, innocent figure partaking in a discrete encounter with the offender is the image that the prosecutor must try to produce if the defendant is to be convicted of any offence carrying that specification. The defence will be trying to break down that image. A 'real' victim will be caught between the image and his own experience. Through the nature of the criminal justice system and the criminal law itself, victims will experience difficulties, additive to those faced by all witnesses. The victims in our study, especially the sexual assault victims, expected some problem in being able to tell their story and in being able to convey their idea of their identity as victim. They took active steps to accomplish this, mostly to their own satisfaction. They thereby became potential problems for the prosecutor, requiring careful management. It was that management, and victims' views of their overall performance, that made the prosecutor the most unsatisfactory courtroom participant as far as the victims were concerned.

Relations with the prosecutor

At court, the case was normally prosecuted, not by the police, but by a prosecuting solicitor or prosecuting counsel acting for the police. Victims who did attend court, whether to give evidence or just to watch the proceedings, found that prosecutors and police officers did not live up to their expectations. Victims who attended but did not have to give evidence were not sure whether they could go into court and were not helped out of their indecision by prosecution or police. Indeed, one victim was phoned up subsequent to his attendance by the police and told that the case was nothing to do with him – it was in the hands of the police. There is, of course, nothing to prevent a victim attending every court appearance should he wish to, though the only occasion that a victim need attend court is if he is called to give evidence.

Even if a victim is called to court to give evidence, the defendant may decide to plead guilty on the morning of the trial, so that no evidence is needed. Unless victims are informed that they can go into the courtroom and hear what is said, they may remain waiting outside in ignorance:

I wasn't called – they told me after two hours I wasn't going to be called. I felt very annoyed. They came out first and said he'd plead guilty but they didn't say I wouldn't have to appear. It was only when the judge was summing up (passing sentence) that a policeman said I could go in.

I didn't know what was going to happen, then a police officer came over and said they may plead guilty – hang on, you might be needed. But we had to ask him all the time. We waited when it started – we didn't know what was going on – then a woman came out and said fill in witness expense forms and go home but you can go in and watch the ending. I thought that was very badly organised. She was ambiguous – I would have liked to have heard the whole thing. Couldn't an usher or police officer have sat us down and explained it beforehand?

If victims do attend court, then, once it has been established that they are not going to be needed as a witness, there should be some means by which they are able to go into the courtroom and hear the whole of the proceedings, should they wish to. At the moment, witnesses are the responsibility of the police officer in the case, but once a victim stops being a potential witness (or if he attends court out of interest), he is no one's responsibility. If the police officer in the case is not there (if, say, it is known there will be an adjournment), then the only people that could help victims would be the prosecutor or court ushers.

If the victim is to give evidence, then he is likely to be worried about what he will have to do in court. The victims in our study felt it would have been very beneficial if someone had explained to them what would happen (which the police very rarely did) and if they had been introduced to the prosecutor beforehand:

I was nervous, frightened because I hadn't been to a trial before. They didn't try and help me in any way – the prosecution solicitor should have explained to me what was going to happen – it would have been easier. I didn't even know there was a solicitor until it started.

Most victims did not meet the prosecutor beforehand at all. This was not an oversight. Prosecution counsel are not allowed by the rules of etiquette (Bolton 1971) to talk to witnesses prior to the case. The prosecution solicitors we interviewed sometimes felt that it might compromise their independence if they were seen to speak to victims (see also Johnson 1977; McConville and Baldwin 1981):

I only see them personally if I need clarification of the evidence. It's exceptional for me. The prosecution is more open to criticism for stage-managing its case. It's legitimate for the defence, not us. (Northampton prosecuting solicitor)

I don't think it would be a good idea to talk to witnesses before the case – we do try to be impartial and if you meet the person to any extent you might find your feelings joining in. (Coventry prosecuting solicitor)

Again, where charges were to be dropped and the victim was present at court, it would seem the ideal opportunity to tell the victim what was happening and to consult with him. That opportunity was not usually taken. It seems extraordinary that highly trained, professional lawyers should fear that their independence or their ability to present a case according to their position as officers of the court could be compromised by seeing and speaking briefly to someone whose statement they have already read and whose testimony they will be hearing. It may be true that seeing a victim has more impact than reading a statement – but trials are based on oral, not written, evidence. Again, hearing from a witness may bring into sharper relief the potential conflicts between State and victim – but these are intrinsic to any centralised prosecution system. If the fear is that prosecutors will be thought to have coached witnesses, then it is strange that such charges are not levelled against the police in England or procurators fiscal in Scotland. As we move towards the adoption of an independent prosecution system, perhaps also we could try to produce a more human and humane system for victims, in which it would be normal for prosecutors to introduce themselves to victims and commonplace for victims to be informed of progress, consulted about dropping charges and brought into the courtroom to hear the case.

The few victims who did meet the prosecutor beforehand commented on his apparent disinterest in the case:

He wasn't particularly interested – he said at the start that he thought the DPP was wrong in saying the case should go ahead.

He seemed to think it was lost before it started.

In general, one has the impression of victims being isolated and confused at court, not knowing what they may be required to do or what they are allowed to do. They do not realise what is happening round them and it is rare for anyone to explain it to them. Police officers, when they were present, did seem to make some effort. Prosecutors did not see it as their job, a finding similar to that of Kelly (1982) for rape victims in the United States. Her victims felt they were denied participation in and information about what they saw as 'their' case. Some also felt their interests were not being represented by prosecutors. In sum, her victims objected to the present workings of the criminal justice system, one which they found, to their surprise, was not geared to their perspectives. What they wanted was more contact with the prosecutor.

In our study, the determinant of victim satisfaction was how the victim was treated by the prosecutor, rather than what the prosecutor said in court. The lack of attention paid to victims' needs at court is perhaps best exemplified by the comment of one police officer victim: 'there's all the probation and after-care for the offenders but none for the victim. That's wrong – we've got the criminal justice system the wrong way round.'

Witness expenses and return of property

There is considerable inconvenience involved for victims who attend court. This may include travel costs, loss of earnings, difficulty in finding replacement staff at work or problems in finding someone to look after children. The total financial cost of being a victim over the whole period until the trial, including going to the police station and attending court, can add up to over £100 for many victims. The only part of this which can be recouped are those costs involved in attending court to give evidence which are allowable as witness expenses (travel expenses and some loss of earnings). Nearly half of the victims who did claim these witness expenses were unsatisfied, either because they were not allowed their total loss of earnings or because the cheque took so long to arrive.

Any property held by the police as possible evidence in the trial also tended to take a long time to be returned to the victim. On some occasions the victims had themselves to go to the police station in order to reclaim their property. Clothes sent for forensic examination were sometimes damaged because pieces had been cut out as samples or because stains had soaked in. No victim knew how to claim compensation for any of these clothes.

Outcomes and sentences

The majority of cases in the study resulted in guilty pleas (66 per cent – see Table 4.2). In addition, the offences against two victims were taken into consideration during the guilty plea hearings of those offenders who were charged with similar offences committed on different occasions. Eighty-four per cent of victims had at least one offender convicted of a charge relating to the assault on them or that offence taken into consideration. There was little difference between Coventry and Northampton victims in the outcome of the case.

When considering sentencing, we must remember that the final charge on which the defendant was sentenced was often not the same as the one initially recorded or charged. In fact, as we saw above, it was quite common for charges to be reduced in the passage of the case

Table 4.2 Outcomes on main charge relating to victim (numbers of victim cases)[1]

	Coventry	Northampton
Magistrates' court guilty plea	34	22
Magistrates' court not guilty plea defendant convicted	7	8
Magistrates' court not guilty plea defendant acquitted	0	4
Magistrates' court not guilty plea directed acquittal	1	2
Juvenile court guilty plea	5	3
Juvenile court not guilty plea defendant convicted	2	0
Juvenile court not guilty plea defendant acquitted	0	0
Juvenile court not guilty plea directed acquittal	0	0
Crown Court guilty plea	24	20
Crown Court not guilty plea defendant convicted	5	5
Crown Court not guilty plea defendant acquitted	7	3
Crown Court not guilty plea directed acquittal	1	0
Taken into consideration	2	0
No evidence offered	4	2
Discharged at full committal proceedings	1	0
Not yet tried	0	1
Committals for sentence to the Crown Court	2	1
Appeals to Crown Court – upheld	0	1
– dismissed or withdrawn	4	0

[1]Where there was more than one charge relating to that victim, the most serious charge is shown. Where there was more than one offender, and those offenders were tried at different courts, the highest court is shown (Crown Court rather than magistrates' court or juvenile court). Where one offender pleaded not guilty and another guilty, on the same charge, the case is shown as a not guilty plea, since this affects the victim most directly.

through the courts (though it was uncommon for the victim to be informed of this). The defendant might also have been sentenced at the same time for other, unrelated offences. These offences might have affected the nature of the total sentence and, hence, the sentence on the charges relating to the victim. The sentences passed on the charges relating to the victims in the study (Table 4.3) do not necessarily convey the total sentences passed nor the sentences as they related to the charges originally recorded by the police (which may have been the only information on charging available to the victim). Table 4.3 does, however, seem to represent the basis on which victims reacted to the sentences passed, apart from those victims who were very unhappy about charges being dropped. Some offenders were also ordered to pay compensation to the victim. Twenty-six victims were awarded compensation orders, fifteen for their injuries alone, six for damage caused to their property or clothing and five for both injuries and property damage. The size of the sums awarded, the reactions of victims and the difficulties facing the courts in awarding compensation to assault victims will be discussed in Chapter 8.

Reactions to sentences

When they were first interviewed, victims were asked what sentence they would like to see the offender given for the offence against them. Of the 134 victims whose offenders were subsequently sentenced, only 40 per cent thought at that time that the offender should receive an immediate custodial sentence. The other answers ranged over all the non-custodial alternatives, with a substantial proportion of 'don't knows'. Victims did not seem to be very punitive even at this early stage in the case. This represents what they thought the offender should be given as a sentence – what they expected the courts to give was often very much lower.

One may compare the sentence victims thought the offender should get with the sentence he actually received on the main charge relating to the victim, using the categories in Table 4.3 which have been ranked from left to right in approximate order of severity of sentence. This shows that in 43 cases victims thought the offender should receive a more severe sentence than he finally received, in 32 the wished-for sentence and the actual sentence were identical and in 23 cases the offender actually received a more severe sentence than the victim thought he should receive.

When victims were told the sentence, if necessary by the researchers at the final interview, they were asked for their reaction. Overall, 47 per cent of victims thought the sentence was right, 38 per cent thought it was not right and 15 per cent did not know. All the sexual assault victims disapproved of the final sentence and all the robbery victims approved.

Table 4.3 Sentences given on the main charge against the victim according to the offence convicted (numbers of victim cases)[1]

Offence convicted	Bind-over	Absolute or conditional discharge	Fine plus compensation to victim			Probation or supervision order	Community service order	Suspended sentence	Suspended sentence + fine	Borstal	Prison or Detention Centre				Hospital order
			Up to £50	Up to £100	Over £100						Up to 6mths	Up to 1yr	Up to 2yrs	Over 2yrs	
Common assault	0	0	1	0	0	0	0	0	0	0	2	0	0	0	0
s. 51	0	0	1	0	0	0	0	0	0	0	0	0	0	0	0
s. 47	3	2	12	7	7	4	3	2	5	3	10	4	0	0	1
s. 20	0	3	5	6	2	2	1	7	3	2	7	3	1	0	0
s. 18	0	0	0	0	0	0	0	0	0	0	0	1	0	0	0
Robbery or assault with intent to rob	0	0	1	0	1	0	0	0	0	3	0	0	3	2	0
Indecent assault	0	0	0	0	0	3	0	0	1	0	0	0	0	0	0
Rape or attempted rape	0	0	0	0	0	0	0	0	0	0	0	0	0	0	0
Affray	1	0	0	0	0	0	1	0	0	0	1	0	0	0	0
Offensive weapon	0	0	1	0	0	0	0	0	0	0	2	0	0	0	0
Breach of the peace	4	0	0	0	0	0	0	0	0	0	0	0	0	0	0
TOTAL	8	5	21	13	10	9	5	9	9	8	22	8	4	2	1

[1]If there was more than one offender, the defendant convicted of the more serious charge or given the most severe sentence has been used. The two cases in which the offence against the victim was taken into consideration are not included.

The views of the physical assault victims were more mixed.

Those that disagreed with the sentence mostly thought it should be more severe – an immediate prison sentence rather than a suspended one or a larger fine instead of a smaller one. These included all the sexual assault victims. Some, however, would have preferred a different non-custodial penalty, such as a community service order or probation. Some complained about the lack of compensation for themselves, feeling that the victim should receive something rather than the State receiving the benefits of all the monetary penalties (see Chapter 8).

It is difficult to draw conclusions from these reactions of victims. Agreement or disagreement with a sentence depends on the nature of the actual sentence imposed. As can be seen from Table 4.3, there was a considerable range of sentencing for each type of charge. This reflects the variety of types of offence that can be subsumed under each legal definition, as well as the variety of circumstances of offenders. One might expect, however, the reaction of a victim whose offender was convicted of wounding or assault inflicting grievous bodily harm (s. 20), but sentenced to an absolute or conditional discharge or a small fine, to be that the sentence was too lenient, particularly if the original charge recorded by the police was s. 18. Victims did feel that some of the sentences for some of the more serious physical assault offences were very low, especially if the offence was committed in a public place or had a domestic background. Magistrates' courts did seem to be sentencing these offences rather more leniently than the Crown Court. In the magistrates' court a fine was the most likely result for a s. 47 or s. 20 assault; but, in the Crown Court, similar offences often attracted custodial penalties.

Victims, unless they are present during the whole of a trial and sentence, will not have the amount of information on the offender that the sentencer has. Their view of what the sentence should be can only be based on the offence itself and any further details, such as previous convictions, that the police may have told them. However, even when victims thought the sentence was too lenient, their proposed alternative was rarely outside the range of sentences that might be thought appropriate for that type of offence by the courts. The present study has confirmed what Maguire (1982) found for victims of burglary and what is suggested in the British Crime Study (Hough and Mayhew 1983) – that victims are not the punitive 'hang them, flog them, lock them up for ever' people that popular myth suggests.

Knowledge of outcomes and sentences

For some victims, the case ended in a trial, with the victim giving evidence. Whether the offender was convicted or acquitted, the victim was usually in court for this outcome and so heard the result. For others, the majority, the offender decided to plead guilty. No trial and no evidence from the victim was necessary and the victim was unlikely to attend the final hearing of the case. He could not learn of the outcome of the case (whether the offender was convicted or not) by being there. Even when victims were present at the verdict, sentencing of any convicted offenders might not take place then, but be adjourned for the preparation of reports. These victims might not attend the subsequent sentencing appearance. Opportunities for the victim to learn of the outcome and sentence by being present in court were, in practice, very limited. The victims found it difficult to learn of the date of the final appearance, as we saw above; they might not be able to take the time to attend unless they were required to give evidence; or they might not wish to attend.

They did, however, very much wish to know what the outcome and sentence was. Not surprisingly, this was the single most important item of information. But, in practice, several victims in our study had no idea of the outcome and many more had only a partial knowledge of the sentence passed. Their sources of information were varied: the police, the newspapers, the offender, friends and neighbours. Police practice in telling the victim the outcome of the case differed in the two police forces in the study, and this produced some differences in the experiences of Coventry and Northampton victims.

In Coventry, of the 50 cases in which there was a guilty plea and a final interview with the victim, 90 per cent did find out eventually about the outcome of the case (and all but one were correct on this). The remaining five victims knew nothing about their case having been tried until they were told by the researchers at the final interview (see Table 4.4). Those told by the police might have to wait a considerable time before being told (several weeks or even months), and some had found out from other sources before this. Five had even telephoned the police themselves to find out what had happened.

Turning to knowledge about the actual sentences, 92 per cent of the victims whose offenders had been sentenced on a charge relating to them (or had the offence taken into consideration) knew something about the sentence passed. Only 67 per cent, however, knew all the salient details of the sentence. (Salient details were defined as the overall sentence (total fines, total length of imprisonment etc.), the sentence on the charge(s) relating to the victim and the amount of any compensation awarded to the victim. They did not include details of costs, legal aid contribution or any other compensation or sentence on any other charges.) Only 48 per cent of those not present at court themselves had received information about the sentence from the police. Many of these were not given sufficient details of the sentence and the delay before they were told ranged up to four months, with the average being about

Table 4.4 Ways of learning about outcomes and sentences (number of victims with final interviews)

	No knowledge	Present at court	Police (eventually)	Newspaper	Offender	Friends	Magistrates' court	Total
Coventry								
Outcomes (guilty pleas)	5	14	21	7	2	1	0	50
All the salient details of sentence	21	9	18	9	0	6	1	64
Northampton								
Outcomes (guilty pleas)	3	11	8	11	1	4	0	38
All the salient details of sentence	25	11	5	4	1	2	0	48

one month. Eighty-four per cent felt they should have been informed of the sentence by the police.

In Northampton, the position was even worse. Ninety-two per cent did find out eventually that their case had been heard, but only 68 per cent knew the correct outcome. Eight were informed by the police, but four of these did not know the full outcome. Three of the 15 who discovered the outcome from the local newspaper or a friend were in some way incorrect. As regards sentence, the most important source of information for those who did not attend court was not the police but the local newspaper. Only 48 per cent of victims knew all the salient details of the sentence. Victims still wished for official notification, however. Ninety-two per cent of Northampton victims who were not present at court felt that they should have received some official notification, 77 per cent seeing this as the responsibility of the police and 15 per cent that of the courts.

At that time, the policy of the West Midlands Police Force, of which Coventry formed part, was that victims should always be informed of the outcome of the case (including any sentence). This might be done at court, if the victim was present, or by a personal visit or telephone call from the officer in the case. The fact that the victim had been informed had to be written on the police file before the case could be closed. This notification might take some time, as the officer in the case would not receive the file back (in order to notify the victim and return any property) until other administrative procedures had been completed. There would be several weeks delay during this administrative step, though not the two months or more that some victims experienced. Supervising officers and, indeed, officers in the case themselves, said that they regarded this notification of the victim as important:

Notifying the victim is the best public relations exercise we can carry out – especially when we're successful.

The complainant should be made aware of the outcome whatever it is – in most cases they are. It's an oversight or sloppy administration if they're not – bad supervision.

For 27 of the 36 Coventry victims who were not present at court, the police file was marked that the complainant had been informed. However, in only 21 cases (including the five victims who telephoned the police themselves) did the victim say that the police had informed them of the outcome. The information was not always full – victims were often not told that the offender had been convicted of a lesser offence than that with which he was originally charged. All the victims said that they would have liked to have been told the full details by the police.

There appeared to be doubt whether there was a specific policy in the Northamptonshire police force at that time as to whether victims should be informed of the outcome of their case. It appeared to depend on the wishes of the Chief Superintendant of the division and the initiative of the officer in the case. No written evidence was required on the police file. As we noted above, significantly fewer victims were told the outcome and sentence of their case in Northampton compared to Coventry. This would seem to reflect police policy.

However, even a policy of informing victims, if it is to be done by a personal visit by the officer in the case, does not seem to produce results. In Coventry, where both policy and supervisory officers stressed the necessity of informing victims, a majority of victims who were not present at court said they had not been informed of the sentence. In Northampton, only a small minority were told. Victims did want very much to be told both the outcome and the sentence. The vast majority placed this responsibility on the police. Where the police did not meet these expectations, victims felt considerable distress and annoyance:

I think the police should have told me. I had to ask.

Following the rules I should have been told – I never have been – I would have liked to have been told. (police officer victim)

I'm angry with the courts and the police. I should have been told.

Studies of victims of other offences have also pointed out the unfavourable reactions of victims to non-notification of outcome and sentence by the police. Maguire's (1982) burglary victims complained that after the first few days, they had heard nothing further about the case. Only 24 per cent had received any notification of police progress. Howley's (1982) victims also criticised police who did not report developments. In America, Kelly's (1982) rape victims wanted both information and consultation.

Absence of information, both at the investigation and at the outcome stage, seems to be felt very keenly by victims. This need was obviously not being met by the police in our study. If the aim is to inform all victims so that their initial satisfaction with the police is to be maintained, it seems that even policy orders and supervisory officers' wishes are not enough. A more foolproof system will need to be devised (see Chapter 5).

The press and the courts
The press play an important role for victims in giving them some immediate information about the results of their case. As we have seen above, for some victims, the press may be their only source for this knowledge. The local newspapers in both towns did give extensive coverage to court appearances for offences in our study. Initial appearances might not be reported, but the majority of outcomes were

covered, whether there was a guilty or a not guilty plea. More than 70 per cent of victims said that they had seen a report of their case.

Victims were less likely to be displeased by newspaper reports of court cases than they were by reports of the offence itself or subsequent police enquiries. Victims saw newspapers merely as the agent through which information on the court appearance was transmitted and so less responsible for any 'errors' or insinuations in the report than as regards reports of the original offence. Even so, 44 per cent of victims who had seen a court report said they were dissatisfied, mainly because they felt it had been written in a sensationalist way, rather than as a 'factual' report. As we saw in Chapter 3, complaints about incident reports concerned the very fact of there being any publicity at all. Complaints about court reports were not about the fact of publicity, but about the accuracy of reporting.

Court proceedings are open to the public. The reporter is describing events that he has seen and heard first-hand (although those events are themselves reconstructions of the original incident according to the various perceptions of the witnesses). Depictions that the victim may not appreciate may be the 'fault' of either witness or reporter. For victims, press reporting of their case is a mixed blessing – appreciated for its much-needed information (even though not the whole result may be given), but sometimes denigrated for its portrayal of the victim and his role in the offence.

Satisfaction with the courts

After the outcome of the case, victims were asked to rate their overall satisfaction with the courts (on a five-point scale, from very satisfied to very unsatisfied). Of those victims that felt able to give such a rating (several felt that they had no idea of what the courts had actually done, since they had not been informed of the progress of their case through the courts), 6 per cent were very satisfied, 47 per cent satisfied, 9 per cent neutral, 25 per cent unsatisfied and 13 per cent very unsatisfied. There was no significant difference between Coventry and Northampton victims, nor over different types of case. Differences in satisfaction ratings and the reasons given by victims concerned both the outcome and sentence and the progress of the case through the courts. Victims tended to ascribe some of the prosecution's decisions to the courts. The courts were seen as being under the control of the judge or magistrates entirely, such that any decision mentioned for the first time in the courtroom by prosecution or judge was seen as the responsibility of the judiciary (the defendant and his legal advisors, however, were not seen as being under anyone's control). Thus, victims were significantly less satisfied where the charge relating to the offence against the victim was reduced during the passage through the courts than where the charges remained the same as those originally recorded by the police (p<.001). Victims' expressed reasons for dissatisfaction included lenient sentencing, not informing the victim of the date of the trial or of the outcome of the case and insufficient warning to attend as a witness in Crown Court cases. On occasions it appeared that, although most victims thought that the police should tell them about the outcome and sentence, some of the blame for this was placed on the courts. The experiences of waiting and of decisions made by prosecutor or sentencer combined to make victims significantly less satisfied with the Crown Court than with the magistrates' court (p<.001).

Although, not surprisingly, victims whose offender was acquitted were significantly less satisfied that those whose offender was convicted after a trial (p<.001), cases with not guilty pleas had higher satisfaction scores than those with guilty pleas (p<.001). It appears to be the verdict rather than the problems of being a witness which caused dissatisfaction. Indeed, victims who were present at court for the outcome of their case were more satisfied than those who were not (p<.001). This increased satisfaction may be due to the greater information that participation brings, to the feeling of being involved in the case, to a greater knowledge of all the factors surrounding the case that the sentencer takes into account or to a better understanding of court procedure. Which is the most important cannot be known on the data from our study. What may be said is that the problems of being a witness do not outweigh the benefits of participation.

The experiences of victims with the courts were dogged by the same lack of information as were their contacts with the police during the investigation of the case. Their opinions of the actual procedures in court, and even of sentencing, were often favourable, whenever they knew anything about what was done. It was the peripherals of the court system – lack of facilities, cramped surroundings, sitting next to the defendant, lack of warning at the Crown Court, inadequate recompense for their costs and, above all, lack of information and knowledge of when the appearance would be and what they would have to do – that caused considerable distress and inconvenience. Most victims did not appear to wish to play a more active decision-making role in the present court system. They did wish to be consulted, particularly on decisions that would make a significant difference to the charges on which the offender would be tried or whether he would be required to face trial on any charges relating to them at all. Most of all, they wanted to be told what they would be expected to do if they had to give evidence and what happened at court if they were not present.

5 Victims, the police and the courts

The decision to prosecute is not a single act, taken at a particular point in time and immutable thereafter. The appearance of a defendant in a courtroom pleading to the charges put to him is the end product of a series of decisions, taken by different actors at different times. It may start with the victim reporting to the police, but it continues through the decisions by the officer in the case to record the crime and to investigate it in particular ways, the deliberations of the police officers supervising that recording and that charging, and the ideas of the police prosecutions department and the prosecutor on how to present the case. Prosecution is a process, occurring over weeks or months, a process in which the victim makes an appearance at different stages, but only plays a peripheral role.

We shall argue in this chapter that victims see their role as continuing throughout this process of prosecution, paralleling that of the police. They wish to follow what is happening and to help where they can, being ready to intervene when they are needed. They expect the police to facilitate this by providing information and by consulting them. In contrast, the police appear to wish to reserve the prosecution process to themselves, requiring victims to jump the hurdle of deciding to press charges as soon as possible and then seeing them as having little further role until the time comes to give evidence in court. The expectations of victims are not matched by those of the police. The result is that victims are not valued and perceive themselves not to be valued.

The role of the courts is different. They are seen by victims as the final adjudicators, pronouncers upon the offender and his offence, not as providing any service for the victim. However, the court surroundings come in for criticism as regards the facilities provided. Victims do consider that, more than other witnesses, they are necessary to the proceedings and so should be accommodated. But their views on judges and magistrates (as opposed to prosecutors) indicate that consideration for the victim in the witness box, or in what is said about the case in court, is a pleasurable surprise, not an expectation.

Satisfaction and expectations
These conclusions about the attitudes of victims to the police and the courts are derived partly from measures of victim satisfaction with the police or court handling of their case. Victim judgements about the

police can be very refined. The actors in the prosecution process may be called, as a whole, 'the police', but they comprise different police officers or prosecutors with different jobs and slightly different perspectives. Victims, equally, make distinctions between the behaviour of all the police officers they meet and have varying expectations of those officers according to the job the victims think they are doing at the time. So, victims will typically make individual comments upon all the officers that they encountered at their first contact with the police and they will also change their opinion as the case progresses:

I'd have liked to have known what was going on – their attitude was great at the time but I'd rather be told so I don't carry on worrying about him coming to court.

Measures of satisfaction with the police or with any other agency are not just opinions created out of thin air at the time of the interview. They are informed by the reactions of victims to events as they experience them and by the expectations of victims as to what they think will and should happen. These expectations are themselves partial products of previous similar experiences and of knowledge amassed from friends, acquaintances and the media. When people were asked to make satisfaction ratings in our study, they appeared to be comparing their memories of the events with their expectations of the action taken by the agency, according to how they themselves perceived their offence. Judgements about satisfaction were judgements of positive or negative confirmation of expectations.

Expectations of different parts of the system were varied and specific to those parts. When victims were asked about their satisfaction with the police handling of their case, their answer was a combination of:

(1) Fine judgements about each police officer encountered, according to their expectations of the particular job he was doing;
(2) Their opinions on and expectations of the result of the case; how they considered the police contributed to that;
(3) Their expectations of the overall police job of catching and prosecuting the offender;
(4) Their general views about the police force as an institution.

Many studies have shown that the public in general is well satisfied with the police and with their mandate (Smith 1983; Jones 1983; Hough and Mayhew 1983). It would not be surprising for our study to find that most victims were satisfied or very satisfied with the police – that would merely replicate the general views held by that public of which our victims form a part. Dissatisfaction, especially growing or general dissatisfaction, would be far more unusual and important. The attitudes of the general public to the courts have not been so well researched.

They appear to be more mixed, particularly as regards sentencing philosophies and levels (Durant *et al.* 1972). Here again, it would be changes in attitudes, rather than attitudes at any one time, that would be the more interesting and important as regards the experience of being a victim in the criminal justice system.

Attitudes to the police

Just as the prosecution process can be seen as a series of decisions, so victim attitudes are also a series of reactions to their continuing experiences. They were asked about their reactions to each police encounter and were also asked to fill in more formal rating scales on the police at each interview. There were three of these formal attitudinal measurements: a rating on a five-point scale of how satisfied they were about the police handling of their case to date (used to provide ratings on the first contact with the police, during the investigation phase, after the outcome of the case and after the end of any compensation proceedings); five-point bipolar adjectival scales about their view of the police in general (used during the investigative phase and after the outcome of the case); and ratings of how well the victims thought the police do their job in general (again on a five-point scale and again used during the investigative phase and after the outcome of the case). Victims were also asked whether they would report a similar offence (or, indeed, other offences) to the police in the future. We must remember that all these methods would, and did, appear artificial to the victims. People are used to giving their impressions and attitudes in words, not to constricting themselves into five-point scales, concentrating on whatever facet the researcher wishes to emphasise and worrying about what assumptions the researcher may be using which they feel they ought to follow. Such measurements are necessary to provide some quantitative means to measure changes in perceptions of the same people over time. The results of any one technique can only be suggestive. If all of them change in the same direction and are consonant with the verbal reasons given by victims for their views, however, the phenomenon is likely to be real, even robust.

As we saw in Chapter 2, the large majority of victims were satisfied or very satisfied with the police performance in their case at the time of the first contact (Table 5.1). As the prosecution process moved through the investigative phase to that of prosecution in the courts itself, the proportion of victims remaining at least satisfied with the police remained high. But, as can be seen very clearly in the table, the proportion of satisfied victims did start steadily dropping. If we compare the ratings the same victims gave at different points in their progress through the system, we can acquire an idea of the changing attitudes of victims towards the police, independent of the numbers of victims taking part in the different interviews. This shows that there was a statistically significant decrease in satisfaction with the police handling of the case in both towns (p<.001 using t-test for paired data from first contact to investigative stage and from investigative stage to outcome in Coventry; p<.05 from investigative stage to committal interview and p<.001 from investigative stage to outcome in Northampton). There was no stage in the process during which victim satisfaction increased – the results show a continuous decline, starting immediately after the initial contact with the police.

Table 5.1   Satisfaction with the police on their performance in the present offence

	Coventry				Northampton			
	Percentage satisfied or very satisfied	Mean rating	S.D.	n	Percentage satisfied or very satisfied	Mean rating	S.D.	n
First contact	78	1.97	0.075	180	89	1.77	0.113	79
First interview	73	2.21	0.079	175	85	1.94	0.114	79
Committal interview	59	2.46	0.221	22	53	2.53	0.327	19
Outcome interview	58	2.60	0.097	144	63	2.37	0.157	63

(Very satisfied = 1;   Very unsatisfied = 5)

When victims were asked to rate how well the police do their job in general on a five-point scale, using the range from 'very satisfied' to 'very unsatisfied', the picture shown was again one of declining satisfaction with the police in both Coventry and Northampton, though in this case it did not attain statistical significance.

The adjectival scales were designed to obtain a more detailed impression of how victims' views of the police changed. The adjectives used were: efficient, impersonal, intimidating, sympathetic, over-worked, oppressive, fair, bureaucratic, pleasant, crooked, helpful and competent. Victims had to rate the police on five-point scales ranging from 'very (adjective)' to 'not at all (adjective)'. The average impressions of the Coventry victims are shown in Figure 5.1. Those of the Northampton victims were almost identical, both in the overall shape of the graph and in the changes in ratings at the different stages of the case. The changes in attitudes were not very positive as far as the police image is concerned. Between the investigative stage and the outcome of the case, the police were seen to become:

– less efficient (p<.01, Coventry)
– less overworked (p<.01, Coventry; p<.05, Northampton)
– more oppressive (p<.01, Coventry)

- less fair (p<.05, Coventry)
- less bureaucratic (p<.05, Northampton)
- more crooked (p<.01, Coventry)
- less helpful (p<.001, Coventry; p<.02, Northampton).

Contact with the police as a victim of violent crime seems to have weakened the image of the conscientious, overworked, efficient but helpful policeman.

In this study, all the formal attitudinal measures point in the same direction – that of a decline in satisfaction and of an increasingly negative view of the police as victims go through the process. Even more surprisingly, it appears that this has broken through into victims' attitudes to the police in general. By the end of the case, only a bare majority of victims were producing the roseate and satisfied view that they held at the beginning and which is typical of the views of the public in general. Nor was this decline a temporary phenomenon. Victims who had applied for any form of compensation and who were re-interviewed between one and two years after the outcome of the case showed the same depressed picture in ratings of satisfaction and still had vivid and detailed memories of what the police had done in their case. There was no sign of recovery in victims' perceptions of the police to the levels just after the offence. These offences of violence were important events in the lives of the victims and shaped their attitudes and expectations for a long time after the legal process had ended.

We saw in Chapters 2 and 3 that police actions at the time of the initial contact were generally satisfactory and that victims were not particularly upset if the police did not catch the offender. What then is the reason for this fairly dramatic decline in satisfaction? What expectation of victims was not being fulfilled? The comments of victims provide a clear answer. Even at the time of the first interview, in the middle of the investigative stage, signs of disillusionment had started to set in. This was almost entirely due to a lack of knowledge of what was happening to the case and, for a few, the consequent feeling that the police did not care and were not doing anything –that the police were ignoring both the offence and the victim.

In the first interview, 51 per cent of victims spontaneously mentioned that they wished the police would tell them more about what was going on. In contrast, most were pleased with what they did know and with the procedures in which they had participated:

My own complaint is that they should have the decency to let me know what's going on.

I'm satisfied with what they've done – they got everything sorted out fast. I'm very unsatisfied with not hearing – they should have the decency to write –it's not my place to do so.

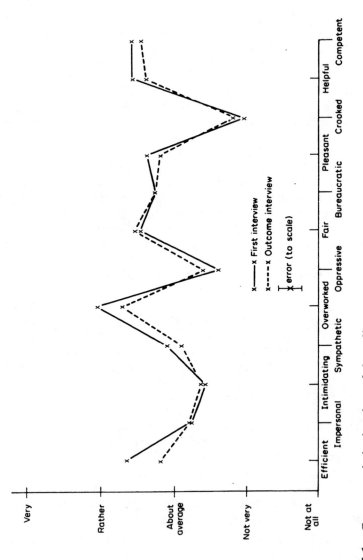

Figure 5.1   Coventry victims' ratings of the police

In 20 per cent of all cases in Coventry (though only in 7 per cent in Northampton), this lack of information had led to such disillusionment that victims felt the police were doing little or nothing about their case:

They've forgotten about it.

Nothing – it's probably stuck in a file.

It's just another case that's forgotten

At the committal interview and at the interview after the outcome of the case, the picture was similar. Lack of information about the case was the prime reason for dissatisfaction:

They should have let me know. I haven't been kept informed about it at all.

I wouldn't say they've handled it very well at all – I haven't heard from them since the statement. I think I as the victim concerned should have known what was going on.

Up to the bloke's arrest I was very satisfied – they were pretty good, then they didn't tell me anything. So I suppose you'd have to put unsatisfied.

At the beginning they were good and sympathetic but afterwards there was no contact. I don't want to know every 10 minutes but let me know I'm not needed at court and what the sentence was. Someone should have told me if I'd bothered to report it.

Apart from not being notified – that would have helped – eased it a bit.

I'm very annoyed – a two minute phone call would do to tell us when the case is on. If they want help they should look after the people who do help them.

Subgroups of victims did, obviously, differ from each other as to their satisfaction with the police. Sexual assault victims, rather surprisingly, were more satisfied than physical assault victims ($p<.001$ in both towns). We thought that this might be due to the concentration in physical assault cases of victims who knew the offender (assaults by a friend or family member) and of cases where the police or victim was unwilling to proceed. Both these factors were associated with greater dissatisfaction with the police handling of the case ($p<.001$ in both towns). It might also have been due to differences in perceptions between male and female victims. We performed a multiple regression analysis, including the variables sex of victim, type of offence, whether the victim knew the offender and whether there was disagreement between police and victim on proceeding with the case. This showed that the type of offence (sexual assault versus physical assaults and robberies) determined the level of satisfaction with the police independently of the other factors (although all the others, except sex of victim, remained significant). In Northampton, in fact, the type of offence was the most significant of these factors in the analysis.

In Coventry and Northampton at that time, therefore, sexual assault victims were more satisfied with the police than physical assault or robbery victims. The clue to this finding again lies in the care taken with victims after the first contact. Both Coventry and Northampton police officers had read and accepted the adverse publicity on police treatment of rape victims. Many tried consciously to be helpful to sexual assault victims, to keep in touch with them and to keep them informed of exactly what was happening in the case, especially if there was any likelihood of them having to give evidence. This was reflected in the appreciative comments of these victims. The victims were being treated and being valued according to their expectations.

These sexual assault victims were, however, those whose offences had been accepted and recorded as crimes by the police. We cannot say anything about the treatment of those whose offences were not recorded. Equally, it is not necessarily true to say that this relatively satisfactory picture in these police forces may be present elsewhere. Chambers and Millar (1983) have shown the distress of their Scottish sexual assault victims at their questioning and treatment by, in particular, CID officers.

Disagreement over prosecution was another major reason for decreased satisfaction with the police in our study. So, victims who did not want the offence reported or who were doubtful (see Chapter 2) were less satisfied than victims who wanted the offence reported (both $p < .001$). Equally, victims of cases in which either the police or the victims themselves were unwilling to prosecute were significantly less satisfied than victims in cases where both pressed for prosecution (both $p < .001$). These findings do reflect on the police handling of the case itself, rather than on the way in which the police treated the victim. They go to the heart of the potential disputes between victim and police concerning police decision-making on prosecution.

We saw in Chapter 2 that the police tend to ask (even put pressure on) victims to press charges at a very early stage. The police wish victims to show active support for prosecution as soon as possible. This support will usually be put in a written form in the statement the victim makes. A verbal decision may be requested at the first contact with the police, within minutes of the offence. The role of 'pressing charges' is quite strange. There is no legal necessity for any police decision to prosecute to be supported by the victim. There is, indeed, no legal requirement for or point in such a statement. Its functions are purely practical and strategic, with the beneficiary being the police, rather than any subsequent court proceedings. The statement is an indication to a senior police officer or prosecutor, trying himself to decide upon prosecution, whether the victim will support police action and give evidence. It may also be seen by police officers as a means by which to justify the arrest of the offender (though, again, only a police decision that there are reasonable grounds is necessary here). It can also be used to put pressure upon a subsequently recalcitrant victim to adhere to his original statement and give evidence. The statement from the victim is being used by the police to justify actions for which, in fact, they alone have the burden of justification. The police hence view the decision of the victim to press charges as one which should be arrived at as soon as possible, and, once taken, as one impossible to change – a threshold to be crossed.

Victims, however, did not appreciate the importance of this threshold. They regarded it as an expression of their views at the time at which it was made. Any subsequent deviation would need justification, they considered, but reasons to change might, and indeed did, arise. They reserved their rights to continue to follow the process of prosecution and to continue to have an input into decision-making. Some, a majority of those who were subsequently in conflict with the police, thought that they should be able to withdraw their wish to prosecute later. But none wished to question the police mandate not to prosecute, or to decide on charges, courts and the value of particular evidence (though they did wish to be consulted and to be informed). There is a discrepancy here between police and victim views of the role of the victim. The victim sees his evidence as his own property and his role as following and paralleling the prosecution process – as still being involved. The police tend to regard a statement that the victim will press charges as crossing a threshold which cannot be recrossed – as marking the point beyond which the police may reserve to themselves the process of prosecution. They see as compatible their use of the victim's wishes as justification and their effective prevention of any subsequent active participation by the victim (unless that intervention is such as to undermine the prosecution totally, such as refusal by a major prosecution witness to give evidence).

Attitudes to the courts

Since victims rarely attended court or knew anything about court appearances until the outcome of the case, it was only possible to ask them to rate their satisfaction with the courts' handling of their case at the final interview (see Chapter 4). Hence, no measure of their change in feelings of satisfaction on this was possible. Victims were, however, asked to say how well they thought magistrates, judges and (court) lawyers did their job at both the first interview and the interview after the outcome of the case on a five-point scale from 'very well' (scored 1) to 'not at all well' (scored 5).

At both interviews, victims thought judges did their job better than magistrates (see Table 5.2). However, their perception of both judges and magistrates became significantly more favourable by the outcome

Table 5.2   How well do magistrates, judges and lawyers do their job?

| | Coventry | | Northampton | |
	First interview	Outcome interview	First interview	Outcome interview
Magistrates				
mean	3.10	2.85	3.02	2.78
S.D.	0.087	0.088	0.132	0.148
n	135	108	64	54
Judges				
mean	2.84	2.57	2.56	2.27
S.D.	0.090	0.085	0.126	0.121
n	119	101	61	49
Lawyers				
mean	2.45	2.58	1.98	2.10
S.D.	0.096	0.101	0.116	0.129
n	122	103	52	49

(very well = 1;   not at all well = 5)

of the case (Coventry magistrates: $p < .01$; all others: $p < .05$). There was no significant change in attitudes to lawyers between the first and outcome interviews.

The more favourable impressions of judges and magistrates formed during the progress of the case may be contrasted with the increasingly negative perceptions of the police and the lack of change in views about lawyers. Increasing familiarity or contact could not produce such divergent results. Nor is it a result of a difference in populations, since it was the same victims who were changing their attitudes to the police, to judges and magistrates and to lawyers. Victims did start with a very much higher view of police capabilities than of the capabilities of magistrates and judges, such that even the first interview scores for the police were higher than the outcome interview scores for magistrates and judges. However, it is not possible to find any one hypothetical 'mean point' towards which all the scores can be seen to converge over time. It appears that both the more favourable view of the courts and the less favourable view of the police post the victims' experiences with them are real phenomena, congruent with the explanations given by victims as to their changes in view. So, for example, victims who were present in court commented favourably on the judge or magistrates, specifying particularly the unexpected time or trouble they took over the case and the attention they gave to it. On the other hand, although victims in general thought lawyers did their job well, many were not sure that that job acted in the best interests of justice:

All they do is twist and lie but they do it well.

They'll say anything in court to get their client off.

Would victims report offences again?

At both the first interview and the interview after the outcome of the case, victims were asked whether they would report certain types of offence to the police in the future. Four types of offence were used, representing serious and less serious assaults and a frequently occurring property offence. They were:

(1) The same sort of offence as the present one;
(2) A burglary in which a lot of possessions are taken;
(3) An attack on the street by a stranger who knocks the victim to the ground and badly hurts him;
(4) An assault at a party in which the victim is punched by someone he knows slightly and falls and cuts his hand.

If one compares the numbers of victims who thought that their present offence should have been reported (bearing in mind that it was not necessarily the victim who actually reported it) with their views about reporting similar offences at the first and outcome interviews, then it seems that slightly more people would report the offence to the police at the time of the first interview but that considerably fewer would by the outcome of the case. There was a net movement between first and outcome interviews of 23 Coventry victims (12 per cent) and seven Northampton victims (8 per cent) in the direction of not reporting and seven Coventry victims (4 per cent) and four Northampton victims (5 per cent) in the direction of reporting.

The experience of the criminal justice process did seem to have swayed some victims towards not bothering with the process again. Given the overall respect for the police and agreement with them shown in the population as a whole, and, initially, in our study, this is a surprising result. The reasons given stressed the part the police played. Most said that in future they would deal with the offence themselves because of all the trouble it had caused them, including the perceived lack of information from the police and fears of retaliation. Others mentioned the negative attitude of the police, sentencing and disagreement with the police over prosecution. These concerns did not, however, affect whether victims would report a subsequent offence of burglary. Burglary would continue to be reported by almost all victims. There was, though, some effect on attitudes to reporting the hypothetical assault examples. So, of the 30 victims who would not go to the police with an offence similar to the present one, nine would also not report the serious assault (example 3 above). The two-thirds of victims that would not have reported the more minor assault (example 4) at the first interview were joined at the final interview by most of the remaining victims.

Previous experience and knowledge

Attitudes and judgements of satisfaction are based on expectations – they can be seen as positive or negative confirmations of those expectations. Expectations, in turn, are to some extent a product of people's prior knowledge about what may happen. Victims were asked some questions in the first interview about the criminal justice system. The first question was: 'Can the police decide whether or not to take someone to court where an offence has been committed?' This tests whether victims appreciate that the police have the ultimate decision-making power on prosecution. Only 56 per cent of (non police officer) victims were aware of this. Most of the others said that it was up to the victim to decide. Where police and victim were subsequently to be in conflict, it is likely that the police power over prosecution was not only unappreciated, but also came as a shock.

The other questions concerned the courts. The majority of victims knew that there were different types of court trying criminal offences (78 per cent) and many went on to list the different courts. Sixty-five per cent knew that not all courts have juries (a slight decrease in the standard of knowledge shown for the identical question in Durant *et al.*'s (1972) study carried out in 1966). Some of the confusion over witness orders may have been due to the belief that there is only one court (so what does a letter notifying transfer from one to another mean?). The final question relates to the need for the victim to go to court and be a witness: 'If someone pleads guilty, do the prosecution still have to call witnesses to prove he committed the offence?'. Only 45 per cent of victims knew that there was no requirement for witnesses to give evidence after a guilty plea. This rather low level of knowledge explains why many victims were still preparing themselves to go to court even if they suspected the defendant would plead guilty.

This level of knowledge implies that the police and the courts must not presume that a victim will know what may happen to his case or what his part in the proceedings will be. Lack of knowledge may also lead to additional distress, which in turn will be exacerbated by lack of information about the progress of the case. There is a need for some general information to be given to victims at the start of the process, setting out what will happen to the case, what they may have to do, what role they can play and where they can obtain help and advice. Such a book (including details of compensation as well) has been produced by the French Ministry of Justice (Ministère de la Justice 1982) and is sold in France at bookstalls at a subsidised price (takings go to victim support organisations). Given the lack of support and advice for the victim within the prosecutorial and court system (there is no solicitor for victims), it is high time for such an initiative to be launched here.

Summary and discussion

Victim attitudes to the police start off at a high level of satisfaction. This is not surprising – general opinion surveys show that the public in general have a high regard both for the police in general and for their mandate. For victims, this general picture of satisfaction, of confirmed expectation, holds up during the first contact. Thereafter, however, there is a continuous and significant decline, so that, after the outcome of the case, around a third of victims were no longer satisfied with the performance of the police in their case. This picture of progressive disenchantment appeared not only in ratings of satisfaction about their own case, but also in general judgements about the way the police did their job and in the picture drawn of the qualities associated with the police. For a few, this disillusionment was sufficiently great to make them say that they would not report a similar offence again and even extended sometimes to the reporting of other assaults. Such a convergence of results is quite rare, given the crudeness and artificiality of current attitudinal measures. It tends to indicate a strong phenomenon.

Yet, at the same time, victims showed increasing satisfaction with magistrates and judges, while not changing significantly their opinion of lawyers. The results cannot merely be the result of the passage of time, or some methodological artefact of using such scales, or due only to continued contact and interaction with such people. It is true that the first ratings of the police showed much higher levels of satisfaction with the police than the courts (and also, one suspects, higher expectations). Then, it is necessary to explain why expectations of the police are not realised, whereas expectations of the courts are more than measured up to. After all, not all contact with the police produces such disillusionment. Although experience of being stopped and searched on the streets, when innocent, does lead to harsher judgements of police actions (Smith 1983; Hough and Mayhew 1983), being stopped when driving does not (Dix and Layzell 1983). Motorists' criticism, in fact, seemed more to be directed towards the courts (though the occasional officious or rude police officer also came in for a share of disapproval).

Victims' reasons for their judgements provide a clue towards an explanation and a resolution of the two paradoxes we have described: first, the contradiction between the importance of the victim to the system and his lack of accepted role within that system; and, secondly, the victim's decreasing satisfaction with the police, compared to his increasing satisfaction with the courts.

The concern of victims is with attitudes, information and consultation. It is an expression of the need to be valued, to be wanted and to be considered as an important participant. That desired status does not extend to taking over the system. Victims were, on the whole, quite happy with what both the police and the courts were actually doing with the case (at least, what they were doing in the study areas at that time). The concern was over process, not outcome. There appears to be a mismatch between the victim's expectations of the system and the system's assumptions about victim wishes. The police have become, in Howley's (1982) words, 'preoccupied with technical efficiency', whereas victims look to the police for support and reassurance. The police believe victims are most worried about outcome (catching the offender, putting together the case) and undervalue their need for consideration, respect and help (see Jones 1983, for a similar view as regards the general public). Prosecutors and court staff are concerned with processing the ever-growing numbers of defendants through the system in the fastest and most economical way. The victim is relatively invisible and is ignored. Despite the dependence of the system on the victim for reporting, detection and evidence, indeed, for much of its workload and existence, he has no accepted role.

Remedying the deficiencies quoted by victims in our study would not appear to pose a great threat to the current operation of the system (we shall consider in Chapter 10 what theoretical effects giving the victim any greater role would have for the operation of a State-run criminal justice system). In general, victims did not wish to have decision-making power over the case.

There were some points at which victims would prefer consultation before decisions are taken – on whether charges should be pressed, on whether charges should be dropped at court and on whether information should be given to the press. But the major requirements were for information and help – not as charity, but in exchange for the very considerable time and effort the victims themselves put in at a time when they were injured or shocked. The need for information was present throughout the process. Victims wanted to know whether the offender was caught, what the charges were, whether he was in custody or on bail (a matter in which the facts were less frightening than fear of the unknown), when the court appearances would be, whether the victim would have to give evidence and what the outcome and sentence was. The most important of these was the outcome and sentence, whatever that outcome might be. This search for information was not just the result of attempts to cope with the shock and stress of the offence, though some might be due to that (as has been found with people undergoing other types of shock). There was considerable worry about what the victim would have to do in the system and real anger at not being informed of the result of the case. Victims felt that they should be considered as having a proper role in the system and interest in the case, a feeling fuelled by the perceived inequity in the amount of help they gave the system, compared to what the system gave them.

This analysis can explain the patterning of the concerns of victims in the criminal justice system. It does not explain why the police are singled out for criticism, while the courts are, relatively speaking, praised. Why should the courts not be given the opprobrium of not informing the victim of the outcome? Though this must be speculative, given the concentration in this study on offences of violence and on the experiences of only a relatively small number of victims, we think that there is a fundamental difference in the ways in which victims perceive the police-victim and court-victim relationships. The police are seen as in some way providing a service to victims. They come when called and then take over the task of catching the offender and prosecuting him. But the idea of service implies a two-way interaction. Victims expect to remain in contact with the case throughout the whole process of prosecution and for that contact to be facilitated by the police. They see the police as independent agents, but agents processing their case, who should, therefore, account to victims (and, occasionally, consult them).

The police see their contacts with victims, however, as required only when they need something more from the victim. Other contacts and helpful attitudes (which do often occur) are for humanitarian reasons or as general public relations, not as of right. The police have a tendency to reserve to themselves decisions on prosecution, seeing as irrelevant (except in their practical effects) the views of 'outsiders'. The police consider themselves the initial validators of victim identity (is the offence a crime, is the victim a victim?). Victims do concede this role to the police – they do construct and maintain their identity according to judgements made by the police. (They also become increasingly confused by alterations to that identity made in the subsequent decisions by supervisors and prosecutors taken for practical reasons.) But victims do not depend for all their expectations on this validation. They retain their own views about process, outcome and sentence. Central to these is their identity as a participant in the original offence and their belief that the police are agents, autonomous agents, but still tied to the victim.

The courts are given a different role. The police may be the original valuers of the victim and the offence, but the courts are seen as the ultimate adjudicators. There is no notion of service as far as judges and magistrates are concerned (though prosecutors are seen as having a similar role to that of the police). Judges and magistrates are not thought of as having any obligation to victims. Any (to victims) especially thorough consideration of the case or kind remarks about the victim's part in the offence or welfare in court are seen not as due, but as a pleasant surprise. The failings of the prosecutorial system are not ascribed to judges and magistrates.

So, the police are judged on their failure to provide a service – an individualised, personal service. Victims do not expect police actions to conform entirely to their wishes – there are both the incompatible demands of others (other witnesses, the offender) and the requirements of the law – thought of as a demand greater than and superior to those of individuals. The police can, and do, justify their decisions according to legalistic rules, even if they may have more pragmatic underlying reasons (see Ericson 1981). Victims may sometimes wonder about police views of the law, but in general they will accept them. Victims do, however, expect a service – some attention paid to, perception of, time taken on, thought given to, their demand. The police may justify their actions through reference to this abstract law, but, in so doing, they must not appear not to have considered – to have ignored the victim.

6 The effects of the offence

It is well known that offences can have serious effects on victims of crime, particularly victims of violent crime. These effects may not be confined to the immediate consequences of the offence – physical injury, shock, loss of property, time off work and financial losses. They can intrude into most of the areas of the victim's life – producing a change in his relationships with members of his family, neighbours, friends or work colleagues.

Maguire (1982), for example, found that 83 per cent of his burglary victims experienced some strong reaction immediately after discovering the offence and 65 per cent still perceived some effect on their lives four to ten weeks later. Brown and Yantzi's (1980) study of Canadian victims of many offences showed that 45 per cent spontaneously mentioned some immediate need that had not been handled properly by the authorities. Crimes against persons (including physical and sexual assaults) showed the highest degree of 'unfulfilled need'. The victims did not appear to forget these immediate problems, but they were soon submerged in later effects, 37 per cent spontaneously recalling some kind of help they could have used in the weeks or months after the incident.

Our study, using a longitudinal design, enables the analysis of effects as they were perceived by victims during the weeks and months after the offence. The victims were asked about the effects that the offence had had on their lives at each interview. They were prompted that they should include effects of injury and changes to their lives at home, work and in the neighbourhood, but no particular effect was suggested to them. Where possible, victims' accounts were compared with police files, especially in relation to levels of injury. The effects were divided into the broad categories of physical effects, financial loss, social effects (at home, at work and in the neighbourhood) and psychological effects. Physical effects cover both temporary physical suffering such as headaches or pain while performing everyday activities and permanent disfigurements such as scars or missing teeth. Financial loss includes any loss of money specified as such by the victim, whether this concerned loss of earnings, damaged or stolen property or medical expenses. Psychological effects include worry, anxiety, depression and their symptoms in the victim or in his relatives.

In addition, three more inclusive categories of effect were used. The category 'any effect' includes all the above-mentioned items. 'Possible emotional need' represents the sum of social effects and psychological effects, since these appeared to be considerably interrelated for individual victims. 'Possible financial need' includes all effects which might have some financial implications for victims. So, those losing time off work, those requiring false teeth or spectacles and those having to replace damaged clothing would be added to those mentioning specific sums of money in the financial loss category.

Persistence of effects

The proportion of victims who said that they had suffered or continued to suffer some effect from the offence was substantial at every interview. At the first interview, only 24 victims (9 per cent) said that they had been entirely free of effects since the offence. At the outcome interview, 75 per cent of those interviewed were still mentioning some effect. Figures 6.1 and 6.2 show the percentages of victims mentioning various effects over time and by stage of the case. (It is possible to calculate the interviews relevant to each time period in two ways – the effects described at the next interview after the time shown (as in the figures) or the effects described at interviews taking place within that time period – but both of these produce very similar results.)

The most striking feature of Figures 6.1 and 6.2 is the persistence and consistency of the prevalence of physical, social and psychological effects over time, compared to the low level and decrease over time of financial loss. It might be thought that this might have been an experimenter effect, in that questions about effects would prompt a positive answer, except that the precise effects suffered changed over time. Pain in moving might be replaced by aching scars in cold weather. Disruption of social life by injury might turn to an unwillingness to go out. Many of the social and psychological effects were also confirmed by relatives. In contrast, financial losses were often no longer important by the second or third interview. It is possible that the points on the graphs representing the fourth interview (or times over 18 months) do concern a sample more likely to say they were suffering from effects, as these represent those who had applied for or been granted compensation. But there is no equivalent reason for suspicion about the earlier points.

There were, of course, differences between the effects suffered by victims of physical assaults, sexual assaults and robberies. Physical assault victims suffered less effects overall, yet the percentages of those mentioning effects were still over 60 per cent at the third and fourth interviews. Physical assault victims were more likely to suffer physical effects, though for the less serious physical assaults, the high initial effect level in all categories had dropped off markedly by the outcome interview. Victims of sexual assaults had both the highest level of effects

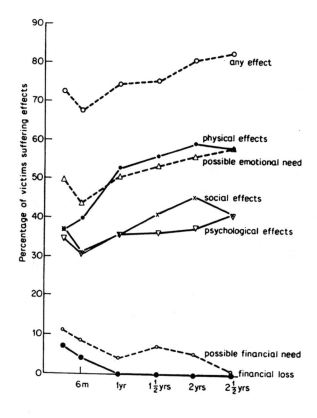

Figure 6.1   Effects suffered by victims at different times since the offence

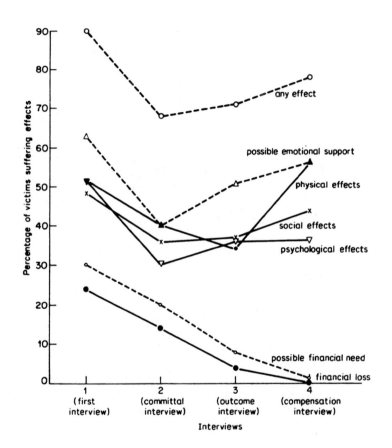

Figure 6.2   Effects of the offence suffered by victims at each interview

at the first interview and the greatest tendency for effects to persist. They were the most likely to describe social and psychological effects. Robbery victims also tended to suffer social effects, particularly a curtailment of social life because of a fear of subsequent attack. This overall summary of the types and persistence of effects cannot, however, specify the types of effect in sufficient detail to indicate needs for support or help. Neither can it show which victims will require that support. For this, we need to turn to the individual types of effect.

Physical effects

The less serious forms of physical assault (such as assault occasioning actual bodily harm) tended to cause only a temporary mark, pain and discomfort or headaches. Though victims found their injuries painful and unpleasant, most were able to bear them. As one put it: 'The bruising soon went down. I still go out, you don't hide yourself just because you've got a few scratches.' Such injuries did, however, cause temporary difficulty coping with activities such as eating (mouth and tooth injuries) or driving (arm injuries). Police officer victims, though having injuries equivalent to those of civilians, were significantly less likely to mention physical effects. They did not appear to consider injuries as important effects (though they were as likely to mention psychological effects).

The assaults or woundings causing grievous bodily harm frequently involved the use of a weapon. Injuries, as would be expected, were much more severe and produced more numerous and more persistent physical problems:

I still can't hear in one ear but the ear doesn't stick out any more.

I've still got no freckles on my face in the middle. I can cover it up with make-up. Most people don't notice it but I do.

There were signs that the upturn in the level of mentioned physical effects over time was due to the unexpected persistence of physical effects after the injuries had healed. So, people would expect scars from knife wounds, but might not realise that their scars would ache in cold weather, make some physical tasks more difficult to perform easily or promote headaches.

Finally, there are the offences where the level of injury may be either slight or severe since the offence is defined both by physical injury and by other harm (robbery and the sexual assaults). Almost all the robbery victims experienced a level of injury that would count as at least an assault occasioning actual bodily harm had property not also been taken. The proportion and incidence of physical effects were similar to these assaults. The sexual assaults involved a wide range of levels of violence and consequences for victims.

The use of medical services
Many victims required medical help as a direct result of the offence. Immediate medical attention might be provided by the hospital casualty department (for 60 per cent of victims), by a police doctor at the police station or at his surgery (3 per cent only saw the police doctor) or by the victim's GP (5 per cent saw only their GP). The police often advised victims to visit the casualty department – both to receive treatment and in order that a statement of the injuries could be provided later by the hospital doctor as evidence. Despite this advice, a small number of victims with quite serious injuries went to the casualty department only reluctantly, left early or did not go at all. Of those who did go to hospital, 19 per cent had injuries which were sufficiently serious for them to be admitted and detained for periods up to 26 days. Three victims spent some days in intensive care and required emergency operations. The sexual assault victims were unlikely to go to hospital, but were seen by their GP or by the police doctor. All but one of the rape victims were examined by a police doctor. A minority of victims also required one or more subsequent visits to hospital (to see specialists, for check-ups and for subsequent operations) or to their GP. A few used other services such as a home nurse, physiotherapist or dentist.

Most victims were satisfied with their treatment at the casualty department (73 per cent of Coventry victims and 91 per cent of Northampton victims). However, a minority were extremely dissatisfied. The major problem in both towns, although considerably worse in Coventry, was the length of time victims had to wait before obtaining treatment. Doctors and nurses were not blamed personally for this, though there were a few instances of perceived unsympathetic attitudes to victims. There was also considerable worry in the few cases where the demands of the police for evidence, for example, photographs of injuries, meant that treatment had to wait.

The other major problem was lack of transport to take the victim home afterwards. This was exacerbated by the fact that many assaults occurred late at night, so that all public transport had stopped by the time that the victim was discharged from hospital. Twenty-two victims either had to walk home (often several miles), take an expensive taxi or call friends out. These victims were still shocked, upset and in pain. They felt that some form of transport should have been provided, especially since they often had no money on them. Many other victims were saved from the same fate by the police, who picked them up, took them to the police station after hospital to make a statement and then drove them home. This would seem to be an area in which volunteers (victim support schemes or car pools) could be of great benefit.

Subsequent visits or sexual examinations by the police doctor are rather different from the above forms of medical services in that their primary purpose is obtaining evidence for the prosecution case rather than providing medical attention for the victim. These procedures involved mostly the sexual assault victims, but some physical assault and robbery victims had samples taken for forensic analysis or were sexually examined. The reaction to sexual examinations was that it was unpleasant and humiliating, but necessary if the victim wanted the case to proceed. The feelings of victims depended largely on the attitude of the doctor. If he was pleasant, friendly and talked to the victim then she was likely to feel that, although it was a very unpleasant experience, she was not (further) degraded:

It was horrible but it wasn't as bad as it could be. The doctor was fabulous – he was friendly and supportive. He almost felt sorry he had to do those things. From what I've gathered I was lucky – the policewoman said my doctor was very nice. If I'd been treated with contempt I'd have dropped the whole thing.

The quality of the medical attention offered by police doctors and the sex of the doctor were not important considerations. Chambers and Millar (1983), in their study of Scottish rape victims, have also found that consideration, support and respect are the most important requisites for the treatment of sexual assault victims.

Holmstrom and Burgess (1978) observe that hospital staff, in the case of rape victims, have two duties – to provide medical care and to collect legal evidence. The aims in these two tasks (care and support as compared to investigation) may be contradictory. We would argue that these two objectives are present, to a greater or lesser degree, in many of the contacts that the medical services have with victims of violence and also dictate the instructions that police officers give to victims to go to hospital. What is important for all offences, but especially in rape and indecent assault cases, is that the collection of evidence should not override the provision of the care and support that the victim needs during a period of crisis. As we have found, and as both Holmstrom and Burgess and Chambers and Millar have also found, it is the attitude of the medical staff and hospital to victims that determines whether they feel they are being cared for. This will include not only whether the staff (including any police officers present) are supportive and friendly, but also whether the victim has to wait for a long time without attention and whether transport is available afterwards. With slightly more fore-thought and training, there is no reason why support for the victim and the gathering of essential medical evidence cannot be combined so as to minimise further trauma and degradation for the victim. Any further medical evidence (such as the taking of blood samples for forensic evidence) could be left until the victim has rested.

Financial and property losses

There is one another possible 'direct' effect of an offence besides injury: the extent to which victims experienced losses of money and property. Among offences of violence, robbery is unique, since, by definition, it involves the loss of property. However, victims of other types of offence may also suffer substantial property loss such as broken windows or damage to a vehicle. These often counted as separate offences in their own right (such as criminal damage), but, in a number of cases, victims referred to damage to clothing, or damage or loss of spectacles or teeth, which were not the subject of further charges. These losses were often not recorded on the initial crime reports made out by the police or in the victims' statements. For example, in only 10 of the 31 cases in which victims mentioned damage to clothing or spectacles was such loss officially recorded. This lack of information in the prosecution documents could arise becuase the victim does not necessarily know the cost of replacing or repairing the item at the time of his statement to the police. The cost involved could be substantial for poorer victims (dental plates, for example, involved a contribution of around £25 at that time). This lack of recording by the police meant that neither prosecution nor sentencer would know of the victim's loss.

Other financial losses stemmed from the injuries caused to the victims. Of the 276 victims, 202 were in either full or part-time employment at the time of the offence. Of these, 78 (39 per cent) lost some time off work and 61 (30 per cent) lost earnings (including overtime or commission). The most frequently experienced level of loss was between £20 and £50, but there were some losses of over £200 (at 1979–80 levels). The most severely affected were the small businessman and the self-employed, who often did not have the requisite insurance:

The business is losing money, I cannot go to the cash-and-carry so friends go and get things. When I was in hospital we paid friends to look after the shop . . . I have no insurance myself because I can't afford £150, we're a small business . . . sometimes I feel confused, very worried. All the time I'm worried, it's very bad for me. What will happen to my wife and children makes me worried.

When considering cost, we need to add on the cost involved in helping the police and going to court. Whenever victims went to the police station to make statements, provide identification evidence and so forth, they paid for their travel costs themselves. In few cases were they provided with transport by the police. On occasions they lost time off work and earnings or had to find someone to look after children. We saw too in Chapters 3 and 4 that victims might also lose the use of any property held for forensic tests. Their costs in attending court would not be met if they were not summoned to give evidence and might only partially be covered even if they were. Over the weeks and months, such expenditure mounted up to many pounds and placed an additional burden on victims at the time when they were covering the costs arising from injuries. There is no scheme for immediate redress for such victims. Indeed, it is debatable whether these expenditures can be recovered at all.

However, most managed to cover the financial losses somehow, often using money put aside for holidays, clothes or children to do so. The majority of costs were incurred soon after the offence and, by the time of the second or third interview, had largely been met and were seen as no longer significant (see Table 6.1). At the time of the outcome of the case, items included within the category 'possible financial need' affected only 7 per cent of victims. Neither of the currently available sources of compensation for victims of violent crime (the CICB and compensation orders from the courts) would provide any assistance before this time. We can also see from Table 6.1 that there is no difference between cases that lead to court appearances and those that do not. A court-based solution to financial loss would not cover many of the victims suffering it.

Table 6.1 Financial loss and possible financial need (percentage of victims)

| | Interview | | | |
	1	2	3	4
Financial loss				
All cases	24.1	14.0	3.8	0.0
Cases involving court appearances	24.8	14.0	3.9	0.0
Cases where offender was not caught or not prosecuted	23.7	*	3.5	*
Possible financial need (special damages)				
All cases	30.2	20.0	7.7	7.3
Cases involving court appearances	30.3	20.0	7.8	5.3
Cases where offender was not caught or not prosecuted	30.5	*	7.1	*

*insufficient number of cases (n<10)

Financial loss, particularly severe financial loss, only affects a few victims and most manage to cope somehow over time. Some, however, are seriously affected, even if the magnitude of the loss is relatively small. For example, a few could not afford to undergo dental treatment necessitated by the injuries they suffered. Some gave up presents for their children at birthdays and Christmas. One could not go back to work or get out of the house because he could not afford the price of new spectacles. These victims are not necessarily the ones that would be thought to be affected. They are as likely to be men as women, young as old. The problem of compensating for direct financial loss is the problem of dealing with relatively small financial losses which happen to a few people forming no obvious category and which affect them normally for a short period of time very soon after the offence.

Social and psychological effects

Victims also referred to a diverse range of effects which may broadly be described as psychological and social consequences of the offence. It would have been ideal if victims had described these in neat categories. In practice, their descriptions of feelings and behaviour were often complex, open-ended and unrationalised. It was clear that, for many victims, physical and emotional consequences were experienced together as part of a complicated process. For example, with some of the victims off work for the longest periods, it was difficult to distinguish the point at which they had recovered from the physical effects of the offence, but had entered a new phase of depression and lethargy in which the memory of the offence and the enforced inactivity of sick leave led to a reluctance to go back to work. No criticism is suggested as these victims clearly wanted to return to normal life as soon as possible. This whole process (coupled with reduced earnings) was clearly very demanding for their families and led to further guilt and anxiety on the part of the victim. In fact, the area of work-related assaults (on, for example, bus drivers, shopkeepers, police officers etc.) produced some of the most severe and long-lasting emotional effects. Although few actually changed their jobs as a result of the offence (though this was a common immediate impulse), there were several whose long-term depression caused an inability to deal with members of the public. Where the victim could depend on highly supportive work colleagues or was employed by an organisation containing an attentive personnel function, it seemed that the process of return to work was greatly eased. Where support from employers was not forthcoming, victims suffered additional problems. It is possible that employers may not be aware of the problems victims face at work after an assault.

Overall, a majority of victims suffered some kind of emotional effect, which often led to changes in their behaviour and social lives. These were usually long-lasting (remaining over periods of months or even years) and commonly took the form of nervousness, anxiety and worry, particularly when alone or out of the house:

I'm still scared. I'm on my own at night. (My husband) works nights so if (the offender) finds out where I live he might come here.

I feel uneasy if I see a group of lads, I was afraid of nothing before, but now I'm uneasy.

When I'm out I get a very tensed-up feeling.

There was no doubt that, for the vast majority of victims, the offence was a very significant event in their lives and also a great shock:

It opened my eyes. I didn't think it could happen to me. If it had been in town I'd have expected it. But not at the end of my own street.

Attitudes to their families, to people that looked like the offender and to their neighbourhood could all change. This could lead to avoidance of certain places or even of going out at all. Fourteen per cent of victims went out very much less frequently than before the offence. These were not only the elderly, but also young men, whose whole lifestyle might change dramatically.

The group suffering the most major psychological and social effects, however, was sexual assault victims. They were also the most likely to suffer from multiple and persistent effects. These tendencies occurred with indecent assault victims as well as with rape victims, even when the victim herself thought that the offence was minor. It might be thought that this reflects the sex of the victim, rather than the nature of the offence, but we found no difference between male and female victims of physical assault as regards either their attitudes and feelings or the social effects they suffered. This is contrary to Maguire's (1982) results with burglary victims, where he found that female victims were more likely to experience severe and persistent effects. It seems that the differential likelihood of suffering emotional effects is specific to the type of offence (or to the effect on the coping process of different societal attitudes to the victims of particular offences).

For indecent assault and rape victims, almost all the effects experienced by physical assault victims were present, though anxiety was more frequent. A unique feature of sexual assault cases was the distress and anger that victims ascribed to their male relatives, who were described as 'very sick about it', 'very mad about it' or 'doing his nut'. One victim said that her husband was 'angry that someone had touched his wife'. Victims also mentioned their own sense of 'being dirty' and in some cases there were marital difficulties or the development of a specific mistrust towards men. While many felt in some way guilty about the offence (though they also acknowledged this as, in many cases, irrational), sexual assault victims could be almost overcome with guilt. Their relatives could unconsciously be encouraging this. There was no doubt that both sexual assault victims and their relatives found it very difficult to cope with the offence and that it might affect many areas of their lives. Though, in fact, no victim did move as a result of the offence, where victims already wanted to move, victimisation was a contributory factor in strengthening their intention to do so. Even small everyday activities might provoke self-doubts:

> I think about it when I wear T-shirts – you're brainwashed about sex and they say about rape victims – they lead them on – so I wonder if I did, then I think, that's stupid. (indecent assault victim)

Knowing the offender

Psychological and social effects can obviously be greater if the victim and offender know each other. In this case, contact will not necessarily end with the offence. Victim and offender may have to co-exist with each other in the same community. Even when the offender is unknown, the victim may be frightened of retaliation or of how to cope with a possible meeting. The problem is not one-sided. The victim may decide to take his own action against the offender.

We saw in Chapter 1 that 39 per cent of victims were assaulted by offenders known to them in some way. Offenders known as relatives or friends in fact produced the highest number of severe or multiple effects on victims, when compared to those known at work, through the neighbourhood or initially unknown. This group mostly involved assaults by men on women and in several there was a prior history of reporting assaults to the police. It is clear that the police had to deal with complicated and emotionally loaded situations and with victims whose expectations might be confused or erratic. This is hardly surprising given the combination of emotional and legal complexities that often surround cases of assaults by relatives or partners. This should not, however, be taken to imply that these victims wanted the case taken out of the criminal justice system. Many actively wished for proceedings to take place, including the 69 per cent of such victims who suffered significant or severe effects.

Actual contact with the offender after the offence was surprisingly frequent in all types of case and involved both offenders who were known to the victim and those who were previously unknown. Fifty-five per cent of victims had some contact with their offender – 53 per cent having direct contact (face-to-face, phone or letter) and 11 per cent indirect contact through third parties (some had both). The vast majority of instances took place in the community, with only a relatively small percentage occurring as a result of police or court procedures. Contact was more likely for the less serious physical assault victims (s. 47 and s. 20 assaults), reflecting the higher proportion of victims knowing their offender and the increased likelihood of the offender being granted bail.

'Unofficial' contact (not under the auspices of the criminal justice system) tended to cause considerable distress. Female victims became upset:

I was in pieces, very frightened at seeing him again.

whereas male victims' feelings tended to be more equivocal or aggressive:

I felt slightly uncomfortable, I think we were both thinking, 'you bastard'.

It bugs me a bit. It's an uneasy feeling to know you can't trust him any more. I try to keep out of his way.

Fifty-four per cent of victims who had contact with the offender expressed some level of upset, of which 28 per cent was judged by the researchers to be severe. The figures refer to cases and not to instances, so that in any individual case, there might be more than one contact with the offender and more than one type of reaction. There were, of course, situations where the victim was initially highly distressed but where differences between victim and offender were finally reconciled, but, in general, victims experienced substantial amounts of distress over contact with the offender at any point in the case.

Retaliation
Retaliation can be by the offender (or people acting on his behalf) because of the victim's participation in the criminal justice system or it can be by the victim (or his relatives or friends) on the offender. Retaliation by victims – at least in terms of direct action or definite threats – was much less common than retaliation by offenders (see Table 6.2, though this is, of course based upon victim reports). Thirty-eight victims (14 per cent) experienced some form of retaliatory behaviour. This was concentrated among the physical assault victims. Unless retaliation occurred immediately following the offence, it was likely to take place somewhere familiar to the victim – his home, home street or a local pub or club. This tended to add to the stresses involved. The most serious form of retaliation was a further assault or damage to the victim's property (six cases). In all of these, the offender was known to the victim as a relative or friend or through the neighbourhood. The nature of each actual retaliation was typically quite unconnected with 'gangs' or 'organised crime', being local or domestic in nature. Furthermore, these cases tended to have a background where victims either initially did not wish to proceed or subsequently changed their minds. Fears of retaliation tended to contribute to this wish to drop out of the criminal justice system and were not helped by the response of the police when retaliation was reported to them.

Explicit intimidation or threats by the offender (12 cases) also scared

Table 6.2   Cases where there was direct or indirect retaliation

Nature of retaliation	Number	Percentage
By offender		
Assault or damage to property	6	2
Direct threat of violence	12	4
Direct threat other than violence	5	2
Threatening letter or phone call	2	1
By person other than offender or on offender's behalf		
Threat to victim's friend or threatening message to victim	8	3
Direct threat against victim	5	2
On behalf of the offender (total)	38	14
By victim		
Victim 'thought about' retaliation	10	4
Victim saw offender and thought about retaliation	9	3
Victim looked for offender	1	0
Victim considered retaliation after talking to police	1	0
Friends or relatives looked for offender with or without victim	5	2
Friends or relatives threatened or assaulted offender	2	1
Friends or relatives thought by victim to wish to retaliate	5	2
On behalf of the victim (total)	33	12

victims and made them worried about going on with the case: 'He asked me if I wanted it done again'. Another example involved a victim who said she would report any further assault by her boyfriend to the police. He replied: 'I'm a vicious bloke and if (you) did I wouldn't mind going down'.

Retaliation by or on behalf of the offender was, therefore, a relatively frequent occurrence for the victims in our study. Less than half the instances were reported to the police. In fact, it was uncommon for the police to discuss with victims what to do if there was contact with the offender and whether it should be reported. The decision whether or not to report was hence obviously a matter of considerable concern to victims, involving much discussion with relatives and friends. Some were very loathe to report in case it exacerbated the retaliation. Others felt the police would not be able to do much. The experiences of those who did report would tend to encourage this belief. Most of those who did finally contact the police were unhappy about their lack of action. Six of the 15 who reported retaliation were not visited by the police. Fourteen were not aware of any action taken by the police. The only cases in which a statement was taken from the victim about the retaliatory action were the four in which a new criminal offence had definitely been committed by the offender (offering of bribe to drop the case, damage to property, burglary and assault inflicting grievous bodily harm). Only the assault case was prosecuted and convicted. Victims felt: 'If the police can't help you, who can?'

The police officers interviewed all said that they would take any intimidation of a victim very seriously and would send someone to see the victim and take a statement and then interview the offender and put the matter to him. Prosecution was a more difficult matter, since the only offences available were the substantive criminal offences (such as assault or criminal damage), or breaking any conditions of bail or perverting the course of justice (which requires the consent of the Director of Public Prosecutions before prosecution). This last is only used for very serious intimidation. The police had no powers to deal with threats. It is entirely possible that, when retaliation was reported to the police, they did go and see the offender and warn him as to his conduct. By not informing the victim of any of the action they had taken, however, they deprived that action of much of its power. Victims were left feeling scared and alone.

Retaliation by victims against offenders rarely proceeded beyond the level of just thinking about it, though victims sometimes surprised themselves by the strength of their reaction:

It turns you more to violence – you think of ludicrous things. (My wife and I) both do archery and you fantasise about keeping the bow permanently strung and nailing them to a tree.

There were only two cases of direct action, both by relatives of the victim rather than the victim himself. In one the husband of an indecent assault victim smashed up the offender's home before the case came to trial. The husband was convicted himself for this. In the other, a serious physical assault where there was hostility between the two families, the victim's brother tried (unsuccessfully) to attack the offender in a local pub and was restrained by others.

Overall, there were 71 instances of either victim or offender retaliation. The total number of victims affected by either form of retaliation was 51 (19 per cent of all cases in the study). In many instances there is probably little the police can do about victim retaliation, except dissuade victims from taking their own action (which they usually do). In contrast, the police do not advise victims what to do about offender retaliation and tend not to reassure victims or inform them about the results of any action taken if that retaliation is reported. This does not encourage either peace of mind for victims or the smoother progress of prosecution cases.

Effects, needs and expressed needs

We have been describing the effects that victims thought were sufficiently important to them to mention in the interview. When we come to look at the provision of support or assistance to victims, we need to consider what status those effects should be given. Van Dijk (1983a) has described how many current efforts at victim support have no basis in criminological or victimological research. Equally, we must not uncritically accept effects as indicating need for any particular type of support.

The effects mentioned by victims are measures of whether victims felt an effect was important enough to mention it to the researcher. They are not measures of the severity (perceived or actual) of those effects. They cannot, therefore, give more than an indication of the presence and possible prevalence of any need. Suffering an effect does not necessarily imply the existence of a need for any particular kind of support. It is impossible to measure actual need and it is an extremely difficult task to predict the extent of need of any individual, although it may be possible to distinguish between groups who seem to have different levels or types of need.

Nor can we use the needs expressed by victims as measuring 'objective' or 'actual' need (if such a concept exists). There may be some large degree of positive relationship. But expressed needs are to some extent culturally based. They are related to the expectations of victims as to the potential effects of the offence and to their knowledge of what remedies exist. If victims do not know that victim support schemes exist, or that compensation may be available from the courts or from the CICB, then they may only be able to formulate a diffuse wish for emotional support or for compensation.

We cannot, therefore, use the effects which victims say they suffer or their expressed needs as representing actual needs. But this is not to suggest that effects or expressed needs are unimportant. The effects which victims said they had suffered were sufficiently immediate for the victims to have presented them as significant to the researchers. They were not prompted about any kind of effect. If the system changes, then the expectations and thus the effects and expressed needs will also change. Some effects will be alleviated through informal support by family and friends. Others form the unfulfilled needs of those victims.

One might consider the effects that victims said they had suffered as marking the outer boundaries of expressed need. They may also be the basis on which victims judge how responsive the system is to them.

The provision of help and support to victims

It has become something of a cliché that modern life has involved a weakening of traditional communities, particularly in large towns. However, our findings do not support the expectation that a large number of victims are likely to suffer from social isolation and an absence of informal support. Almost all the victims (95 per cent) referred to the intervention of some other individual at some stage of their case. At the time of the offence, it was very rare for people who were present to ignore what had happened. When victims had to visit hospital they were frequently accompanied by friends or relatives. Most victims received some practical or emotional support from relatives, friends or work colleagues.

Many, however, did mention that they would have found the experience of victimisation much more difficult if they had been living alone or had been socially isolated in some other way. There were a few victims who did seem totally isolated. One was an elderly man living in hostel accommodation. He described how lads from the local council estate used to beat up and rob the hostel residents if there was an opportunity, but accounted for his own difficulties with a fatalistic patience. Another was an elderly West Indian victim living above a boarded-up shop. He was already in poor health and had been robbed at home by two white men. He apparently spent his days staring out of the window of his flat at passers-by and wondering if any of them intended him mischief. It was only after several visits to interview him that he was eventually confident enough to open the door.

It is difficult to judge the social isolation and need for informal support of victims, since many described themselves as 'independent' or 'looking after themselves', though this itself might be part of the coping process. Even if they did have concerned friends and relatives, this might not be enough. Several sexual assault victims and some physical assault victims referred to the difficulty of discussing their feelings with relatives. The researcher was seen as a sympathetic stranger with whom the victim had no emotional ties and, therefore, someone with whom he could talk without provoking any adverse reaction. Despite the prevalence of informal support, there did seem to be a need for other, outside support, both to isolated individuals and to victims who felt unable to talk about their offence to their family.

Victims rarely made use of any outside agency, apart from the police. Twenty-three had approached a solicitor, for information on compensation, for general advice on the case or in 'domestic' cases in which there were concurrent civil proceedings. Fifteen had used another agency such as an information centre, women's refuge or rape crisis centre. For most, the police were the agency seen as providing the major practical and emotional support. Those who had received help and support from the police were pleased that this had been available. The police were also the agency most frequently mentioned when people were asked what help victims need.

However, there are material constraints on the support the police can provide, particularly on the amount of time they can spend with victims. In serious cases (especially those of rape), if the police officer in the case can spend a lot of time with the victim, this will be of great help. In less serious cases, all the police may be able to provide is a sympathetic attitude during the time they are there.

Recognising this, victims did often try and describe another body, as far as they knew not in existence, which could give practical and emotional help:

There should be a separate body apart from the police, to come round in an advisory capacity . . . (it) would advise on the problems of work, let the police know, let's face it the average person doesn't know what to do. The Samaritans would do but who wants to get the Samaritans? It should be social welfare people. Under them circumstances I think they'd be accepted. Some old biddy who gets burgled, someone to tell them about insurance claims. The police is like someone who's never had it happen to themselves.

There ought to be a police social worker, a policeman not involved in the case (or) not a policeman, someone suitably trained, they'd have to have knowledge of police procedures to come under the police umbrella.

There should be a statutory agency, a place where people could go and talk so that the (mental effects) were not so serious . . . a place run by people who've had similar experiences, like there is for alcoholics and attempted suicides.

What these victims were describing was an organisation very similar to a victim support scheme. These use volunteers to visit and offer practical and emotional support to victims of crime, with close police liaison. The first was set up in Bristol in 1973 and there is now a considerable and growing number of schemes. Recently, the National Association of Victim Support Schemes has been founded to provide links between schemes and to co-ordinate training and so forth. At the time of the study, there was no scheme in Northampton but there was one in Coventry (in addition to a rape crisis centre). However, only five victims had been contacted by any scheme and all of these had not wanted to pursue it. Indeed, only 17 per cent of Northampton victims and 30 per cent of Coventry victims had heard of the idea of victim support schemes at all, even though, in Coventry, there was considerable publicity throughout the period of the study. As has been found in other areas of crime prevention and offering of services (see Riley and

Mayhew 1980), people do not take in and remember information about agencies unless they themselves are currently being affected. To contact victims of crime, victim support schemes will need to go out to the victims (as indeed they do), rather than waiting for the victims to come to them. This proactive approach is especially necessary because of constraints imposed by the victims themselves. There was little reluctance to use information services or practical help, but a number seemed to feel that to ask for emotional support would be somehow shameful, or that agencies offering emotional support only would be intrusive rather than supportive.

In both Coventry and Northampton, the overwhelming majority of victims approved of the idea of such a service (84 per cent overall). Both practical help (including the provision of information) and emotional support were thought important. Victims were fairly evenly divided between favouring voluntary or professional workers, though both training and having passed through the experience of victimisation were stressed. The majority felt the schemes should be separate from the police. Very few of these victims were actually hostile to police involvement, most seeming to favour a formal independence which would not exclude the police.

Slightly more than a third of victims said that they would have liked help from a scheme during their own case. The kind of help they wanted was more frequently practical than emotional. The victims were not concentrated among those offences that would be presumed to produce high emotional stress (such as sexual assaults).

There appears to be some stereotyped idea of the 'needy victim' in the media and even among some police officers and some of those providing help to victims. The sterotyped victim is elderly or female or living alone (or even all three). His needs are primarily emotional. In contrast, the victims in our study who said they would have benefited from a victim support scheme were often young, male and in work. Nor could one judge need for support from the seriousness of the offence. As the National Association of Victim Support Schemes has stated, there is no direct relationship between the apparent 'seriousness' of the offence and the degree of impact on the victim. Victims' ideas of what was serious seemed to be highly subjective and dependent on the victim's temperament and attitudes.

Effects and their remedies
It is possible to summarise the effects that victims described over time as follows:

(1) Immediately after the offence, victims suffered considerable physical and emotional effects. Some obviously required medical attention, during which care and support for the victim was as or more important

than evidential needs. Almost all expressed a need for emotional support and reassurance. The role of friends and relations was significant here, but some victims were isolated or the offence was such that they found it difficult to talk to those they knew well. In initial contacts with the police, which took place at this time, the manner of the police was very important. Victims wished the police to be considerate and supportive and to give the impression that they were taking the offence (and the victim) seriously.

(2) The proportion of victims mentioning a need for financial support (apart from social security benefits) was small. These needs also appeared to recede in importance after a few months. The few victims who did suffer these hardships, however, felt them very deeply and there was considerable hardship.

(3) In contrast, mental effects, physical effects and effects on the victim's home and social life affected a considerable proportion of victims and often persisted over a long period. Again, some coped with informal support. Others would have wished for more help from the police or the services of a victim support scheme. These were the major effects suffered by the time at which victims received any compensation. Financial needs had normally already been satisfied by this time.

(4) Victims saw no contradiction between a wish for emotional support and for help, a need for information and practical guidance and being treated with respect by those in the criminal justice system. They did not want to be patronised, to be treated like children or to be offered charity. They wanted both respect and the acknowledgement of their state of crisis and emotional upset.

Many of the effects mentioned by victims cannot be ameliorated by the kinds of provision that are made at the moment. While victims tend to have financial, emotional and informational needs at the same time, the agencies that exist to cater for each of these tend to be separate (compensation agencies and courts, victim support schemes and the police). There is no overall co-ordinating body to consider how all the needs of victims might be met. There is no single telephone number to ring for assistance. Although victim support schemes may, one day, come the closest to providing this co-ordination, at the moment they do not exist in all areas and they do not have the resources to take on the vitally important work after the first few days (for example, at court, dealing with the police or helping with compensation). We shall consider practical recommendations in Chapter 10, but it seems very unlikely that any one agency can fill all these roles. The task seems one for co-operation between several agencies, with the co-ordination being supplied by the agencies, not by the hapless victim. In the context of the many and serious effects with which victims attempt to cope, the provision of help at present looks scattered and scanty.

7 Applying for compensation

Direct financial losses related to the offence appear to affect only a minority of victims of violent crime, though expenses related to participating in the criminal justice system are more widespread. The major effects are physical, psychological and social. Compensation for victims of violent crime, however, is not restricted and is not intended to be restricted to direct financial losses. In Britain, at least, it has always been regarded as relating to all the injuries suffered by the victim, as well as to direct financial losses. This, indeed, is what is seen as differentiating compensation from welfare benefits (such as sick pay or disability benefits from the Department of Health and Social Security), which are not tied to victimisation as a result of crime, but are available to all those who are sick, disabled etc. regardless of the reason for that disability.

In fact, the payment of compensation to the victim is one of the oldest means for settling disputes. Lenman and Parker (1980) describe the use of such an arbitrated settlement, usually involving the payment of money, in most primitive and feudal societies. They give examples from Tokugawa, Japan and medieval Britain. This compensation or restitution was restricted, however, to payments by the offender, often on a scale which represented the seriousness of the offence rather than the effect on the victim. Later, State law and explicit criminal law, with their emphasis on punitive justice and concentration upon the offender, gradually came to take over from the more informal community law. Elements of compensation or restitution still persisted, however, and have recently been accorded a greater role.

Compensation from offenders (and the older words restitution and bote, or boot) has the meaning of 'to make amends for, make reparation, recompense, remunerate'. So Petty (1662) enquires, 'It will be asked how manifold restitutions should picking a pocket (for example) be punished?' (*Taxes* 58). And Stephen, in his description of the eleventh-century laws of England quotes, 'If the great toe be struck off, let twenty shillings be paid him as bot' (in *Edin. Rev.* 1884 April: 339). The idea is that the victim should be paid back for what he has lost or suffered, because he has experienced injury or wrongdoing. The amount is related to the seriousness of the offence. The harm done by the offence may of course itself be related to some extent to the victim's suffering, but the amount paid would not necessarily take into account the individual reaction of a particular victim. Similarly, it would be sufficient to show that that offence was committed against that victim. There would be no minimum quantum of suffering or expense necessary to qualify.

Although there are several schemes being set up in various parts of the country to include the payment of compensation as part of diverting the offender from the criminal process or as part of a probation order or community service order, the major provision for compensation by offenders is for the criminal courts to make compensation orders as part of the sentence received by the offender. This was the only possibility for compensation by offenders within the criminal justice system for the victims in our study. (Note, as a matter of terminology, that the word 'compensation' will be used in this book to refer both to compensation or restitution by offenders and to compensation from public funds.) The idea of compensation orders comes from the view of the Advisory Council on the Penal System (1970) that compensation must form an integral part of sentencing and must be seen in the context of the whole sentence. They considered that, even where difficult issues of liability or assessment of the amount of compensation arise, it may be practical for a court to order some measure of compensation. These provisions, enacted in the Criminal Justice Act 1972, allow the courts a general power to order compensation for any offences resulting in any kind of loss to any identifiable victim and replace the previous patchwork of highly specific powers tied to different offences and modes of trial. The scope and power of compensation orders has, since the study finished, been extended even further by the Criminal Justice Act 1982. Compensation orders may now be given as a complete sentence in their own right, rather than just as an ancillary order. Like all other financial penalties, they are subject to the means of the offender. However, since the 1982 Act, they are to take priority over the imposition of fines.

The role of the State in paying compensation is of much more recent origin. State provision to pay compensation to victims of violent crime was first enacted in New Zealand in 1963. The CICB, which covers England, Scotland and Wales, followed in 1964 and the idea has now become worldwide. State compensation has been justified in several different ways (Miers 1978; 1980; Burns 1980; Thorvaldson and Krasnick 1980; Harland 1978). Some of these are apparently victim-centred. It has been argued that the State should, on humanitarian and social welfare grounds, compensate those who suffer hardship occasioned by criminal violence. Others have suggested that the Government, or even society, is responsible for its failure in preventing the crime against the victim and so has some moral obligation to reimburse him (Burns 1980). The notions of equitable justice and of reciprocity in social relationships have also been raised. These are based on the premise that the victim has suffered through no fault of his own. A sense of injustice or even of 'outrage' may then arise in the population which can only be satisfied by compensation of the victim (Thorvaldson and Krasnick 1980). The Working Party which recommended the establishment of the CICB (Home Office 1961) appeared unable to find any clear reason for setting up such a system and fell back on what they termed practical considerations:

We can find no constitutional or social principle on which State compensation could be justified, but we think that it could nevertheless be based on the more practical ground, already in the minds of its advocates . . . that although the Welfare State helps the victims of many kind of misfortune, it does nothing for the victims of crimes of violence as such, notwithstanding that they are largely deprived of the means of self-protection and in most cases have no effective remedy at law. There is an argument for filling this gap, based mainly on considerations of sympathy for the innocent victim, but falling short of acceptance of any bounden duty to mitigate the victim's hardship; and we think this argument more likely to appeal to the public than any more abstruse principles that might be formulated.

The reason finally adduced in the setting up of the CICB seemed to combine two elements: compensation would show 'social solidarity or the desire to express public sympathy for the victims of crime' (Home Office 1978).

Other reasons for setting up State compensation schemes have not been so seemingly victim-centered. American schemes have been advocated to improve the satisfaction and promote future co-operation of the victim with the criminal justice system. Alternatively, Miers (1983) has argued that most schemes are essentially 'political' – they play on the desire of the public to compensate victims but merely state the desirability of compensating victims rather than setting up any effective means to produce such compensation. They 'make a public statement about crime and the values which are embodied in criminal justice and welfare programmes'.

All State compensation schemes stress the need to consider and compensate the particular harm suffered by the individual applicant (although it is not clear why this follows from any but the social justice model). Hence the applicant is asked to provide details of his expenses, losses and suffering. The decision-making process is, however, one-way. The scheme decides who is eligible and what expenses may be claimed in each case, according to the guidelines used to set it up. (The applicant usually has the right to appeal if he feels that the guidelines are not being followed, as with the CICB.) There may be, however, no consideration of what harm victims do suffer, or whether the compensation scheme is meeting any need expressed by victims. State compensation is given by State to victim, according to rules devised by the State. It is not the negotiated settlement of medieval times, nor the symbolic expression of a wrong having been committed seen in later restitutive processes in the courts.

Strangely, modern compensation processes (both those using State funds and those concerning the offender) appear to have arisen without any direct reference to victims and what they themselves see as important. For all except the 'political' purposes of compensation, this enquiry would seem to be necessary. If we never look at the reactions of victims, how can we discover whether suffering is alleviated, expenses or losses recompensed, moral status restored, or co-operation with the criminal justice system increased? Even if we have only a 'political' purpose (and this is itself predicated on one or other of the alternative purposes being supported by that society), we may find that public statements about the worth of the schemes to victims, which are later shown to be hollow, may rebound on any who set up such ineffective schemes.

The obtaining of compensation, as far as most sources of money are concerned, depends upon the victim making a personal application. State social benefits, the CICB and insurance claims all require the victim or someone acting on his behalf to take active steps. The exception to this would appear to be compensation orders from the courts, which may be made without any application, but it will be argued in Chapter 8 that, in practice, applications play a crucial role here too.

In order to take such active steps, victims need to know about the existence of the sources of compensation and to decide to take action. They need to wish to claim and to believe that it is worth applying. The low take-up rates for all forms of compensation, including the CICB, have been known for some time (Genn 1983a; CICB 1976). The reasons for those rates, as the CICB acknowledge, have remained speculative. in their Twelfth Report (1976), they discuss the possible effects of both lack of knowledge of the scheme, and of victims not wishing compensation either because they prefer to place emphasis on retribution or protection from future attack or because they wish to forget the incident as quickly as possible:

In the case of the Old Bailey bomb explosion, a very high proportion of the victims knew of the existence of the Scheme, yet only 103 out of 186 applied. Until suitable research is undertaken, we can only speculate as to the real reasons why some victims choose not to apply for compensation.

Our study, with its longitudinal nature, may be able to provide some answers to this, although it must be remembered that the sample is small and taken from only two towns in the Midlands. We did not ask victims specifically about compensation until the interview after the outcome of the case, in order to avoid artificially influencing any applications. By that time, victims would have received any advice or help from the police or other bodies. At the outcome interview, we asked victims: 'Do you think you should have compensation for what was done to you?'; 'Do you know of any way that you could get compensation (whether or not you want it in this case)?' and 'Have you applied for any form of compensation?'

There were 217 victims who took part in this final interview, 152 from Coventry and 65 from Northampton. Of these, only 74 (34 per cent) had actually applied for any form of compensation (42 from Coventry and 32 from Northampton). It is very unlikely, in the experience of the compensation agencies, that applications would have been made after this time. The CICB, for example, comments in its Seventeenth Report (1981) that:

during 1980/81 the number of applications made within three months of the incident amounted to almost 70% of our intake. A further 20% of all applications were received between three and nine months after the incident. There has been very little change in the pattern during the last few years. . . .

The task in this chapter is to explore the reasons for this low take-up rate for compensation of around a third of victims. We shall look at whether victims wanted compensation; whether they knew of any source of compensation; why they decided to apply or not to apply to particular sources; and whether there were any other personal factors that appeared to differentiate between those who applied and those who did not.

The wish for compensation

The numbers wanting compensation were much larger than those who actually applied. Fifty-seven per cent of victims said that they would definitely have liked some compensation, 7 per cent were doubtful and only 35 per cent did not want compensation.

Though victims sometimes found it difficult to articulate the exact reasons why they wanted compensation, the reasons that were given were dominated by a concern with recovery of special damages (stated by 62 per cent of those giving reasons). This might include recovering the costs actually paid out for damaged clothing, medical or dental bills or travel costs to doctors and hospitals (38 per cent) or loss of earnings (24 per cent). Where, in the course of an assault or robbery, property had been stolen or damaged, victims also felt that this should be compensated. The effects of injuries (especially any permanent scarring (18 per cent) and mental suffering, anxiety and inconvenience (16 per cent)) were also relatively frequently mentioned. These findings accord with those of Elias (1983) about claimants to the New York and New Jersey compensation boards. Forty-seven per cent of his claimants said that they had applied for compensation in order to receive redress for specific losses (medical, property, lost income or out-of-pocket expenses).

This particular focus on special damages is against the general trend of concern about general damages on the part of compensation agencies. From the point of the view of the victim, it may reflect the relative ease of assessment of special damages, compared to that of general damages. Alternatively, such an emphasis may come about because special damages represent money that the victim had to pay out, or lost the use of, during the time of crisis immediately after the offence. At that time, general living expenses were also likely to be higher than normal. The perceived need for such compensation may, therefore, be particularly great.

When we look at the reasons given by those who did not want compensation, the major one was that the offence was too trivial (said by 85 per cent of those giving reasons). This might either be because the injuries were considered too trivial or because there were no specific expenses (loss of earnings or out-of-pocket expenses). Such reasons might be given even where the offence was classed as serious by the police (for example, where a physical assault was considered to involve grievous bodily harm, or in a rape case). This mismatch between victim and police perceptions of seriousness has occurred at several points in the study. It seems to be related to the disruption caused by the offence to the victim's daily life, which, in its turn, will depend (at least as far as psychological and social effects are concerned) on the victim's personality. Victims of offences more likely to lead to serious injury (rape or the grievous bodily harm offences) were no more likely to feel that they wanted compensation than the others (actual bodily harm, robbery, indecent assault). There was also no significant difference between the numbers of sexual assault victims and other victims thinking that compensation was appropriate, though sexual assault victims did give rather different reasons why they did not want compensation:

I wasn't hurt physically. What happened you can't compensate.

Not for a sex assault.

It would appear that the type of harm which some victims consider merits compensation, or at least the type which they think would be compensated, involves the infliction of physical injury or specific losses rather than mental suffering.

Victims found it very difficult to estimate the amount of compensation they thought they should be awarded – only 46 per cent of those wishing compensation being able to put even a minimum figure on the amount. This problem was not just a result of the difficulty of assessing general damages, but also because the amount tended to be related to the preferred source of the compensation. The amounts which were suggested were often small – 29 per cent of those giving an amount requested £50 or less and 19 per cent between £51 and £100 (1980 prices). These small amounts (less than the minimum award from the CICB at that time) were either because they wished the money to be paid by the offender and appreciated his possibly low means or because the victim linked the amount to specific costs (loss of earnings or out-of-pocket expenses). One victim made this distinction very clear: 'It should be £50 from the court or £200 from the CICB'. In fact, 22 per cent of all victims interviewed commented spontaneously that they would prefer compensation to be from the offender rather than from any other source. We shall discuss this further in Chapter 8.

Several victims commented that they did not think their claim would manage to come within the scope of the CICB because of the size of the minimum limit (now up to £400 or £500 for cases of domestic violence):

I don't really expect anything from them if the minimum is £150.

I don't know if I'll get bugger all 'cos it says £150 minimum – I had no loss of earnings.

If it was £150 I'd be more than happy.

The CICB minimum figure represents an overall total of general damages and specific damages, less any sums obtained from other State sources. It is, therefore, difficult to estimate which victims would or would not qualify for an award on purely monetary grounds. Given the severity of many offences, however, it seems probable that many victims were underestimating rather than overestimating their possible compensation from the CICB and so may have been deterred from making an application.

Knowledge, eligibility and wish to apply

Knowledge of a compensation scheme is obviously a prerequisite for an application to that scheme. Comparing victims' knowledge of the different compensation possibilities is, however, a difficult exercise, as some types of compensation are only available to certain victims. Potentially, all victims are entitled to make a claim against an identifiable offender in the civil courts. All victims whose cases lead to a conviction might be awarded a compensation order by the criminal court. Many victims are likely to fall within the provisions of the CICB. These three, therefore, are types of compensation of which one might hope all victims have heard. On the other hand, employers' insurance schemes and personal insurance schemes (usually for the self-employed) are restricted to those who subscribe to them. In the field of criminal injuries, they are rare and tend to apply only to those receiving injuries at work (such as bus drivers). One might not expect all victims to know of these possibilities.

Victims were asked at the outcome interview whether they knew of any way in which to claim compensation, should they wish to. The results are shown in Table 7.1 (State welfare benefits are not included as they were assumed by most victims not to fall under the heading of 'compensation').

Table 7.1   Types of compensation which victims knew about[1]

| | Percentage of victims | | |
	Coventry	Northampton	Total
Civil action	3	5	4
Compensation order	19	15	18
CICB	31	54	39
Employers' insurance/donation	4	0	3
Private insurance	4	0	3
No method known	56	39	51
Total number of victims	152	65	217

[1]Victims might know about more than one possibility.

The most striking feature is the high percentage of victims who knew of no means of obtaining compensation. A few of these said that, had they wished to pursue the matter, they would have taken steps to find out:

I would have gone to a solicitor.

I would go to the Citizens' Advice Bureau to find out.

But the vast majority were ignorant of how to obtain help, expected the police to provide information or simply had no idea that any form of compensation existed:

I've heard of the CICB since from someone – he said you should have got it – nobody pointed it out.

I didn't have a chance. The police didn't give me any chance.

I know nothing about it at all except I'm the sufferer.

I don't know where – I'd apply but where?

Seven per cent of Coventry victims and 10 per cent of Northampton victims specifically mentioned that they felt the police had failed in not providing them with information about any possibility for compensation. On some occasions this appeared to be due to ignorance on the part of the police: 'But I asked the police if I could get compensation: they said no, I'd have to claim. They couldn't tell me anything about it.' On others, it appeared that the police had mentioned the possibility of compensation at an early stage and the victim had understood that the police would do something about it (obtain addresses or forms etc.), but nothing subsequently materialised.

There is, unfortunately, no study in this country which has attempted to assess the knowledge of the general population as to how any form of compensation might be obtained. The lack of knowledge about civil actions (replicated in our study) has been documented several times. Genn (1982), for example, describes a scheme to increase knowledge of the possibility of civil compensation for accident victims, given the finding in Genn (1983a) that only 12 per cent of all seriously injured accident victims obtained damages through the tort system. None of Vennard's (1976) small sample had sought damages from the offender in the civil courts.

There are slightly more data available on the CICB. Genn (1983b) found that eight of her 20 victims seriously injured during a criminal offence obtained some compensation – seven from the CICB and one from, apparently, a civil claim. (Note that these were the only criminal injury victims who had suffered two or more weeks of incapacity out of 35 085 members of the general population sampled – showing the rarity of serious criminal injury.) The reasons given by those who made no effort to claim were similar to those in our study. Some did not know what to do and expected the police to help them in some way. Others misunderstood the operation of the CICB and thought the offender had to be apprehended in order for a claim to be allowed.

Other previous studies have only used small samples. In Vennard's (1976) study of victims of selected indictable offences whose offenders were convicted at magistrates' courts, only one third (11 victims) had heard of the CICB and six had applied. The others either felt that their injuries were too minor or else were unsure how to apply. In the United States, statistics compiled by the New York compensation board indicate that less than 1 per cent of all victims of violent crimes reported to the police were applying for an award (see Elias 1983). Elias himself found that over half his victims claimed that they had never heard of the state compensation schemes. Almost one-half of those that did know failed to apply. The main reasons were feeling that they were ineligible (11 per cent), thinking a claim would be futile (11 per cent) and being unsure how to make a claim (9 per cent).

In our study, those who had heard of the CICB but decided not to apply were asked why. Interestingly, no victim cited the bother or work involved in claiming. This does not appear to be a relevant factor. The triviality of the offence, the concern with specific losses and a belief in compensation from offenders were mentioned here, just as they were in the context of wanting any form of compensation. They were joined, in the case of the CICB, by a belief that the police would take a more active role, occasional misinformation by the police and the deterrent effect of the minimum limit.

Turning now to compensation orders from the courts, Vennard (1976) found that most of her victims of property offences had heard of the ability of the courts to make such orders, but that only half her assault victims knew this. From the evidence of our study, the position has not improved. Knowledge on the part of the victim is not so essential for compensation orders, as no application is necessary (see Chapter 8). However, if victims are not aware of the possibility, they may be less likely to give relevant details to the police.

Applications for compensation
We have seen that several factors may be important in determining whether a victim applies for compensation – such as whether they want compensation or whether they know about particular methods of compensation. We can now draw these threads together and consider whether these factors are independent and how important each is.

Direct applications by the victim for compensation might be to the CICB or to the various forms of employers' insurance. No victim made any civil claim against the offender. We performed analyses to see which of the many variables known about the victims and their cases would best predict whether a victim would apply for any form of compensation and also whether they would apply to the CICB (stepwise discriminant function analyses using both Rao's V and Wilk's lambda criteria). Numerically, however, applications for compensation were dominated by applications to the CICB. The results of both analyses (shown in Table 7.2) are, therefore, similar and will be discussed together.

Much the most important factor in both analyses was whether the victim knew about any form of compensation. The amount of compensation wanted and whether any compensation was wanted at all were also significant but played a much smaller part. It would appear that it was lack of knowledge rather than any lack of a wish for compensation that was preventing applications.

Other less important but significant factors which predicted applications are shown in Table 7.2. Where the offender is known well, compensation agencies tend to look more carefully at applications. The CICB, for example, has a higher minimum limit for cases where offender and victim are members of the same family. It is unknown, however, whether victims were deterred by this or whether they did not think compensation should or could be awarded in such circumstances. Equally interesting are the variables which do not appear to affect applications for compensation. Perhaps surprisingly, the nature of the

Table 7.2 Applying for any form of compensation

Variables predicting whether victim would apply for any form of compensation (in descending order of significance, all significant at <.00001 level):

	F to remove
Knowing about any form of compensation	75.3
Wanting a larger amount of compensation	12.9
Wanting compensation	5.9
Not knowing the offender well as a friend or relative	3.9
Case involving court proceedings	2.9
Being of lower socio-economic status	1.6

(The above variables would predict the actual grouping of victims into those applying or not applying for compensation 82.5 per cent correctly. Percentage variance accounted for by variables = 45.3.)

Applying to the CICB

Variables predicting whether victim would apply to the CICB (in descending order of significance, all significant at <.00001 level):

	F to remove
Knowing about CICB	133.9
Wanting a larger amount of compensation	15.3
Wanting compensation	5.9
Being female	3.2
Not knowing the offender well as a friend or relative	2.9
Case involving court proceedings	2.3
Being of lower educational attainment	1.5

(The above variables would predict the actual grouping of victims into those applying or not applying to the CICB 86.6 per cent correctly. Percentage variance accounted for by variables = 57.0.)

offence and the age and marital status of the victim appeared to have little effect. Again, it was whether court proceedings occurred, rather than whether the offender was caught, or the nature of the plea or the kind of court which was important.

A similar analysis was performed by Elias (1983) to distinguish between his applicant and non-applicant groups for state compensation in New York and New Jersey. The most important distinguishing variable was whether the applicant had heard of the scheme (this accounted for 45 per cent of the variance). Another 13 per cent was determined by whether the victim had been helped by a victim service centre (equivalent to a victim support scheme). Such centres in the

United States, however, routinely tell victims about the state compensation programmes. So, as in our study, knowledge of the possibility of compensation was the most important factor. All others were much less significant.

Sources of knowledge about the CICB

Given this major influence of knowledge, it is important to consider how victims did find out about the CICB or other possibilities for compensation and what role the existing publicity has played. The words 'finding out' are very much applicable here. It was extremely rare for any victim other than a police officer (and not all of them) to have anything other than a vague awareness of the possibility of existence of some compensation body prior to victimisation.

The ways in which victims did come to hear definitely about the existence of the CICB are shown in Table 7.3. The major initial source was, as might be expected, a police officer who was working on the victim's case. However, some of the cases included in that category resulted from victim enquiries or initiatives in visiting the police station. In others, the police, while informing the victim that such a scheme existed, did not provide the address or told the victim that he would need to use a solicitor in order to apply. Rarely was the full information necessary for an adequate consideration of whether to apply provided. The influence of police colleagues and of trade unions was largely confined to the police officer victims, these sources for civilian victims being of the same order of magnitude as that of newspapers. It is clear

Table 7.3   Sources of knowledge about the CICB

Source	Percentage of victims knowing about the CICB (N = 83)		
	Those who applied	Those who did not apply	Total
Police officers on the case	29	5	34
Colleagues or friends who are policemen	5	13	18
Trade unions (including Police Federation)	13	1	14
Friends	8	2	11
Citizens' Advice Bureaux, law centres etc.	5	1	6
Newspapers, magazines	2	2	4
Unknown	4	9	13

that the police officers working on the case were far from being the main source of knowledge about the scheme. A similar plethora of sources by which victims heard about the existence of compensation schemes has been found in the United States (Carrow 1980; Elias 1983).

The failure of the police to inform victims is hardly surprising, given the state of knowledge of some police officers about the CICB. As far as the researchers were aware, the existence and mode of operation of the CICB were not included in either recruit or CID training for either of the police forces in whose areas the research was undertaken. That there is such a body is part of the informal knowledge acquired from colleagues in the police station. It is normal, however, for police officers to apply to the CICB through the Police Federation, which will handle all the correspondence. They may, therefore, not be aware of the mode of operation as it applies to civilian victims nor even that the Board will compensate, say, sexual assault cases. The position is best summed up by the following comments from police officer victims:

You must advise every person that they can claim and that it does exist. Only the police can do this. I wasn't told about it at training school – I only learnt from experience. It should be taught at training school and there should be leaflets.

The majority of the public are ill-informed. The police officer should help out. Often they do. There should be more advertisements about the CICB, more information.

When you're looking after a victim, you don't think about the CICB. Until I had my business, I didn't realise the CICB is for anybody – not just police officers.

The CICB itself has made great efforts to spread knowledge widely. Both leaflets and posters are printed and distributed to all possible agencies which may deal with victims, whenever a change is made in the scheme. They are sent not only to police stations and courts, but also to Citizens' Advice Bureaux and other information-giving bodies, hospitals, victim support schemes and Government bodies such as the DHSS. The CICB has also made considerable use of the media and encourages any initiative to publicise the scheme (CICB 1980).

Yet the victims that took part in our study found it very difficult to learn about the scheme, let alone to obtain any such publicity material. Only one victim was given a leaflet. This was reflected in the suggestions made by those victims who were re-interviewed following an application made to the CICB. Forty-four per cent spontaneously mentioned the difficulties in finding out about the Board.

The most difficult thing was finding out they existed. I went to a couple of police stations and then had to write away. The first police station didn't have the address. Why not posters in public places where you'd expect to find them? I knew you could claim money from somewhere but I'd have passed it by.

Even knowing about it – that it existed – was the most difficult.

The most difficult thing was finding out – I found out from the Citizens' Advice Bureau and friends. Why didn't the police tell me? Perhaps I didn't qualify (to be told). You could instruct bobbies that there is such a form available and it is part of their job to have the address available and to inform victims about it.

There appear to be three factors which militate against victims acquiring knowledge of the CICB. The first, and most major, is that becoming the victim of a relatively serious crime of violence is a comparatively rare event for almost all groups of citizens. As a consequence, only a few will be personally interested in any publicity about such a scheme prior to their own victimisation. This is borne out by the lack of knowledge of the victims in our study prior to the offence. Sums spent on overall media coverage would, therefore, have to be large to make any impact and their effectiveness is likely to be small. In other countries, such public information campaigns, because of their simplified nature, have also been found to produce misconceptions as to eligibility and consequent bitter disappointment. (This has occurred in the Netherlands (van Dijk, personal communication) and in the United States (Carrow 1980)). The task, therefore, is the very difficult one of informing a very small group of people during a specific short period in their lives.

Such a task can probably best be accomplished by activating those agencies and groups that deal with victims of such crimes. This requires two processes to occur: there must be knowledge of the scheme and willingness to inform victims among the personnel of such agencies; and publicity material must be available to victims so that they can consider whether to apply. While a victim is in a state of crisis at hospital or during the first contact with the police, he may not be able to comprehend or think logically about verbal information on compensation.

The most obvious agency is the police (particularly since reporting to the police is considered important for eligibility for compensation). Here the second factor comes in – the present rather haphazard way in which police officers acquire knowledge about the CICB and by which they inform victims. Both are symptomatic of the rather low priority given to victims in the criminal justice system, despite a willingness on the part of the police to perform these tasks. The first is remediable by training. The second is more difficult to change. Given the very large number of tasks that police officers are required to perform when seeing victims, remembering to inform victims about compensation is difficult. In the United States, some states have introduced legislation requiring law enforcement agencies to notify victims. The level of compliance, however, seems to be extremely varied (Harland 1978; Lynch 1976).

The most efficacious method would probably be to include such notification in the routine administrative tasks required to be performed on each case. In Scotland, procurators fiscal routinely send all identifiable victims a leaflet about compensation orders from the court (see Chapter 8). This leaflet also gives the address of and brief details about the CICB. It should ensure that at least all victims whose offenders are prosecuted should learn about the CICB. There will shortly be a national prosecution system for England and Wales. This notification system (which has also been commended by the Parliamentary All-Party Penal Affairs Group (1984) in their report on victims) could then easily be introduced. It would still be necessary to mobilise the police to deal with victims whose offenders are not caught or not prosecuted. This requires an input into training, a realisation that aiding victims is an important part of the police task and an adequate supply of publicity material.

It is in the supply of publicity material that the third factor militating against knowledge of the CICB comes into play. The CICB send out a large number of leaflets and posters whenever the scheme is changed. However, the responsibility for reordering such materials when they run out is left to the recipients (such as the Home Office and police force headquarters). It seems that police stations and other bodies are not necessarily reordering supplies of leaflets, nor asking for more posters when these become tatty and are taken down. When the researchers asked for leaflets at some of the police stations in the study, none were available. Some police officers interviewed claimed never to have seen any. Considerable improvements could be made in the distribution and replenishment of publicity material.

We have seen that knowledge of the existence of the CICB is the most important factor determining whether victims apply. It is likely that similar factors will be found to exist for any other generally applicable scheme concerning victims (for example, the provision of victim assistance and support by volunteers or court services to victims and witnesses). The challenge of devising a system for the efficient notification of victims has not been met. As far as State compensation is concerned, such a system is required by the Council of Europe Convention for the Compensation of Victims of Violent Crime (1983), already signed by nine states, including the United Kingdom.

When this system is devised, or even moderate progress is made, it is likely that applications to State compensation schemes (and their cost, if the scheme is not altered) will increase considerably. In the United States, publicity campaigns have been stopped when they resulted in too great an increase in eligible applicants (Elias 1983). Such a return to a reliance on information distribution mechanisms which are known to be faulty is antithetical to the purpose of a compensation scheme – to compensate all eligible applicants according to the rules laid down in the scheme. It shows up such schemes as wholly 'political' and as having had little intention of actually compensating victims. A better solution is to anticipate and to prepare for any increase in applications.

Meanwhile, as we explore, in Chapters 8 and 9, the experiences of victims with the different mechanisms for compensation, we need to remember that over half of the sample did not know of any way in which to obtain compensation. Many of them were victims of serious crimes of violence. They were, in many cases, deprived of compensation not because of their own actions or inactions, but because they had no idea that any such system might exist. No one in the criminal justice system had told them anything about it.

8 Compensation from offenders

An award of compensation to the victim from the criminal courts occurs by means of a compensation order made against the offender at the time of sentence. Unfortunately, when such orders were introduced, no clear guidance was given to the courts as to how they should be used, nor how compensation should fit in to the aims of the penal system. Viscount Colville, in the House of Lords debate upon the Criminal Justice Bill 1972, stated that the Bill should not be too precise as to the circumstances for compensation (see Softley 1978a). The power of the court to award compensation was consolidated in the Powers of Criminal Courts Act 1973 and at the time of our study stated that:

a court by or before which a person is convicted of an offence, in addition to dealing with him in any other way, may, on application or otherwise, make an order requiring him to pay compensation for any personal injury, loss or damage resulting from that offence or any other offence which is taken into consideration by the court in determining sentence. (s. 35(1))

Hence, as originally enacted, compensation orders were merely ancillary orders and had to be given together with another penalty. As modified by the Criminal Justice Act 1982, since our study, they may be given either as ancillary orders or as sentences in their own right. In addition, if the offender has insufficient means to pay both adequate compensation and a sufficient fine, compensation is to be given priority.

There has been disagreement among legal commentators as to the proper role of compensation orders since their introduction into the criminal justice system. Some commentators have stressed the civil nature of compensation. Its position in the system is then merely to enable the victim to obtain reparation from the offender more swiftly, more easily and with less potential cost than he could through the civil courts (though a subsidiary aim has been to improve co-operation with the criminal justice system). The Dunpark Committee (1978) in Scotland cited this as the primary reason for introducing compensation orders to Scotland. Such a position can produce an apparent tension between the supposed demands of the victim for civil damages and the penal nature of the award, particularly in respect to offenders (Duff 1981). This tension has been shown in seeming inconsistencies in the offences for which the victim may obtain reparation in the civil and criminal courts (Atiyah 1979); in the difficulty in adjusting compensation to the offender's means (for example, Wasik 1978; Brazier 1977); and in the problems experienced by the criminal courts when dealing with cases where the sum of compensation or the liability of the offender is in dispute.

Others have taken the view that compensation is an appropriate aim for the criminal justice system. Compensation may be seen as part of the punishment to be meted out to the offender or as merely one aim among many others for the sentencer to take into account. In the latter case, the sentencer is required to consider the needs of the victim as well as those of society or the offender (see Gandy (1978) for support for this view among the legal community in South Carolina). It has also been seen as having a rehabilitative effect on the offender. However, there are many proponents of this view, but few concrete findings as to its effectiveness (see Harland 1983; Hudson and Galaway 1980; Bonta *et al.* 1982). Some have gone further and argued that punishment in its utilitarian aims implies the necessity for the promotion of social justice in order to encourage law-abiding behaviour. Such social justice would then demand the use of reparative sanctions by the courts so that offenders, having been shown to be responsible for their actions, may repair the harm they have done (for example, Thorvaldson 1980; 1982).

These differing opinions have reflected the presence of so much theoretical confusion that it has been said that it is unclear whether compensation from offenders is intended primarily for the benefit of the offender or the victim (Harland 1981b). It is the thesis of this chapter that the confusion over the aims of compensation, unresolved at the time of the introduction of compensation orders and growing since, has caused practical problems in its operation in the courts.

In particular, two problems have arisen:

(1) There is a conflict between the perceived need to repay to the victim all his losses (according to civil criteria) and the penurious state of many offenders.

(2) The apparently sudden re-emergence of compensation has introduced another actor into the process, one who is now rarely seen in the criminal process of trial and sentence but is commonly present in the civil courts – the victim. In fact, as we have seen in earlier chapters, the suddenness of the appearance of the victim at the point of sentence is illusory. However, due to administrative reasons (which have a basis in the lack of an accepted role for the victim), he is rarely visible in the courtroom. The seemingly unexpected emergence of the victim when compensation is considered can give rise to worries on the part of the professional participants as to what he may say or do in the courtroom and how he may bias the deliberations of the court. It may also produce possibly misleading and unhelpful comparisons with civil procedures.

The desire for compensation from offenders

This list of theoretical and practical problems might lead to the expectation that compensation by offenders has been a relatively unappreciated measure, one which is the subject of worried and negative comment by Governments and by the general public. Nothing would be further from the case. Both in Britain and in North America, there appears almost to be unanimity in the desire for compensation from offenders.

In Britain, Government policy is to encourage the use of compensation orders by the courts. This has been enunciated several times in the last few years and forms part of the recent strategy for a new deal for victims. One of the clearest passages is:

It is all very well to speak of an offender paying his debt to society: it is also important, in my view, that he should pay the very real and personal debt he owes to the victim of his crime. . . . It is encouraging that the criminal courts continue to make greater use of their powers to order offenders to pay compensation. . . . It is so often the case that the offender has insufficient means to pay full compensation. In these circumstances it is obviously not essential for the courts to establish the precise value of the loss incurred. Having heard the submissions of the prosecution and the defence, a court should usually be able to order an amount of compensation it considers reasonable in all the circumstances. (The Home Secretary's address to the second Annual General Meeting of the National Association of Victim Support Schemes, 23.2.82)

The Parliamentary All-Party Penal Affairs Group (1984), though enumerating the disadvantages of obtaining compensation in this way (such as the penuriousness of offenders, the inability to make orders when offenders are not prosecuted or are given a custodial sentence), still calls for an extension of their use and their improvement by means of a prison earnings scheme.

In the United States, Gandy and Galaway (1980) found that 80 per cent of their sample of the general public of South Carolina favoured the idea of compensation, though this was linked more to property offences than to assaults. Gandy (1978) has also shown that 82 per cent of the legal community (judges, solicitors and attorneys) were favourable to the idea. There is as yet no research study of public opinion in Britain, but a recent opinion poll (*Observer* 21.3.82) has suggested that 66 per cent of those interviewed favoured offenders compensating their victims instead of being sent to prison. Despite the fact that it was not a specifically mentioned outcome, 10 per cent of victims identified in the British Crime Survey (Hough and Mayhew 1983) wanted compensation to be the sanction for their offender. A survey of victim support schemes (NAVSS 1983) found that 33 out of 46 local schemes wanted increased use of compensation orders from the courts beyond their already quite common occurrence.

In fact, the courts in England and Wales have steadily increased the number of compensation orders being made since their introduction in 1972. In 1980 (the fieldwork time for the present study), just over 120 000 persons were ordered to pay compensation by magistrates' courts and 6200 persons at the Crown Court (other than for summary motoring offences – *Criminal Statistics* 1980). Such orders are given in a majority of criminal damage cases at the magistrates' court – and indeed all property offences show considerable use of compensation by sentencers. The figures for offences of violence are very much lower and have been so from the introduction of the provision (Vennard 1979).

In our study, 60 victims (28 per cent of those receiving final interviews) spontaneously commented that they would have liked to have received compensation from the offender. Given the low proportion actually knowing about the possibility of court compensation (18 per cent – see Chapter 7), and the fact that no specific question about compensation from offenders was included, this is a surprisingly high figure.

Compensation orders made in the present study
Only 26 victims from our study were actually given compensation orders by the courts, 13 from Coventry and 13 from Northampton. This represents just under 20 per cent of the cases sentenced at court. Even though all these cases were originally recorded by the police as crimes of violence, only 15 were made for injury alone. Six of the orders were solely for damage to property occasioned during the assault and five were for both property damage and injury.

The amounts of compensation awarded were fairly low. Five awards were under £20, ten between £20 and £40, eight between £40 and £60, two between £60 and £100 and only one over £100 (awards were made in 1979–80). The total amount awarded for injury was £878.50 (an average of £43.93 per victim) and for property damage £238.51 (an average of £21.68 per victim).

Since transcripts of the court appearance at which sentence was passed were collected during the study, we can attempt to calculate the level of compensation that might have been awarded if the Magistrates' Association guidelines relevant at that time had been followed (Magistrates' Association 1978). The total amount for all cases in which transcripts were made, calculated on this basis, comes to about £1400 for injuries and effects of injuries alone (loss of earnings should be added to this). However, the amount actually awarded for both injuries and loss of earnings in these cases was only £665. It might be objected that the comparison is not fair, since the awards must take into consideration the offenders' means. However, for 50 per cent of the compensation orders made, the main sentence was a fine, and, in almost every case, the amount of that fine (not counting any costs, legal aid contribution etc.) was considerably greater than the amount of the compensation. Only one award reached the then minimum CICB limit of £150.

These findings are not unusual. Indeed, the proportion of compensation orders made in our study was higher than the national percentage for offences of violence against the person at the time (17 per cent at magistrates' courts and 9 per cent at the Crown Court). In the same year, 76 per cent of orders for violence against the person at the magistrates' court and 52 per cent at the Crown Court were for amounts of £50 or less. Previous studies have also commented on the paucity of compensation orders and the relatively low level of awards for offences of violence (Softley 1978a; Vennard 1978). The phenomenon is not confined to England and Wales. Smandych (1981, citing a study by Standerwick) has commented that although Canadian judges have recently shown much greater willingness to employ compensation, this has mostly been for property offences. Both Hudson and Chesney (1978) and Harland (1978) have found that compensation by offenders in the United States has been mainly restricted to less serious offences involving property loss, though here it is common for full restitution to be ordered (though not necessarily paid).

Factors affecting the making of compensation orders

The question arises, therefore, given the apparent public and political willingness for orders to be made, why so few orders are passed in cases involving offences of violence and why these are for such small amounts. We analysed all the cases in our study in which sentence was passed to see which factors appeared to predict whether a compensation order would be made (using discriminant function analysis). Unfortunately, we could not include those personal details of the offender which were known to the court (such as his means), as these were to be found in those parts of the antecedents or social enquiry report that were not referred to in open court. However, we did include details of the victim (age, sex, social class, education etc.), the offence (physical or sexual assault, whether the victim knew the offender well or very well (as a relative or friend etc.), the court case (type of court, plea etc.) and what was said in court about compensation and the losses suffered by the victim. The results are shown in Table 8.1.

It can be seen that one of the most important predictors of the making of a compensation order was whether the prosecution mentioned the word 'compensation' during the court appearance. Such a reference might have been in any context. Some mentions were a specific application for compensation, but others involved merely reminding the sentencer of his powers or even citing the making of a compensation order in the sentence for a previous conviction. Other important factors

Table 8.1   *Factors affecting the making of compensation orders*

Most important variables predicting whether a compensation order would be made	Standardised canonical discriminant function coefficient (direct analysis)
The prosecution mentioned the word 'compensation'*	2.30
The prosecution mentioned the injuries suffered by the victim*	0.41
A custodial sentence was not passed*	0.36
The victim knew the offender well as a friend or relative*	0.25
The victim knew of any means of compensation	0.22
Greater age of victim*	0.21
Lower socio-economic status of the victim*	0.18
The offence was a physical rather than sexual assault	0.18

The non-availability of a computer program for discriminant function analysis which includes pairwise deletion of missing data, the small number of cases in which compensation orders were made, and the extent of missing data due to the longitudinal nature of the study, made stepwise analysis very unstable. The table, therefore, represents direct discriminant function analysis. The variables that appear to be the most significant (F to remove > 1) after several stepwise analyses are starred. The starred variables would predict the actual grouping of cases into those with and without compensation 68.8 per cent correctly.

were whether the prosecution gave any details of the injuries suffered by the victim and whether a custodial sentence was passed. These have all been cited as relevant factors in previous research (Softley 1978a; Vennard 1976; 1979). In this analysis, however, it appears that factors concerning the court process are more important than personal attributes of the victims or the type of case. Obviously, some of the remainder of the variance will be accounted for by the attributes of the offender.

The importance of the prosecution mentioning compensation, and, indeed, the advisability of making an application rather than leaving the matter up to the initiative of the magistrates or judge, suggests that it is important to examine not only the views of victims about compensation but also the views of those who conduct the prosecution (police and prosecution solicitors) and those who advise magistrates as to their powers (justices' clerks) (see below).

Attitudes of victims to compensation orders

We have already pointed to victims' general approval for the idea of compensation from offenders. But did the low levels of compensation orders awarded to victims in practice produce a diminution of this enthusiasm? Those victims who were awarded compensation orders were significantly more satisfied with the way the courts had dealt with their case than those who were not ($p < .001$). Compensation was seen as the province of the courts and any satisfaction or dissatisfaction was directed towards them and not the police (as opposed to, for example, informing the victim of the sentence, the responsibility for which was placed by most victims on the police). Receiving a compensation order, then, increased satisfaction with the courts, but did not affect either current views of the way the police had handled the case or the likelihood of reporting to the police in future. The study gives no support to the idea that compensating the victim will increase general co-operation with the criminal justice system. It does show, however, that victims appreciate and approve of the award of compensation orders and consider it to be right and proper that compensation should be part of the sentence of the court.

Views as to the amounts of the orders made were rather more mixed. Of the 22 victims interviewed after sentence, 12 considered that the amount given was sufficient:

I didn't expect anything – it was enough compensation. (robbery) victim

Enough came. It's like saying how much is your right hand worth. I can't answer – it's satisfactory. (wounding victim)

I was pleased about the compensation – enough – it was fair. (victim of assault occasioning actual bodily harm)

Seven victims thought that the amount was too little, but qualified their disapproval in some way. Many found it very difficult to suggest what would be a fair sum for compensation for injuries and in fact suggested figures of the same order of magnitude as that awarded by the court. Victims also took the view that the means of the offender should be taken into account:

Injuries should be recompensed. Make the offender pay if he has ways and means of doing so – if he hasn't got anything then it should be the government.

Property damage, on the other hand, did not cause such problems of assessment and there was little dissatisfaction:

For the glasses it was enough – for everything else – suffering, sickness things, many difficulties in my ways – no not enough – it's very difficult to put a figure on it.

It was possible to trace 12 of the victims who were the recipients of compensation orders and re-interview them two years after the court outcome (the remainder had moved and were untraceable – the result of the high mobility and increasing unemployment in the areas over this period). This small sample can give us an idea as to whether any added difficulties in enforcing orders had affected their judgement of the merits of compensation orders. Surprisingly, they had, if anything, become more satisfied with the amount of the orders and remained in favour of the principle of compensation coming from the offender. A few commented, however, that they would have preferred that it should initially be paid by the State, with the offender paying back the amount gradually into a central fund.

Other studies have also found a welcome for the principle of compensation from offenders, but some concern about the amounts awarded. Vennard (1976) found that half of her victims who received compensation orders described outstanding financial losses greater than the amounts received and that this 'naturally produced dissatisfaction on the part of the victim'. The North American studies have shown more positive results. Smandych (1981) cites a study of 146 Canadian victims who had participated in negotiating an agreement to receive compensation as part of the offender's sentence. In general, victims were 'extremely positive' in their initial reaction to the value of making offenders compensate their victims. Chesney (cited in Newton 1976) found that 60 per cent of Minnesota victims awarded compensation from the offender as a condition of a probation order thought the restitution awarded by the court was fair and a similar percentage considered this to be the proper method for victim compensation. Interestingly, 62 per cent of the offenders interviewed also thought the compensation they were ordered to pay was fair. Fifteen per cent of Elias' (1983) victims who had applied for *State* compensation complained that they would have preferred compensation from the offender (as did several of our victims – see Chapter 9).

This almost unquestioning acceptance of the appropriateness of the principle of compensation from offenders, its place in the criminal justice system and, particularly, the preference for it among those who received such orders is striking. It contrasts vividly with the doubts of legal commentators.

Police, prosecution solicitors' and justices' clerks' views of compensation orders

A compensation order may be made 'on application or otherwise'. However, in order to make such an order, the courts need, first, to have the relevant information put before them and, secondly, to realise that they have the power to make the order. The victim himself, if he were to attend court, could theoretically provide this information himself. We have found, however, that, except in the case of not guilty trials, victims are rarely informed or able to discover when the relevant court appearances are (see Chapter 4). Nor, unless they are required as a witness, will they be paid expenses to attend hearings. It tends, therefore, to be up to the police to provide the necessary information about the effects of the offence on the victim and up to the prosecution to bring it to the attention of the court. Do they see this as part of their role?

The 32 police officers interviewed, although sympathetic to the idea of compensation in principle and willing to help in whatever way they could, did not feel that they had time to gather together the detailed and up-to-date information necessary to give the sentencer the full picture of victim losses. Much of this would either not be available at the time witness statements were taken or would not necessarily be appropriate for inclusion there. The initial statement from the victim could not cover, for example, persistence of physical effects, loss of earnings, contributions by victims to NHS treatment, estimates for repairs to damaged property or damage to teeth resulting in extractions or dentures. Further contact between victim and police would be needed to establish such details. We have already described the paucity of such further communication and the difficulties involved for victims who wish to contact the police (see Chapter 3). Difficulties in providing the police with further information will be exacerbated if victims are unaware of the possibility of obtaining compensation from the courts and so do not appreciate the necessity of passing on such information to the police.

In fact, details of injuries and losses were rarely given to the courts in the cases we studied (see Table 8.2). As a comparison, the percentage of cases from the overall sample in which victims said they had suffered the equivalent effects is given. It seems extraordinary that in some cases no details of injuries suffered were cited at all in court. Persistence of any physical or mental effects was very rarely reported, while not one case of financial hardship was cited. Even where not guilty pleas were entered, so that the victim was present at court and available in the witness box to give evidence about such factors, the prosecution did not always attempt to elicit evidence on this. The courts were being provided with hardly any evidence from which to consider the amount of a compensation order, let alone a complete or up-to-date account of the victim's injuries and losses. As Vennard (1979) says: 'guidelines assume that the extent of injury and loss is ascertainable whereas in fact magistrates are often constrained by lack of such information'.

Whether the sentencer is given the necessary information depends not only on whether that information is available to the prosecution, but also on whether it is presented to the sentencer. The sentencer's

Table 8.2   Percentage of cases in which information about victims' injuries or losses was given to the courts

	Guilty plea cases	Not guilty plea cases	All cases	Victims suffering these effects in overall sample
Any information on injuries given	78	93	81	91
Any mention of time off work	9	13	10 ⎫	
Length of time off work given	3	7	4 ⎬	28
Amount of loss of earnings stated	0	0	0	22
Any physical or mental effects on the victim mentioned occurring over 24 hours after the offence	16	38	20	>75
Any post-casualty medical treatment mentioned	1	1	1	25

awareness of a wish for compensation will also depend, in the absence of the victim, on the prosecution. His knowledge of his powers in this respect in a particular case may be influenced by whether compensation is mentioned by the prosecutor or by the clerk (if a magistrates' court).

Some of the prosecution solicitors interviewed were extremely dubious about putting forward an application for compensation on behalf of the victim. They felt this might compromise their position of independence. A few solicitors felt that the courts should not award compensation for injury at all, but that complainants should apply to the CICB. They often did not appreciate the size of the minimum requirement for the CICB. Only one of the solicitors made a practice of reminding the courts of their powers to award compensation in injury cases. Some examples of the varying views were:

It's not my business to suggest anything to the bench – it's the clerk's job to remind the magistrates. The magistrates can ask me for any details they need.

We don't mention the possibility of compensation for injury to the court because we're not the one making the application. We might mention the amount of time lost off work – but from the point of view of showing how serious the assault is, not for compensation.

I do suggest it – because it's compensation, not punishment. In my last place we had standing instructions we were to draw the attention of the magistrates to their powers to award compensation for injury. One didn't do it for football hooligans or husband/wife disputes but for unprovoked assault or assault on a police officer, yes. So I tend to do it here.

The sentencer might be expected to think of the possibility of compensation whenever a suitable case arises. However, during a court appearance for one of the cases in our study, a circuit judge queried in open court whether he was able to make a compensation order for injury. Again, the justices' clerks who advised magistrates in our study tended to feel that it was up to the prosecution to make any necessary application:

Before the Criminal Justice Act (1972) there was a requirement to apply for compensation – so the prosecution accepted the onus and made sure the victim was there to give a first-hand account. Now, when we have a guilty plea, the prosecution tells the victim he needn't come and all the prosecution has is a bald statement about three windows and their estimated cost or a casualty officer's statement – not how many days they've had off work or dental bills. It seems the victim is no one's responsibility – he's only important in as far as he's necessary for the Crown's case for conviction.

Most clerks we interviewed did consider that the victim had no right to make an application for compensation himself orally in open court. They would stop any victim trying to speak and suggest that he talk to the prosecution solicitor. Any information that he might be trying to impart would then perforce be filtered through the prosecution who, as we have seen, do not always agree with the idea of compensation, let alone with their playing an active role in its procurement. It is respectfully submitted that this ruling is contrary to the wording of the relevant statute (Powers of Criminal Courts Act 1973), which states the possibility of an application being made – 'a court ... may, on application or otherwise ... make an order requiring him to pay compensation ...'. The victim, then, should be able to make such an application to the sentencer.

Here we come to the nub of the problem – and the reason why the prosecution mentioning the word 'compensation' in court is an important predictor of the making of a compensation order in our study. The rewording in the Criminal Justice Act 1972 and the Powers of Criminal Courts Act 1973 to make sure the victim does not *have* to attend court to apply for compensation did not put that responsibility on any other participant. Consequently, the police may not see it as their job to collect the necessary information; prosecution solicitors may not make any application or put forward that information on behalf of the victim; and clerks may wait for the prosecution to mention it first.

Payment and enforcement of compensation orders

The making of a compensation order against the offender is only the first stage towards the receipt by the victim of that compensation. The victim also needs to be informed of the order; the offender must pay the money and the court must (if necessary) enforce the payment; and, finally, the court must pay the money to the victim.

Although the sample of compensation orders made in our study was very small, we did search the magistrates' courts records to trace details of payment and of enforcement action on the orders. We also interviewed the justices' clerks and administrative staff of the two magistrates' courts which administered the compensation orders made in the area of the study (an order made at the Crown Court is administered by a magistrates' court, normally the one for the area in which the offender resides).

We managed to trace details of 24 of the 29 orders made against offenders (to the benefit of the 26 victims). Nineteen (79 per cent) had been paid off in full, over periods of time ranging from 15 days to 374 days (with an average of about five months). This includes a delay between payment by the offender to the court and payment by the court to the victim of between five and 93 days (with an average of 34 days). Courts in the study area only paid out cheques to victims once a month or every three months, to cut down on time and administrative costs. Some action had been taken by the court on the five orders which had not been paid.

The figure of about 80 per cent of orders paid in full is similar to that found in Softley's (1978a) larger study of compensation orders and also that in his (1978b) study of fines. In both of these, around 75 per cent of orders had been completed within 18 months. Default and enforcement problems are not confined to this country – indeed we seem to have lower default rates than many others, possibly because account is taken of the defendant's means. Both in Canada (Bonta *et al.* 1982; Smandych 1981) and in the United States (Elias 1983), much larger default rates of between 40 and 60 per cent seem common.

One might expect that victims subject to non-payment or delayed payment would become disenchanted with such a means of compensation. However, victims' dissatisfaction seemed to focus instead on lack of information from the courts as to the progress of payments and what enforcement action was being taken. They expected payments by instalments over a substantial period, because of offenders' (generally) limited means:

It took a bit of time – it was paid by instalments. That was OK. I knew the bloke wasn't working so I expected a long time.

The court can't help it – the boys can only pay so much. But I didn't know what was happening.

Nobody contacted me at all even to apologise. I'm very unsatisfied but at the non-enforcement rather than him. They should have taken enforcement action. (no payment made – the offender was still paying off old fines at the rate set by the court – a fact of which the victim was unaware)

As we saw in Chapter 5, the principal complaint of victims about their involvement with the criminal justice system up to the point of sentence was that of lack of information about the progress of the case. Information about the making of compensation orders was no exception. Only one of the courts in our study (a Crown Court) informed victims that a compensation order had been passed. The others only contacted victims if money had been paid in by the offender, but did not bother if it was not (unless the court wished to write off the order completely, which, at that time, required the consent of the victim). Victims, however, were annoyed if they were not told that an order had been made and even more dissatisfied if payments suddenly dried up without any explanation:

If the bloke (offender) hadn't told me, I wouldn't know it had come to court. I haven't had the £20 yet. I don't think I'll get it. Someone told me they don't have to tell you anything – you have to go to the office to find out. That's very bad. It's not the police, it's the court's fault.

I had to go to the police station to find out. I felt a fool although they were sweet, but no one tells you what's happening.

Similar problems have been noted in the United States (Hudson and Chesney 1978).

Victims who did not receive payments started to become concerned if the length of time over which they had heard nothing passed the time limit in which they expected the order to be paid. They then tended to assume, probably incorrectly, that the court was taking no enforcement action and did not care about them or their needs:

As far as getting money out of the bloke, they never seemed to press it – they should have took action.

I'd like to know why it wasn't paid at once. Just let me know I'm getting it and it'll take a long time.

At one court, the situation was made almost comic by the fact that, when money was paid to a victim, just a cheque in an envelope arrived, without any letter of explanation. This produced considerable mystification in most victims (and some considerable worry as to whether they were really entitled to this unexpected money from the Clerk to the Justices). Since all the victims in the study had been informed of the sentence (if only by the researchers), most guessed what the cheque represented, and only two rang the court or the police. Both the police and the court in that area were, however, used to victims ringing up in considerable puzzlement:

Something came – £14 in two envelopes. We thought it was so funny no letter came with it – only a cheque with a counterfoil. We didn't know what it was. We took it to the bank – they accepted it and gave us back the counterfoil.

An envelope came containing a cheque for £50 from the clerk to the justices – no letter – nothing. Well, I knew what it was – but you shouldn't have to guess.

The lack of information to victims seemed to be a result of concern on the part of the justices' clerks interviewed that, if victims were to be told that a compensation order had been made, the clerks would be bothered continuously by victims contacting them to discover why the money had not yet been paid. In courts which do inform victims, however, this problem does not seem to be significant. The Crown Court in our study which was informing victims did not seem to perceive any problem. In Scotland, under the rules accompanying the introduction of compensation orders by the Criminal Justice (Scotland) Act 1981, the clerk of the court is required to write to the victim to inform him that an order has been made and then to account at regular intervals (once a month at the time of our study) for the progress of the order. This frequency seems somewhat excessive, and is certainly greater than that expected by victims in the present study. Adopting the principle of informing victims of the progress of the order whenever sums are paid out and, if nothing is received from the offender, say also every three or six months, would probably do much to increase the level of victim satisfaction with the courts.

Why are so few compensation orders made?

We can now draw together the strands of evidence provided by the attitudes of those involved with compensation orders, and consider why so few are being made in cases of violence, and why those that are made are of such low value.

We have seen that those involved with the prosecution of the case have tended to take the view of the legal commentators cited at the beginning of this chapter – that the inclusion of compensation for victims within the criminal justice system is problematic. In particular, they do not necessarily consider that it is part of their job to advance this process. The lack of specification in the statutes as to whose job it might be, and the lack of an accepted role for the victim during the previous stages up to conviction have added to this problem. If more orders are to be made, then both attitudinal and procedural changes may be necessary. In particular, a way will need to be found to provide the courts with sufficient information to consider the making of an order. In the terms of the second practical problem cited at the beginning of this chapter, information about the victim will have to become more 'visible' to the court.

The low value of the orders made, however, is a much more basic problem. There are several reasons why this may occur – the limited means of offenders, lack of information presented to the court about the extent of the victims' injuries and losses and the necessity at the time of the study (now removed by the Criminal Justice Act 1982) to prefer an adequate fine to sufficient compensation, where there is insufficient money to do both. The new legislation, if given effect by the courts, now enables the available money to be directed towards compensation. There are also some proposals for restitution schemes in combination with probation orders and for prisoners' earnings (Parliamentary All-Party Penal Affairs Group 1984) which could increase the number of sentences with which a compensation order could be combined and, hence, the proportion of offenders who could pay at least some compensation. No legislation, however, can easily increase the ability of offenders to pay. As we mentioned at the beginning of the chapter, compensation by offenders can never reach the full civil scale in all cases.

But does this matter? If one holds the view that compensation in the criminal courts is merely a simpler or quicker way of obtaining civil damages for the victim, then it must. It may even be, as Softley (1978a) has suggested, that the 'perceived incongruity of harnessing to criminal proceedings a procedure for compensating the victim or loser' may ensure that no compensation order at all is made. If, however, compensation orders are thought of as a means of working towards 'social justice' and as compatible with a penal sanction, then an award which takes into account the means of the offender (and, therefore, often an award below the level of civil damages) would be not merely possible, but correct. The position would be identical to that of a fine, the amount of which, according to the Magistrates' Court Act 1980, must reflect the offender's means. Given such a view of compensation orders, there would not necessarily be an identity between a scale of civil damages and a scale of compensation orders, since the compensation orders would reflect a differently weighted set of priorities. It would appear that many victims in our study were adhering to the second position, whereas the professionals were more divided in their views. This fundamental split explains why there is little advocacy of such orders from the prosecution and why victims may feel let down by the prosecution.

Whichever point of view is held about the place of compensation in the criminal justice system, there can be no dispute that the court should be provided with sufficient information about the victim's losses to be able to consider what the magnitude of an order should be if it wishes to make one. Several different means for ensuring this have been set up in different countries. Various states in America have legislated to require probation officers to include victims' losses, offenders' proposals for compensation and recommendations based on these in their pre-sentence reports; to grant victims the right to make a statement to the court relating to the extent of their injuries and financial losses; to require the prosecutor to investigate the possibility of compensation; and to set up schemes whose staff provide an assessment on behalf of the victim to the court (Harland 1981a and b; Harding 1982).

The system most likely to be compatible with that of England and Wales, however, is the Scottish one. A systematic process for obtaining the relevant information from the victim, presenting it to the court and keeping the victim informed about the enforcement of any court order was introduced in Scotland soon after compensation orders became available to the courts. When the procurator fiscal (the independent prosecutor) receives the file of a case from the police, he scans it to see if there is an identifiable victim. That victim is then sent a form to fill in about the extent of his losses, together with a leaflet which explains about compensation orders and also mentions the possibility of applying to the CICB. The victim completes the form and returns it to the procurator fiscal, who hands it to the sentencer at the time of sentence. We interviewed some of those involved in the operation of this scheme about one year after its introduction. At that time, it did appear to be working, with very little dissent about increased workload from those who had to operate it and with no apparent problems generated by possible inaccuracies in the information on the form despite the fact that it is not normally checked by the fiscal. Interestingly, some of the higher awards appeared to be being given in injury cases. This was ascribed to the provision of more information to judges; to increased awareness of judges about victims; and to the contact established between prosecutor and victim. For a case involving a black eye or bloody nose, orders of the level of £100–150 (at 1982 prices) might be made. Loss of earnings and travel expenses (especially important in rural areas) are also included on the form.

It has been suggested that higher compensation orders might lead to greater failure in payment and so to more prison sentences in default. It is difficult, given the limited time the scheme has been operating in Scotland, to know at what level default will stabilise, but the trends do not appear to suggest there is a problem. The only major problem in the operation of the scheme as far as prosecutors are concerned seems to be the disparity between areas of the country in the numbers of orders made. This is probably due again to differing opinions about the philosophy behind the orders, in this case on the part of sentencers (see Duff 1981; 1982). Prosecutors in a few areas were sending out and submitting forms to the courts for large numbers of victims, without, they felt, adequate 'return' in the form of compensation orders being made by the courts.

The Scottish system has the additional advantage that it furthers contact between prosecutor and victim (seen as important by victims in our study – see Chapter 4). Such a scheme, involving both prosecution and court staff, enables adequate gathering and exchange of information both prior to the court case and after any order is made. As we discussed in the last chapter, it may also go some way towards relieving victims' lack of knowledge about compensation. Following the original report of our study, the Scottish scheme has been commended by the Parliamentary All-Party Penal Affairs Group. The introduction of an independent prosecution system for England and Wales would seem an ideal opportunity for its initiation. It would facilitate contact between victim and prosecutor (the lack of which is one possible disadvantage of a prosecution service separate from the police); allow the victim the opportunity to state the effect the offence has had on him without requiring implied comment on the part of the prosecutor and relieve the extraordinary shortage of information currently being given to the courts.

The debate about the role of compensation in the criminal justice system will continue and we take it up again in Chapter 10. Given the apparent popularity of such orders and the extension of the courts' powers in recent legislation, however, it would seem necessary at least to produce a system by which such powers can effectively be used. This implies, at a minimum, first, the introduction of a new system to provide information to sentencers about the effects of the offence on the victim. It is not possible to produce this within the framework of the prosecution case for conviction. Secondly, the courts need to become more aware of their powers to make such orders. The development of case law regarding the suitability of cases, the kinds of losses that should be covered, the possibilities of making an ancillary order in particular circumstances together with a community service order, probation order or custodial sentence and the use of instalments would be beneficial. In personal injury cases, guidelines as to quantum and the necessity of covering other losses (consequent damage to clothing, spectacles and so forth) could be more comprehensive. Thirdly, the victim should be informed of the making of the order and, at regular intervals, of the progress of repayments and of any enforcement action taken.

9 The Criminal Injuries Compensation Board

The major source of compensation for victims in our study was not the courts, but the Criminal Injuries Compensation Board (CICB). The success rate for receiving at least some money was very high. Fifty-four victims applied to the Board and 45 (83 per cent) received either a full or a reduced award (see Figure 9.1). The sums of money involved ranged from £154 to £3000, with a mean of £611. Only one applicant appealed against a decision by the Board not to grant an award and no applicant appealed against the quantum of any award.

It would appear from these figures that the CICB is operating in many respects as a model organisation. The proportion of ineligible applicants is low, so little organisational time is being wasted and few applicants are being disappointed. Applicants tend to accept the results of the lowest stage of the decision-making process (appeals are from a single member of the Board to two or three sitting together). This suggests a high degree of concurrence by applicants with the Board's rules and method of operation and of satisfaction with the level of the awards. The sample in our study is not untypical. The national figures for the period over which most of the decisions on the sample were being made (1979–80) show that 83 per cent of those English applications which were resolved resulted in some award being made. Ninety-one per cent of decisions made by the single member were accepted by applicants (CICB 1980).

This experience is not common in other countries. In the United States, Canada and in some European countries, the proportion of applicants who receive some money from State compensation schemes is often below 50 per cent, in some cases much lower (Elias 1983; Doerner and Lab 1980; Council of Europe 1978; Cozijn 1984). It is not surprising that the CICB have, for some time, taken the view that

this would seem to indicate that a very high proportion of applicants were satisfied with the way that their claims were dealt with by the single member. (CICB 1972)

In this chapter, we shall explore the views of the applicants to the CICB from our study to see whether the high level of acceptance of the Board's decisions is in fact correlated with high levels of satisfaction

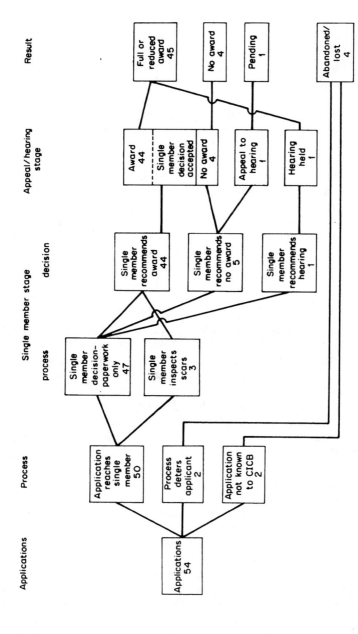

Figure 9.1 Results of applications to the CICB

with the process, the amounts of awards and the principles on which the Board operates. The information we have available includes interviews with all the victims as to why they had or had not applied to the CICB; interviews with all 54 applicants after the outcome of the case (normally a few months after sending in the application form); further interviews with 35 of these applicants approximately two years later; analysis of the CICB files of the 54 cases, and interviews with the administrative officers of the CICB.

The process for claiming compensation

The process of applying to the CICB starts when the victim fills in an application form. This asks for details of the offence, whether and how the circumstances of the injury were reported to the police; the extent of the injury and treatment received; earnings lost and out-of-pocket expenses incurred; social security, pensions, gratuities, compensation and insurance payments received; and particulars of any previous application. The applicant also signs a certificate authorising the Board to obtain any details they may require from medical practitioners, the police, the social security or other public benefit authorities, the applicant's employer and government-sponsored training or rehabilitation units. When the Board receives an application, it is acknowledged and standard enquiries are set in train with those of the agencies mentioned above applicable to that case. Each agency is asked to give a report about the victim's contact with them. The police are also asked whether, in their view, the injuries were due to a crime of violence, arrest of an offender or prevention of an offence (all three categories being eligible for compensation); whether the injuries resulted to any extent from the applicant's own conduct; whether there were any other material facts about the applicant's conduct, including his conduct before and after the incident and his background; whether the applicant has previous convictions; and the result of any prosecution. At this stage the victim may also be contacted to supply further information or clarify details on the application form.

An application will not normally be submitted to the single member of the Board for a final decision until all the relevant details are available and have been checked. This requires that the agencies mentioned above should have returned their reports completed correctly, that a firm medical prognosis should have been given and that any court case should have reached the point of conviction and sentence. If the application form or medical reports show that the victim is still suffering from injuries or effects, or that he has scarring, or that the applicant might be eligible for industrial disablement benefit, then the applicant will be sent a further form (a 'CS1A') asking whether he has fully recovered and, if not, what his present symptoms and treatment are. If the applicant has scarring, he may be asked to submit black-and-white photographs of the scars. A contribution of up to £1.50 (£2.70 as from 1 April 1982) is paid towards the cost of photographs. The administrative officers of the Board also say that the applicant's agreement to the loss of earnings figure to be included in the award is obtained if it is very different from what he is claiming.

If it appears that it will take a considerable time for a firm medical prognosis to be made or a decision to be reached in a court case, the papers may be submitted to the single member for consideration of an interim award.

It is standard for enquiries and contacts between Board and applicant to be by means of letters, rather than by telephone or personal contact. There will normally only be personal contact prior to the decision by the single member if the member decides that he needs to inspect the extent of any scarring. The administrative officers of the Board felt that such a paper system is sufficient, becuase it is their practice to obtain an expert opinion from a consultant when there is any doubt.

The single member may decide to make an offer of a full or reduced final award, to make no award, or to refer the application for a decision by two or three members of the Board at a hearing. If the applicant appeals against the decision of the single member, the application will also go to a hearing, at which the applicant must appear in person. The applicant accepts the decision of the single member by signing and returning an acceptance slip. Any award will then be paid by cheque to the applicant.

Making an application

1. The application form
The application form itself appeared to present few victims in the present study with problems. Although the form that victims used was not the modified, simplified, multi-coloured version now available, it still seemed to stand out as a rare example of an intelligible official form. The following comments were typical:

It's not complicated – one of those mugs' forms.

The form was easy really – presumably they asked about everything to check up.

Nothing complicated. It was in reasonably good English – strange for a government form.

However, the application form does not ask specifically about the mental effects of injuries. The question is phrased: 'What injury did you suffer?' Victims found it difficult to express such effects in the context of the question asked:

It's not possible to say it to the Board. It's just a piece of paper you got it down on. 'I was bottled three times etc.' I don't care about the injuries, but you can't say the mental effects.

The form was very easy and straightforward. But I rabbited on about the psychological aspect – I didn't know how to write it down.

It is possible that the only source of information about mental effects will be the applicant, as hospitals and general practitioners tend to confine themselves to details of physical injuries, except in sexual assault cases. It was certainly true that the percentage of applicants mentioning mental effects on the application form was far lower than the 51 per cent of victims who had complained of psychological effects during previous interviews (see Chapter 6).

2. Further enquiries – the work involved

The amount of contact between victim and CICB varied considerably. In 52 per cent of cases there was only one letter from the CICB to the applicant apart from the standard acknowledgement, decision and, where applicable, cheque. Seventeen per cent of applicants, however, received four or more communications – one having as many as eight. The number of communications the other way, from applicant to CICB, followed very much the same pattern. Almost all were responses to enquiries from the Board. The present study does not seem to bear out the CICB's observation that victims often produce 'unnecessary enquiries . . . about the progress of their application within a short time of their applying to the Board' (CICB 1977).

The most common enquiry received by victims (91 per cent) was the 'CS1A' form, asking about the progress of recovery from injuries and suggesting the submission of photographs for cases involving scarring. The photographs caused two problems – the embarrassment felt by some victims at having their scars photographed by a commercial photographer and the necessity to pay for the photographs with the expectation of only receiving part of the cost back some time later. Thirty-nine per cent of victims sent photographs at an average cost of £4.90 per victim. The average amount paid to victims was only £2.85. It is not clear why victims should need to bear this cost (and, indeed the cost of postage) until the time the award is made, or why the full cost is not met.

A small number of victims were told by the CICB to apply for permanent disability or industrial injury benefits from the DHSS. This arises under paragraph 19 of the Scheme:

If, in the opinion of the Board, an applicant may be eligible for any such benefits the Board may refuse to make an award until the applicant has taken such steps as the Board consider reasonable to claim them.

Unfortunately, such claims can involve the applicant in a great deal of work, time and trouble, with no direct benefit to him, since the amount of the benefit is merely subtracted from the amount of the award:

I had to go for a medical examination for the CICB – he looked at the scars – it wasn't difficult. Then the company solicitor told me I also had to claim DHSS benefit which would be deducted from the CICB. I had to do the leg work – I went to the DHSS, waited one and a half hours, got two forms. I filled in the forms and went back to the DHSS to give them the form. I received a letter from them saying OK, it's an industrial injury, now you can claim for it. Get another form. I went back, waited, got the form, sent it off. Then I had to have another medical for DHSS – it's a hell of a long rigmarole – two medicals is ridiculous. You shouldn't have to wait for months until another Board decides they need to have you seen. Then the DHSS decided what to pay me and the other bunch, the CICB, knocked it off and I got the residue.

Two applicants were actually deterred from pursuing their applications by the enquiries they were sent. As they were unable to produce the papers and documents required (detailed estimates of loss of earnings while self-employed), they just gave up. Another two applications appeared to have been mislaid by the Board somewhere in the process. The applicants had not queried the long delay but were patiently waiting for the Board to make the next move. This is a possible danger for a scheme based entirely on paperwork, with no personal contact with applicants. Some applicants do not feel competent to express themselves on paper. Rather than feel they are making a nuisance of themselves, they will, with some bitterness, abandon their application:

I didn't write back 'cos it was a waste of time. I can't put pen to paper. I'd rather talk to someone.

For the majority, however, the process was not difficult. Applicants did not see the amount of work they had to do as too great or too difficult, though they did complain about the long delays when nothing seemed to be happening. They did not seem to be aware that the bulk of the CICB's workload during this initial enquiry stage is with other agencies, checking up on what the victim has said. It was the lack of information given to victims about the process that tended to encourage the feelings that:

They seem to do it at their leisure.

Then there was just a long wait with nothing happening.

Ages and ages passed.

3. *The influence of lawyers*
There has been some pressure recently for victims to be able to obtain

legal aid for applications to the CICB. It has been argued (Miers 1978; Vennard 1978) that legal advice should be made available to victims to assist them in preparing their application, to advise them on any award offered and to represent them at hearings. Legal advice up to £25 in value is available on the 'green form' scheme. The CICB's position, however, is:

many applicants welcome the assistance of a solicitor, their trade union or trade association, the Citizens' Advice Bureau or other bona fide agent when making application to the Board. However, we must stress that the procedure of application and the presentation of claims to the Board is kept as simple as possible so that those who wish to deal with their claims themselves can do so. (CICB 1980)

The administrative officers of the Board commented that where an applicant applies through a solicitor it is not so easy to form a picture of that person, since all contact is through a third party. This slight preference for personal applications has been echoed in other countries, for example by the members of the New York and New Jersey compensation boards (Elias 1983).

Victims' reactions were equally positive whether they had gone through the process without expert advice or whether they had used a solicitor or trade union. Those victims who had not used any official source of advice felt that they had found it all perfectly easy on their own. On the other hand, those who had used solicitors or trade unions tended to find their help essential.

A few victims found that their advisers were not, however, prepared to help them on what was to them the most important point – whether to accept the award offered. In fact, some advisers did not seem to be aware of all the provisions of the scheme. It was obvious that for solicitors, as opposed to trade unions, advising on applications to the CICB was a rare event. Some victims had in fact only used a solicitor because they thought, often as a result of police information, that that was the way applications to the Board had to be made.

The services of trade unions were free, or rather included in the benefits paid for by membership. The charges made by some solicitors caused dissatisfaction among some applicants:

I got £1000 but not when the solicitor had finished. He charged me about £200.

£150 they said, but when they heard what I got they raised it to £300. That's what I was worrying about – she said that she'd keep it down but I was being taken advantage of. I had to pay back the £25 green form.

It is impossible to know whether the apparently equivalent satisfaction with the CICB of those that did and those that did not use such sources of advice is due to differences in the types of case or applicant or whether it is that both systems work equally well. It would seem that an applicant who likes coping with forms would be capable of taking an application through to the single-member decision stage himself without discovering too many problems. Some applicants, however, will need either help or support. The few applicants whose cases proceeded to a hearing were adamant that they needed advice at this stage, though not necessarily representation at the hearing.

4. Delays and reasons for delay

The most important period of time, as far as applicants were concerned, was that between sending off the application form and receiving notification of the result, i.e. the offer of an award or the decision that no award would be made. The cheque, where applicable, followed closely on the acceptance of an offer. This period of time varied from 124 days to 734 days (over two years) with a mean of 289 days (just over nine months). One case was still waiting for a hearing at the end of the study period. However, these figures are very considerably better than those in some other countries. In the Netherlands, for example, delays of several years are common (Cozijn 1984).

The CICB, in their report for 1981, state that for several years there has been an upward trend in the time taken to resolve cases. They ascribe this to the increase in volume of applications to be processed each year and the delays which occur in completing enquiries of the police, hospitals, employers and other persons. Delays, as in our study, occur in the processing of applications prior to submission to the single member, rather than during that decision-making process.

For each case in our study which took over six months from application to offer, an attempt was made to work out which factors might have contributed to the delay (see Table 9.1). The most important

Table 9.1 Factors affecting the time taken to process application (for cases in which time from application to offer was over six months)

	Percentage of applications (n = 41)
Medical situation unclear	90
CICB probes/investigates information supplied by applicant	22
Delay due to incorrect form-filling by agency or body other than applicant	20
Delay in reaching verdict in court case	17
Delay by applicant/applicant fills in form incorrectly	15
Other reasons (administrative process)	66

factor occurred where the medical situation did not appear to be clear at the time of receipt of the application form and when this was not resolved by the time of receipt of the answers to the initial enquiries made of hospitals and GPs. These are the cases in which a 'CS1A' form would be sent. The next most important factor was delay apparently inbuilt into the system. It seemed that cases only came up for review at set time intervals, even though all the information might have been gathered some months previously. This may be a function of the number of cases being handled, but, equally, such time limits do require to be reconsidered at frequent intervals and justification made. If the number of applications to the Board increases, perhaps as a result of more effective publicity, it is possible that delays of this kind may become much worse. The third factor, and one which accounted for some long periods of time, though it only affected a minority of cases, was where the staff of the CICB decided to make extra enquiries to check information supplied by the applicant. There was no doubt that, in these cases, the staff were concerned about the possibility of fraud, and considered it very important that all the details the applicant gave should be checked with other sources, even though comparatively small amounts of money might be involved (often under £20). Since CICB funds come from the public purse, it is difficult to prescribe that a balance should be set between the possibility of fraud and the costs investigation. However, it did seem that CICB staff were overestimating the likely amount of fraud and underestimating the effects on the process and the victims of rigorous searching for such fraud in almost every case. Interestingly, delays by the applicant himself were the least frequent reason we found. It would appear that applicants are, in general, coping well with the forms sent by the CICB and providing adequate information.

The applicants themselves were resigned to the delays. The warning on the acknowledgement letter had been taken seriously. Fifty-five per cent had expected their case to take as long as it did. Sixteen per cent had expected it to take even longer. However, 52 per cent thought that the whole process was slow or very slow and deplored the length of time involved.

Nearly one-fifth of applicants had found themselves in financial difficulties as a result of the offence and would have appreciated some form of fast financial aid. However, as we have commented before, it is doubtful whether the needs of these cases of real hardship can be met at all in the context of a large-scale bureaucratic body like the CICB. It is likely that a different system for immediate aid is really required.

5. Hearings

Only four applicants from our study had taken part in a hearing or inspection of scarring by the end of the study. All of these resulted in a positive outcome, in that an award was offered. It is impossible to attempt to measure applicants' satisfaction from such a small sample but it is interesting that all four victims had the same reaction – an initial dread of the hearing being a formal court process, followed by appreciative comments about its informality:

He was all right – a gentleman. It was very informal – better like that – not like a court again. I was quite relaxed. I thought it would be three people – that's what I was told. I thought it would be like a court hearing.

It seemed as though some of the literature sent to applicants prior to the hearing had made them fearful about the process, while the applicants themselves based their expectations on their model of the criminal trial. If applicants are told that they will have to make out their case themselves and, in the case of an appeal, that the hearing may decide to award them less than they have already been offered, then their anxieties may be heightened and they may, for example, decide not to appeal (see below).

6. The 'personal touch'

The CICB was seen by many applicants as an impersonal system – a result of the entirely paper nature of the interaction between the Board and applicant. Several of the applicants commented spontaneously that they would have preferred a personal dimension to the process:

They're so remote with letters. People there don't remember what it's like out on the streets. It needs to be less impersonal.

It would have been nice to have had someone actually come round and see you rather than doing it at a distance, for them to talk to you.

I think you should personally see people. On paper it's just a number. It's not made clear to them how many injuries you have – both the mental effects and the injuries.

There were several elements to this desire. One was the difficulty that applicants experienced in describing the mental effects, which by the time of the award were often seen as longer lasting and more severe than, for example, financial effects (see Chapter 6). It is in fact likely, as we have seen, that if the applicant does not mention these on the application form or the 'CS1A' form (and there is no special space for this), then they may not be mentioned in hospital or other medical reports.

Another facet is the difficulty faced by some applicants in dealing in general with a centralised, remote agency. This is acknowledged by the administrative officers of the CICB (though problems will not be confined to the types of victim mentioned):

The main problems arise in communicating effectively with elderly or mentally unstable applicants. It is sometimes necessary to telephone an applicant rather than write a letter if we are not having any success in obtaining the information we require.

Yet another element is the applicant's desire for his suffering to be recognised and acknowledged by the system. Here the CICB is being treated as a part of the whole criminal justice system – as, indeed, the Board and, recently, the Home Secretary have described it: 'the Board is now a substantial and useful part of our system of justice' (CICB 1980). Applicants do not see the Board as an agency offering welfare payments, or as being there solely to relieve expenses incurred as the result of being a victim of crime. They see it as, to some extent, a body judging their victimisation. They wish to be able to make their explanation and to receive a personal consideration.

The Board is not now organised so as to be able to provide this personal service to applicants. It sees itself as offering a professional service with the aims of producing an efficiently-run system and giving out consistent awards which yet take account of the individual circumstances of offences and victims. It does not appear to regard itself as having any other dimension than a monetary one – it would not necessarily see itself as in the business of providing symbolic or personal comfort. Some of the problems mentioned above could be ameliorated by using other agencies (such as victim support schemes) to help applicants with the process of claiming compensation, where this is necessary. This would not, however, give applicants personal contact with the CICB staff. That would only be achieved by the employment of staff trained for such personal contact and based in local offices, in a similar manner to local tax offices.

Awards and reactions to awards

1. Awards received and awards refused
The great majority of applicants did eventually receive some money from the Board. Only four were rejected. Another one received a reduced award. The reasons why the Board may disallow applications have been the subject of extensive and sometimes hostile comment by legal writers (for example, Miers 1978; 1983; Burns 1980). They may be divided into two groups – cases in which the victim or the offence do not fall within the criteria adopted by the Board as denoting appropriate cases for compensation (for example, that the victim is not an 'innocent victim' or the crime is not a 'crime of violence'); and cases where demands of a more administrative nature have not been met (for example, that the proposed award should reach a minimum limit, or that applications should be made within a certain time span).

Two refusals of awards and the one reduction of award (by 20 per cent) fell into the first category. The victim was thought, either because of his conduct during the offence or because of his previous character and conduct, not to fit the 'image' of the victim who should receive compensation. The CICB will only compensate victims who have played the part of an 'innocent victim' – who have not provoked or in some other way caused the offence to happen and who are suitable people to receive public funds. These criteria are set out as: not possessing a 'record (showing) that he is a man of violence and has himself been guilty of serious crimes of violence' or not being 'a victim who has persistently obtained his living by committing offences of dishonesty and has not made a serious attempt to earn an honest living' (CICB, The Statement). This last is the most controversial. It was only introduced in 1969 (years after the inception of the CICB) and is intended to 'exclude the person whose conduct is undeserving of public sympathy' (Home Office 1978). It is clear from the Report of the Inter-departmental Working Party on the CICB, however, that the original reference was to victims with a reputation (or criminal convictions) for violence. The Board, however, considers that a substantial record of convictions for dishonesty would also debar applicants. It appears that this bar might continue to operate for a considerable period of time, which might not be thought to be in accordance with the spirit of the Rehabilitation of Offenders Act 1974. The victim who was denied an award because of his previous convictions felt this keenly:

There were too many records against me. It's unfair – anything what you do, like, it's always against me. It was never for weapons – I've paid for what I did. I think it's silly, because when you go to court for your crimes you pay for it. You get into trouble they bring it all up. I've been out of trouble for three years – you're being a goody and they treat you like dirt.

Five other victims, however, obtained awards even though they did possess one or more previous convictions (the criminal records of a further 17 were not checked by the police).

The issue of provocation or victim responsibility for the offence has caused less controversy but is an equally difficult matter on which to lay down rules, as the Board and the Working Party have acknowledged (Home Office 1978). The CICB's information on the offence comes both from the description provided by the applicant and from the answers to specific questions put to the police, on blame for the offence and the moral character of the applicant. In the judgement of the researcher, the total information available to the Board showed that in six cases the victim was the first to use violence and in seven he was abusive to the offender. However, in only two cases was an award refused or reduced for this reason. The amount of provocation necessary to produce a reduced award or no award at all seems, therefore, like the extent of previous bad character, to be a matter of judgement. Given the unwillingness of victims to appeal against the decision by the single member (see below), perusal of the few cases reported by the CICB in its annual reports cannot provide an accurate guide to what is allowed. The model of the 'compensatable victim' with which the Board is working, the way in which they build up this picture and the information they use to decide whether a particular case fits into this category are very important matters. Our study, which concentrated on the 'average' case, could not pursue them further. There is a need for their investigation, particularly since it is now likely that the CICB will be put on a statutory basis, after which time its criteria will become much more difficult to change.

The two cases where awards were refused because the amount would be below the minimum limit (£150 at the time, now £400) also point up an area of possible difficulty. Both victims were police officers. All the civilian victims applying in fact had general damages over the then minimum limit (without including any special damages). There were thus no applications from civilian victims which were rendered ineligible by this factor. This makes it much more likely that some (eligible) victims were being discouraged from applying by the prominent mention of the minimum limit in the original publicity they received, as we suggested above. The recent raising of the minimum limit to £400 (above the level expected according to the rate of inflation at the time) makes this possibility even more likely.

2. *Amounts of awards*

The amount awarded to successful applicants comprises several elements. General damages (awarded for pain and suffering) accounted for by far the largest part of the awards (see Table 9.2). Special damages include all those expenses for which the victim might be able to account in detail, that is, be able to specify the precise amount lost. On the principle that applicants should not receive 'double payment', State welfare benefits, income tax relief and offender compensation already paid to the victim by the time of the award are deducted. The offer received by victims stated the net award, detailing the sum awarded for general damages and special damages and the amount deducted for offender compensation (if any). However, no details were given as to the make-up of the amount for special damages (lost earnings, out-of-pocket expenses of various kinds) or the amounts deducted for social security or income tax relief.

Victims' reactions to these offers varied considerably, both in their initial feelings and on later, more reflective consideration. About a quarter were extremely pleased at the amount of the offer and remained

Table 9.2 Elements of awards paid

Element	Cases in which applied (percentage)	Minimum £	Maximum £	Mean £
General damages	100	150	3000	594
Total special damages	72	1	856	102
Loss of earnings (without deducting social security benefits)	39	8	1522	286
Out-of-pocket expenses	54	1	60	19
Deductions				
Social security benefits	37	9	553	122
Tax relief	22	3	156	32
Offender compensation	7	25	60	48
Total awards	100	154	3000	611

so up to the time of the interview:

I was quite happy – very pleased. A bit of luck really. I thought I would get the minimum.

I was quite pleasantly surprised. It was more really than I'd expected.

It was £300 more than I was expecting so I said yes.

Another quarter were always disenchanted with the amount:

I didn't agree with the sum because I still feel a lot of pain from the scar now.

The amount was not enough – it's something that affects you for life. I still think about it every day. But it's not the *money* – you don't want (to receive) a large amount.

But the main impression was that victims did not know how the sum had been worked out, were wearied by the long process and so, having no basis on which they could decide whether or not to appeal, decided just to accept the offer made. Later, some became more satisfied. Others remained neutral or unsure:

By the time I'd gone through all this rigmarole I thought to hell with it, take it and run.

The letter doesn't mention nothing – it doesn't say whether it included my trousers or my earnings so I don't know what it included.

With hindsight it wasn't very good. Because although I didn't lose money from work, I have still got a lump. With hindsight I would have appealed it – but it is such a long-drawn-out procedure – I couldn't be bothered.

When victims were asked to rate their satisfaction with the CICB's award on re-interview, 22 per cent said they were very satisfied, 28 per cent satisfied, 9 per cent neutral, 28 per cent dissatisfied and 13 per cent very dissatisfied.

It is not surprising that some degree of confusion is experienced by victims. The Interdepartmental Working Party itself acknowledged that: 'on quantum, it must be remembered that within fairly broad bands there is usually no "correct" figure of compensation or damages for a particular injury' (Home Office 1978). This was compounded, for victims, by their lack of knowledge of what the CICB had included in the overall figures given and, particularly, by their concern about special damages and the lack of any breakdown on this:

They didn't say how it was worked out. I would like to know how.

They didn't specify what it was covering. I suppose it covered my clothes. The way they worked it out is a complete mystery. I did it myself and couldn't understand it. I would have been curious to know how they did it.

They didn't say what was taken into account. The offer was accept or reject – just that. They didn't split it down. I would have liked to have known.

3. Concern about special damages

Special damages formed a very small proportion, financially, of the total award. To those victims who applied for loss of earnings or out-of-pocket expenses, however, they were extremely important. They represented money that the victim had actually lost or had to pay out. Yet it was almost impossible for the victim to work out whether he had received all that he had applied for. Out-of-pocket expenses were particularly difficult to relate to those claimed, because no breakdown of such expenses, as calculated by the administrative staff of the CICB, was provided to either the single member deciding on the claim or the applicant when he was asked whether he would accept the award offered. It seemed, therefore, impossible for either to tell which of the various expenses had been included in full, which reduced and which not allowed.

The administrative officers of the CICB indicated that the following expenses would be allowed:

(1) Clothing if beyond repair, otherwise cleaning or repair costs (clothing valued at new cost minus wear and tear element);

(2) Travel expenses to hospitals, doctors or dentists for treatment, including expenses incurred after application to the Board;
(3) Expenses incurred in attending medical examinations or hearings required by the Board;
(4) Cost of false teeth, spectacles etc. damaged, lost or required as a result of the offence.

However, the CICB relied on applicants to notify the Board of any expenses incurred after the initial application.

The following would not be allowed:

(1) Clothing damaged through being held as evidence by the police or tested by the forensic department of the police;
(2) Travel expenses involved in helping the police or attending court;
(3) Postage in applying to the Board or answering its queries (although prepaid labels were provided for use by doctors, employers etc.);
(4) Property (such as money or jewellery) lost, stolen or damaged during or as a result of the offence.

Seventeen per cent of victims attempted to claim for items that would not have been awarded, but 13 per cent of victims did not claim all the out-of-pocket expenses to which they would have been entitled, mainly because they were not aware that they could do so: 'I didn't put in the clothes. I don't know if they allowed the earnings. I don't know what they included.'

It is not clear why some expenses (such as travelling to the doctor) should be included in an award whereas others (such as travelling to the police station) are not, particularly if one of the aims of State compensation is to promote co-operation with the criminal justice system. It is even less clear why victims should have to incur more non-awardable expenses in applying to the Board (for example, postage or the excess cost of photographs). Such measures may exist to cut down administrative costs or to discourage fraudulent applications. They represent, however, very small sums in the content of the total award.

Special damages were very important to victims. It is crucial to realise that no victim was suffering from financial need due to the offence at the time the award was made. Any such needs had been made up by scrimping and doing without during the period immediately after the offence. The money had been found from that set aside for clothes, holidays, children's presents, even food; or borrowed from friends and relatives. Victims, therefore, felt very strongly that such losses should form a clear part of the award.

Ideas about the general damages part of the award, however, seemed to differ considerably between the legal view, influenced by civil criteria and incorporated in the CICB, and the views of victims. As far as the legal system is concerned, within broad limits, loss is loss however it occurs. In terms of awarding damages, it matters not whether the loss has occurred through fault or malice. What is important is to investigate the nature of the loss (the precise injuries and damage suffered by the individual victim) and to compensate for the effects of the act. To victims, however, general damages had a symbolic status. They were seen as a symbolic expression of what the State felt that the victim's suffering was worth and as a judgement and acknowledgement of the victim's status as a victim, and hence his right to recompense. Their monetary nature – as cash to spend – was not important. This fundamental difference in the way of looking at compensation will arise again later, when we discuss whether State compensation should be put on a statutory basis and the balance between compensation from the State and from the offender.

4. The scarcity of appeals

It was suggested at the beginning of this chapter that the CICB appeared to be functioning as a model administrative scheme – with few ineligible applicants and few appeals. We have seen that a considerable minority of applicants were dissatisfied with the awards made. Yet no appeal was made by any applicant who received an award. Why was this?

The reasons given by applicants fell into three different categories – those concerned with procedures; those founded on an inability to understand what was included in the total award and how it had been made up; and those based on the difficulty of reconciling a legalistic appeals machinery with an *ex gratia* system of awards.

The procedural factors included the delays already experienced by applicants; the prospect of further forms, difficulties and inconvenience; the fear that any offer might be reduced on appeal (this possibility is stated in the literature given to applicants); and the worry that a hearing might involve the difficulties already experienced or feared as a witness in a criminal trial:

Delay works to the government's benefit – you're actually grateful to receive anything at all by that time and it allows any sense of injustice to settle down to a more objective estimation of what you deserve and so on.

The last thing you want to do is fight for a claim – I've been assaulted, I've been hassled. Why am I getting hassled still filling in forms – thinking about the value of clothes, photos etc.? What did the offenders have to do?

There was also no doubt that victims' lack of knowledge of how the award had been made up contributed to a decision not to appeal.

A more fundamental reason, however, was the feeling that it would not be correct to appeal – that since compensation was stated to be *ex gratia* (translated by victims as meaning a gift), one could not 'look a gift horse in the mouth':

> I didn't refuse it – it's their suggestion so I accept it. I felt I couldn't go on fighting and fighting so I accepted it. It's help not a right so it's up to them to say how much.

Who was I to argue?

The CICB itself, although the scheme is discretionary, considers that it has a legal duty to give compensation to all eligible victims:

> The Board's view of its legal obligation and duty under the scheme is that, if an applicant's entitlement to compensation is established there is no power to withhold compensation. (CICB 1979)

Unfortunately, the wording of the statement of the scheme sent to all applicants (including the words *'ex gratia'* and 'the Board will be entirely responsible for deciding what compensation should be paid in individual cases') seemed to be giving applicants an entirely different impression.

Some of these problems could be resolved quite easily. It would be possible to make it clear to applicants that they do have a right to appeal against the decision of the single member. It would also be possible (though slightly more costly in administrative time) to give a greater breakdown of the special damages offered. It could be argued that applicants should really have some knowledge of what is included in the offer they are being asked to accept. The procedural aspects are much harder to change. If there is any increase in knowledge about the existence of the CICB, it is likely that the resulting rise in applications will create greater backlogs and problems. However, it might then be viable to set up local or regional offices, which might be able to offer a more personal service to applicants.

Should State compensation be a right for all innocent victims?
There has been considerable discussion about the current *ex gratia* nature of State compensation and as to whether the CICB should be put on a statutory footing. In that case, applicants deemed to fall within the scope of the scheme would have a legal right to such compensation as the scheme might provide. Recent Government announcements seem to have brought this possibility much nearer.

Those victims re-interviewed after application to the CICB were asked whether compensation should be a right or whether it should be at the discretion of the Board. Eighty-one per cent of victims thought that it should be a right, with a few qualifying this by saying there should be safeguards against abuse:

> It should be a right – if you're asking for help you can't argue, you can't appeal, you don't know where you are. You can't have a concept of 'fairness' with a gift.

There was no doubt that victims thought of compensation as an entitlement rather than as a welfare payment. They were not to be compensated because they were needy, or poor, or to be pitied, but because they had suffered as a result of a wrong committed with malice against them. Compensation was a means towards social justice, towards the righting of a wrong, towards recompense for a criminal deed. It was qualitatively different from civil damages. It represented reparation from the State on behalf of or in place of the offender. Hence, they felt, the amount of compensation should be related to the seriousness of the offence and should also make up any direct losses. The system should be set up on a legal, not a welfare, model such that it would acknowledge their victimisation and their status as people who had had a crime committed against them.

However, although obviously victims were already classing the CICB as part of the criminal justice system, it was not the case that their experiences with the CICB significantly affected their attitudes towards other parts of the system, such as the police or the courts. There was no difference in victims' views on the police and courts when interviewed immediately after the outcome of the criminal case and when interviewed after the final result of their application to the CICB. It seems that victims are quite sophisticated in distinguishing between the various parts of the system and in attributing credit and blame to each part separately.

The evidence on this from other countries is rather mixed. Doerner and Lab (1980) found very similar results to those of our study. Receiving an award did produce a more favourable impression of the Compensation Commission itself, but had little effect on attitudes to other parts of the system. Elias (1983) also found that his New York and New Jersey claimants would be no more likely than his non-claimants to participate in the criminal justice system in the future, but those claimants who did not receive an award showed much more negative attitudes. In Britain, of course, the percentage of applicants not receiving awards is much lower. As long as this pertains, it is likely that making the CICB a statutory body will not affect victims' future co-operation with other parts of the criminal justice system, though it may increase their satisfaction with the CICB itself.

Should compensation come from the State or from the offender?

Linked to the question of the nature of compensation is the question of its source. The majority of victims who had received awards of State compensation would have preferred at least some of the money to come from the offender. It is well known, and was also obvious to the victims, that they could not expect such large or rapid payments from offenders.

On a welfare model of State compensation, this would be strange. On a justice model it is not so surprising. As some of the victims put it:

If the offender does have it they should pay the full amount, because it's their fault. The government is just covering up the offender's mess.

The offenders should have been involved with the payments. At least half. It doesn't matter that the money would come in bits. It's a principle. Even if it took them 10 years to pay.

It would have been worthwhile if the offender had to pay the Board back.

But justice does not mean that offenders should be the whole source of payments. Some offenders will never be caught; most offenders could not be expected to pay the sums involved. Eighty-two per cent of the victims thought there should be a State compensation scheme – only 18 per cent would have left the whole responsibility to the offender. However, almost all the victims would have liked to have seen a greater emphasis on compensation from the offender than at present and, when informed of them, applauded the proposals in the Criminal Justice Act 1982 as a step towards this.

The idea that gained most favour was that the CICB should act as a back-up system both as to amount of compensation (suggested spontaneously by 42 per cent of victims) and as to speed of payment (suggested spontaneously by 21 per cent). The CICB should pay the victim and then reclaim what remained unpaid from the offender. This is, of course, the system currently in operation when a court compensation order is made, though very few victims knew of this. The victims were, however, envisaging that compensation would play a much larger part in sentencing than at present and that the sums awarded would form a significant part of the CICB award.

Implications of a statutory State compensation scheme

Financially, the CICB is the most important source of compensation for victims. Those who apply are very likely to succeed both in obtaining an award and in obtaining fuller compensation from this source than from any other. This is a much more successful record than that of the State compensation scheme of any other country.

Yet it is clear that the CICB is not exactly the State compensation scheme that victims would like to see, nor does it necessarily, in its present form, possess the structure or processes of review that would allow it to change. While so many victims that do apply feel unwilling to appeal awards with which they are dissatisfied, it is difficult to examine how consistent or correct are the decisions of the single member. It is unclear to victims that they can appeal against awards offered without incurring penalties or offending against the *ex gratia* nature of the awards. While hearings (appeals) are *de novo* and remain, on matters of fact, within the aegis of the Board itself, it is unlikely that any coherent and systematic body of case law and decisions about particular kinds of cases will arise. The Board has wide discretion about the matters that would fall under the heading of allowable special damages, for example, and it is very difficult for applicants (or anyone else) to discover what these are and how they are being applied. It is possible that insufficient weight is being given to mental effects, though the extent of this remains unknown, as the concept of general damages is a gestalt one in civil law. The paperwork-based nature of the system causes some applicants to abandon their applications and others to feel alienated.

If the CICB were to become a statutory body, then some of these problems would disappear automatically. That would also be the wish of victims – a move towards a justice model of State compensation, where compensation is a right for all eligible victims. However, such a change would also have some fundamental implications for the structure of the system and would provide a unique opportunity to consider carefully what form of system we want and what consequent image of victimisation and of society's response to it we wish to convey.

The first implication of a statutory right to compensation for eligible victims is that it would become essential to take all possible steps to inform potential applicants of their rights. It would also be necessary to be prepared for the likely increase in applicants (and cost of the scheme) that would result. Any backtracking on the amounts of awards or cutting down on the scope of publicity would be interpreted as showing a very half-hearted 'political' commitment. We shall return to the question of how compensation should be calculated in the next chapter, when it will be possible to discuss the possibilities for compensation from all the different sources together.

The introduction of a statutory scheme would also have fundamental implications for the determination of eligibility. It is, of course, still possible to include the presence or absence of provocation or other factors relevant to the victim's conduct at the time of the offence, even, possibly, conduct prior to the offence. Equally, offences would need to be classified as crimes of violence and fraudulent claims resisted. However, other aspects are far more difficult to justify. Why should conduct after the offence and unrelated to it affect whether an award is obtained? Why should the applicant's general character and conduct be relevant, if they did not affect the facts of the offence? How can the administrative constraints on eligibility be retained? If receiving compensation is a right, does it become less of a right if the effects of the offence are judged to be worth less than the minimum limit? Surely, compensation could only be restricted to offences of violence or, perhaps, to certain categories of offences of violence, not to the monetary equivalent of their effects.

The opportunity which legislation would provide is that of examining the basis of the current operation of the scheme. One element in this, which is ripe for reassessment, is the way in which the idea of an 'innocent victim' is created and used.

The principle that compensation should only be given to 'innocent victims' has been prevalent since the start of the CICB. The Report of the Working Party on compensation for victims of crimes of violence in 1961 (Home Office 1961) stated that any scheme should be 'based mainly on considerations of sympathy for the innocent victim'. Two assumptions have flowed from this. The first is that there are undeserving victims whom the State has no 'moral' obligation to compensate (for example, if the crime 'arises directly from undesirable activities of the victim'). The second is that there will be fraudulent claims: the scheme should 'provide as many safeguards as possible against fraudulent or exaggerated claims'. Both of these have been amplified by the fact that State compensation is public money, which has to be accounted for. The results have been both the inclusion in the scheme of descriptions of various categories of undeserving victims (who are to be denied compensation or given only a partial award) and the feeling among those administering the scheme that everything an applicant says should be checked. As the administrative officers said: 'all information given on the application form is checked'. From considering the files, there seemed to be almost a presumption in some cases that applicants would tend to or try to exaggerate. Considerable correspondence could take place over small sums.

Miers (1983) has argued that this requirement for innocent victims is due to the political nature of the process setting up compensation boards and the resulting necessity to make value judgements of the worth of the victim – to attach a social label to him (the politicisation of the victim of crime). He has gone so far as to argue that the principal goal of State compensation schemes is symbolic – to reaffirm a set of values about particular kinds of suffering. It is thus not necessary for schemes to reach all or the vast majority of eligible victims or even to compensate victims at all.

The process of setting up compensation schemes has been a highly political one in many countries (see, for example, Elias 1983). Some schemes do not appear actually to compensate many victims, nor to worry about this. The problem comes, though, when a scheme set up in the way or for the symbolic purposes that Miers describes also attempts to provide a real service to all those who apply to it. That is the position that we would argue pertains in Britain today. The problem is that victims are not in practice like the stereotypical victim, particularly in the case of crimes of violence. There has often been some previous interaction with the offender, in which the victim may have been slightly provocative. Many victims of assault know their offender. A significant minority will have one or a few (unrelated) previous convictions. The distinction between victim and offender is one of shades of grey.

Existing legal and sociological categorisations do not help much here. The notion of fault in civil law does not give any guidance in ascribing the status of 'undeserving' to the victim of a crime. The doctrine of provocation in criminal law is only relevant to the determination of guilt in murder cases. In criminal law, as well, the standard of proof is 'beyond reasonable doubt', whereas the CICB operates on the civil law standard of 'balance of probabilities'. Nor is there much case law regarding how these issues might affect the making of compensation orders at the time of sentence. The social sciences have started to provide some clues, in the development of attribution theory and in experiments to elicit what factors lead to the attribution of blame (see, for example, Walster *et al.* 1976). But most of the experiments have involved rather artificial situations and few cover offences of violence. We do not know the limits the public would put on the idea of a deserving victim.

If we are to consider State compensation as forming part of a criminal justice system, as Bottoms (1983) has argued and as both the CICB and the Government have suggested, then one needs to develop a coherent body of principles and practical guidelines for dealing with these issues, both for State compensation and for compensation orders. We shall attempt to draw up the beginnings of such a scheme in the next chapter, according to the ideas that victims themselves felt to be relevant for the calculation of compensation. For now, we can only stress that it is unfair to leave the question to those who, at present, have to decide on quanta in individual cases.

It is, however, necessary to proceed from knowledge of the situations in which offences of violence occur. Otherwise, it might appear strange that many applicants are young working-class men who have been assaulted in public places or places of entertainment. It might be thought that they were 'trying it on'. It seems less abnormal if it is realised that this category forms a large proportion of victims of physical assaults. Those who have to administer the scheme need to have an appreciation of the type of people their applicants are and what their needs are. A paperwork-based scheme with no possibility of face-to-face contact, except at a hearing, will tend to encourage the production of stereotypes and a belief in the 'fraudulent nature of victims', if only as a defence against the pathos in application forms. This might be resisted with a scheme more attuned to the real nature of victimisation and with staff who have the possibility of contact with victims, both in training and in the resolution of difficult cases at a local level.

The time during which legislation to make the CICB statutory is being considered is a period of unrivalled opportunity to review the working of the scheme and to shape it for the future. There is no doubt that, in many ways, the CICB is one of the most effective State compensation schemes in the world. It also possesses the unusual virtue that applicants seem to find it easy to cope with the process of application. Yet there are still faults and contradictions, stemming from the fact that we have not yet really decided on the purpose and place of such a scheme and hence on the types of victim we wish to compensate, the way in which we wish to calculate that compensation or the information we need to acquire from applicants in order to perform that task.

10 The role of the victim

The place of the victim in the criminal justice system has not always been the minimal one it is today. Prior to the introduction of the Metropolitan, borough and rural constabularies in the 1820s to 1850s, the entire system of the criminal law depended upon prosecution by the individual victim:

> In the nineteenth century the burden of prosecution really did rest on private individuals. . . . It was up to the individual who had been harmed by an offence to ensure that the offender was prosecuted; the state would control and to some extent arrest the process, but the eventual responsibility for carrying through the prosecution rested with the aggrieved citizen. (Philips 1977: 96).

In the Black Country in 1836, 80 per cent of offences were prosecuted by the victim, 10 per cent by someone on behalf of the victim and only 7 per cent by the police.

The task of the victim as prosecutor was not an easy one – he had to pay the expenses of the constable, gather witnesses, take time off to attend the preliminary examination in front of the magistrates, be bound over to pay money if he failed to give evidence or prosecute the case at the higher courts (the forerunner of witness orders), travel to the county town and stay there during the hearings of the higher courts and pay the fees of the various officers of the courts and any solicitor or counsel he might employ. The time, money and trouble all this took caused great inconvenience and was one of the major reasons for the formation of police forces and the establishment of an official prosecuting system (Philips 1977; Shubert 1981). However, by 1826, it became possible for prosecutors to recover many of their costs – indeed, a higher proportion of their costs than the present-day victim can claim. In the Black Country, at least, these costs and expenses did not appear to deter many working-class and unskilled victims from prosecuting persons who committed thefts, burglaries and assaults against them.

A similar position pertained in colonial America:

> Unlike the criminal, the victim was better off before the Revolution than he is today. . . . He once was the central actor in the system and stood to benefit both financially and psychologically from it. Today, he is seen at best as the 'forgotten man' of the system and at worst as being twice victimised, the second time by the system itself. (McDonald 1976: 560)

By the late 19th century in both England and America, the present-day pattern was firmly established. Prosecution was the province of the police or prosecution authorities and the victim was relegated to being regarded as 'just another witness'. In England and Wales, however, the legal position, then as today, is that police officers prosecute as private citizens. There is no special power in law conferred on the police as prosecutors (Royal Commission on Criminal Procedure 1981). Nevertheless, in practice, it is the police who take the decisions on whether and how to prosecute and the private individual's powers to start a criminal action are rarely used. It is also very unusual for victims to use their power to start a civil action. Such a trend towards the 'professionalisation' of the criminal justice system has not been confined to the prosecutorial function. Nils Christie (1977), in his article 'Conflicts as property', suggests that the original conflict between offender and victim has been taken away – stolen – from them by the professionals of the system – the police and lawyers.

The victim is a particularly heavy loser in this situation. Not only has he suffered, lost materially or become hurt, physically or otherwise. And not only does the State take the compensation. But above all he has lost participation in his own case. (Christie 1977: 7)

Nevertheless, as we have seen, the victim has a crucial role to play in the criminal justice system. Not only is he active in reporting the offence to the police, he is also the major agent in detecting the offender. In offences of violence the victim is the chief prosecution witness, providing evidence of the circumstances of the offence, identification of the offender and injuries and losses sustained. If he does not make a statement to the police, there will be little chance of a guilty plea and probably no prosecution. If he does not give evidence at court in a contested case, the defendant will almost certainly be acquitted.

This is not a new position, though it may strike some as surprising. In Philips' (1977) detailed account of the role of victims between 1835 and 1869, victims are shown to have played all these parts, almost to the same degree as today. In the interim, the necessity of securing the co-operation of victims for the continuance of the criminal justice system appears to have been forgotten. Even in 1981, the Royal Commission on Criminal Procedure, set up to consider possible prosecution systems, failed to examine whether victims should have any greater rights to make decisions on prosecutions or to be consulted by the police. This is despite its findings that:

There is, then, a crucially important relationship between the police and the public in the detection and investigation of crime . . . The success of the police depends upon public support and this should be reflected in the arrangements for investigation. (1981:20)

The same neglect is seen in the absence of reference to victims in the subsequent documents designed to lead to the setting up of an independent prosecution system (for example, Home Office *et al.* 1983). The victim is truly the 'forgotten man'.

The need for a respected and acknowledged role

Throughout this study, one theme has been apparent in the responses of these victims of violent crime to their experiences with the criminal justice system. This is their wish for respect and appreciation – their wish for recognition as an important and necessary participant in the criminal justice system. It is not an appeal for help or for charity, because they have suffered, but a desire that those who are running the criminal justice system – a system that, in general, they support and admire – should take notice of their right to be involved and to continue to be involved throughout the operation of the system.

This wish for respect is shown in all their experiences with the system. It is the basis of the emphasis upon the attitude of the police officers both at the initial contact with the police and subsequently. In the initial stages, during which the great majority of victims were satisfied with the police, victims looked for a caring, supportive, interested attitude from the police and a reasonably fast response time. The later significant decline in satisfaction with the police was due largely to their failure to tell victims about the progress of the case (particularly the outcome and sentence) and to consult them about giving information to the press, cautioning the offender, deciding not to prosecute or deciding to change or drop charges. Thus, the major reason for dissatisfaction was lack of information and a consequent feeling that the police did not perceive it necessary to keep in touch with the victim. The decline in satisfaction was large enough to affect general attitudes to the police and even, for a few, the likelihood of reporting similar offences in the future.

At court, the complaint was again not about what was actually said and done to the offender (views about judges and magistrates improved significantly over the progress of the case), but about the way in which the victim was treated if he did attend court. The waiting list system at the Crown Court did not seem to be designed for the benefit of lay participants. Facilities at all courts were largely lacking. There was no place for the victim to sit in court apart from the public gallery, often with the defendant's relatives. If there was a guilty plea, there was no one to direct the victim where to go, or tell him when he might go into court. Prosecutors often did not meet victims and were seen as uninterested, though the actual experience in the witness box did not seem to cause great distress to the majority of victims. There was inadequate recompense for costs incurred in attending court.

Even if the police did not manage to catch the offenders, victims often remained satisfied with the performance of the police, provided that they felt that the police had been interested and kept them informed. Neither were victims particularly punitive in the sentences they wanted their offenders to receive. But they did want compensation from offenders to play a much larger role than it does at present for offences of violence. They wanted the sentencer to be informed about the victim's losses and to consider whether he should be compensated.

Victims saw compensation as a proper aim of sentencing and as an integral part of the criminal justice system. For this reason, they preferred compensation from offenders, rather than from the State. They appreciated that they might obtain much less compensation in monetary terms from impoverished offenders and agreed with this. State compensation was seen as, ideally, a back-up system for cases where the offender was not caught or could not afford sufficient compensation. The amount of State compensation (and whether any was granted) was seen as a judgement upon the victim and his victimisation by the criminal justice system. State compensation, they thought, therefore, should be a right for all eligible victims. It should be given to acknowledge the losses suffered by the victim and the necessity for their remedy by a criminal justice system, rather than as charity or as an *ex gratia* 'gift'.

This desire to be treated with respect and as an integral part of the system and the symbolic valuing of compensation did not, however, remove the wish for help and support, providing that help was given with this in mind and victims were not expected to feel grateful for spontaneous handouts. So, victims sought and appreciated support from the police; from friends, relatives and neighbours; and from those few official agencies and persons who were available to them at that time.

The experiences of victims outlined above show the presence of two paradoxes within the criminal justice system. The first is the contradiction between the practical importance of the victim and the ignorance of and ignoring of his attitudes and experiences by the professionals within the criminal justice system. The system is not geared to the perspective of the victim. There appears to be a mismatch between the victim's expectations of the system and the system's assumptions about his needs. So, despite individual police officers' misgivings, the police seem to have become, as Howley (1982) has suggested, 'preoccupied with technical efficiency'. Prosecutors and court staff are concerned with processing the ever-growing numbers of defendants through the system in the fastest and most economical way. We are not suggesting that these are not laudable aims, merely that, if pursued to the extent of ignoring victims and witnesses, they become self-defeating. It is not as though the system is ignoring the victim because he is perceived as a threat. Indeed, the victims in our study were not expressing a desire to take over the criminal justice system. They were requesting a limited degree of consultation, information and support. That consultation would imply that victims' views should be ascertained before particular decisions are taken by the professionals, but would not affect the primacy of the professionals' powers to take the decisions. We shall return to the question of what a victim-oriented criminal justice system would look like, the implications of this and specific recommendations for change later. First, however, we need to look at the measures which have already been taken for victim aid and support and the basis on which these have been offered.

The philosophy behind the victim movement
The second paradox is that the major projects aimed at fulfilling victims' needs have been set up without regard to, or even investigation into, victims' expressed needs. They include State compensation for violent crime, compensation or reparation by offenders, victim support schemes and mediation or conciliation schemes. The result is that some of these may be based on a view of victims or their needs which does not correspond with reality and which may lead to a product which does not satisfy victim needs.

Van Dijk (1983a) has described most of the products of the victim movement as strongly action-oriented – their objective being not so much to discover as much as possible about victims but rather to do more for them. He has called these 'victimagogic', to distinguish them from the victimological literature, which is primarily directed towards acquiring knowledge. He has distinguished four victimagogic ideologies: the care ideology, the resocialisation or rehabilitation ideology, the retribution or criminal justice ideology and the radical or anti-criminal justice ideology.

The care ideology is based on the principles of the welfare state – that the community should take as much as possible of the burden of serious material hardship suffered by individual citizens as a result of misfortunes such as illness, accident or unemployment. Provisions for victims based on this do not stress the criminal nature of the act committed against them but emphasise their welfare nature (for the poor and needy). Victim problems are seen as one facet of more general problems such as stress, psychological trauma or economic need. The moral aspect of the crime and any moral harm the victim may have been left with after the crime are not thought to be particularly relevant, provided his injuries and hardship have been allayed. Examples of facilities justified under this head are State compensation schemes, refuges for battered wives, and some victim support schemes and rape crisis centres. However, there are still some overtones related to the moral aspect of crime, notably in the restriction of some of these facilities to crime victims and the concentration on particular types of victim.

The resocialisation or rehabilitation ideology has as its focus not aid for the victim, but understanding of the offender and a hope for his constructive resocialisation. The prime examples of this are restitution programmes and some mediation programmes, which have been justified (mainly in the United States) more for their presumed rehabilitative effect on the offender, than for their practical effectiveness or retributive fairness in compensating the victim (see Harland 1983).

The retributive or criminal justice ideology has grown rapidly recently, in concert with the burgeoning disillusionment with the results of a rehabilitative or deterrent penal policy (for example, von Hirsch 1976). It stresses the necessity to compensate the victim according to the seriousness of the crime committed against him and also accommodates the notion of giving the victim a stronger position in both the criminal justice system and in sentencing (see Sebba 1982). Action towards victims is to be taken, however, firmly within the constraints of the criminal justice system. Compensation from offenders within the criminal justice system, particularly as part of the sentence (such as compensation orders in England, Wales and Scotland) would be part of this tradition. A right of audience for the victim, at least at the point of sentence, and limited rights of consultation on prosecution would also fall within this ideology.

Proponents of the radical or anti-criminal justice ideology, having noted the declining role and power of the victim in modern criminal justice systems, see the solution not in terms of modifying the present system (as above), but in setting up an entirely different one, based on civil law principles (for example, Hulsman 1977). North American experiments with conflict mediation (see Garofalo and Connelly 1980 for a review of these) and the recent English moves in this direction are the major practical expression of these views. The official criminal justice authorities should concern themselves as little as possible with criminality, leaving aid to victims, reparation and crime prevention to neighbourhood groups.

It will be apparent by now that the victims in our study saw themselves mainly in the retributive or criminal justice tradition. They stressed the criminal nature of the act committed against them and wanted compensation, aid and support to come within the framework of the criminal justice system. Indeed, they focused upon the symbolic nature of compensation, preferring compensation from offenders wherever possible and seeing State compensation as a judgement of their victimisation by the system. However, they did not see why the criminal justice system and the criminal law should emphasise just two parties – the State and the offender. They thought that victims should also have an acknowledged role.

This would also be the view of the original victimologists, such as Schafer (1968) and Nagel (1974), who pleaded for the reorientation of the criminal process towards a trilogy of State, victim and criminal. Both the care and the radical ideologies are entirely alien to this idea (even though many practical schemes for victim aid have been set up under their auspices). The results of studies of victims (particularly victims of serious crimes) in several countries confirm their desire to be located within a criminal justice system and to play a greater part in it (for example, Maguire 1982; Holmstrom and Burgess 1978; Kelly 1982; Dümig and van Dijk 1975; Baril *et al.* 1984).

However, victims also support strongly the efforts of victim support schemes in providing practical and emotional help and information (though they consider that these should liaise with the police, as they do in Britain). In as far as mediation might be accomplished within a criminal justice system, there was some support in our study for this as well. Fifteen per cent of our victims said that they would like to meet the offender again and find out what he was like and as many as 18 per cent said that they would like to have worked out the sentence together with the offender and a judge. This was despite their complete ignorance of the idea of mediation at that time, so that the suggestion was completely new to them. It seems that there was support for such a form of mediation or arbitration:

> If they made it clear you weren't to act on malice, I think that might help. The court needn't necessarily take any notice. One thing, it would give the magistrate some idea of what the victim feels and wants. Now it don't give any opportunity to talk about the feelings.

A victim-oriented system

A victim-oriented system, constructed according to the views of the victims in our study, would not show many major structural differences from the criminal justice system of today. As we have seen, victims were not expressing a desire to take over and run the system and they did not want decision-making power. They were happy that the decisions to charge, to prosecute and to sentence, should be left to those who are taking them now. They did feel, however, that their evidence was their own and that they should not be pressurised into pressing charges or giving evidence in court, should they decide this was not correct. This feeling was particularly strong among victims who did not wish a prosecution to be pursued, including victims of domestic violence. However, they appreciated that the police would need to prosecute in certain instances, for example, to prevent intimidation. Victims' views, though inconsistent with the principle that the State has an absolute power to decide to proceed, represent in fact only a slight shift in emphasis from the present position in practice. The Attorney General's new guidelines allow for non-prosecution on the grounds of public policy or because the victim expresses a wish that there should be no prosecution. With better consultation between police and victim, less insistence on the supported finality of a statement by the victim concerning 'pressing charges' and swifter and more obvious action where there is retaliation by the offender, it is likely that the area of disagreement will narrow.

Victims did wish for active consultation before decisions were taken – on whether charges should be brought or the offender cautioned, on whether charges should be dropped at court and on whether information about victims should be given to the press. But the major requirements were for information and for help, not as charity but in exchange for the very considerable time and effort that the victims themselves put in. Very similar desires were expressed in a study of victims and witnesses in Montreal (Baril *et al.* 1984).

The changes in the prosecution system necessary to bring this about are not structural ones but are primarily attitudinal (though this can be reinforced by the use of professionals specially charged to promote the interests of victims – see below). The victim's problems with the criminal justice system may be seen to stem from his lack of an accepted role within that system. If he is a non-person in the eyes of the professional participants, at least as far as the day-to-day functioning of the system is concerned, he will not be informed or consulted as a matter of course. Even if those participants accept the desirability of retaining his goodwill, because of his possible evidential usefulness, any information flow will still tend to be one-way. The victim will be told what it is deemed necessary or helpful to tell him, not what he wants to be told. It is only if the victim is seen as an important partner in the criminal justice system that the flow of information will become automatically two-way and consultation will occur. This also implies a move towards a service orientation by the police – that the police, while remaining autonomous agents, should recognise and service the victim's needs as another essential partner within the system.

Changes in sentencing, victim aid and compensation again do not involve the wholesale demolition of the existing system, but its reorientation towards a retributive ideology which still encompasses and encourages the provision of help and support. This was also a principle adopted by the Hodgson Committee:

We believe that too much attention is paid to punishment and too little to redressing the wrong done and that nothing like enough consideration is given to the victim in the criminal process. We find much wisdom in the writings of Jeremy Bentham. 'Compensation,' he wrote, 'will answer the purpose of punishment but punishment will not answer the purpose of compensation. By compensation therefore the two great ends of justice are both answered at a time, by punishment only once.' (1984: 6)

Our suggestions pertain only to victims of violent crime. The relevant research has not yet been attempted for victims of property offences, though there is no theoretical reason why the same principles should not apply. The first requirement is for co-ordination of the whole system for victim compensation and support, such that victims learn about all the facilities available (and, for the reasons discussed in Chapter 7, this task can only be performed by the police). Co-ordination is also vital in another sense. It should not be the victim who has to wrestle with the complexities and vagaries of claiming money from different funds, only to find that the different funds each subtract their contributions from the others', leaving him with the same amount which he would have obtained had he only been eligible for one. We need to overhaul our system of historically separate parts (DHSS benefits, compensation orders and CICB payments), so that a victim is required to fill in just one form and attend only one medical.

More importantly, if compensation is to be based on a retributive, criminal justice model, then compensation from offenders should take prime place, with the State acting as back-up. Victims do see compensation orders as part of the sentence and do not expect 'full' compensation from impoverished offenders. They do, however, expect the courts to make such orders a priority in sentencing, requiring the courts to consider whether a compensation order would be appropriate in every case, as has been recommended by the Hodgson Committee (1984). The Committee's suggestion of a Victim Compensation Fund, into which would be paid compensation from all offenders, fines and the proceeds of forfeitures or any new power of confiscation, would, however, destroy the individual basis of reparation between victim and offender and seems to be derived from a care or rehabilitative ideology rather than a retributive one. The present system, whereby sums *already* received by a victim under a compensation order are deducted from any CICB award, but the CICB receives directly any subsequent money paid in by the offender, would seem to be the best compromise between individual reparation and the practicalities of obtaining money from impoverished offenders. It is of course open to the State to transfer monies between its own different funds, for example, from fines to the CICB.

The adoption of a retributive ideology would also affect the tariff for compensation. At present, CICB awards (and possibly compensation orders as well, though this is less clear) are based on awards in the civil courts. If compensation is to be a criminal matter, then, rather than following the care ideology which equates criminal victimisation with accidents, a criminal scale should be used.

Such a criminal scale would pay more regard to mental effects than, historically, the civil courts have done. It would be based on a concept of the 'seriousness' of the offence from the point of view of the victim – not that of the individual victim in a particular case, but what victims might be expected to suffer as a result of that type of offence.

It may be useful to go into more detail about this concept of a criminal scale, as it is still unusual to think of criminal matters from the point of view of the (average) victim. It would involve different elements and weightings of the contributing factors from those derived from the point of view of the offender or of society. From the point of view of the victim, the relevant perception might be 'I might have died as a result of that offence', whereas a consideration of the offender's culpability would have regard rather to 'he should have considered the possibility of the victim dying as a result of the offence'. The seriousness of the crime from the point of view of the victim would include not only the actual consequences to the victim but also the symbolic gravity of the offence and the fact that the victim has been the victim of a crime (rather than an accident). Intentional violence may be considered more hurtful and, therefore, harmful by its recipient than negligent or accidental violence. Being cut with a knife is more serious than being punched in the mouth, even if similar injuries result. The victim might also be said to have been brought unwillingly into contact ('stained') with crime and so to have suffered moral harm as a result of being exposed to conduct prescribed as particularly reprehensible (criminal) by the society in which he lives.

The constituent elements of a criminal scale of compensation for victims – actual consequences, symbolic gravity and the fact of being a victim of crime *per se* – bear a considerable resemblance to those currently being used in determining the seriousness of the offence from the point of view of the offender or society. This is hardly surprising, given the cultural continuity between offenders, victims and those adjudicating on the seriousness of the offence. However, the combination and weighting of those elements in individual cases will be different.

The way in which compensation is calculated in civil proceedings, however, is very different. Here, the only important consideration as to quantum is the actual consequences of the offence on the victim. Potential consequences are immaterial. The viewpoint here would be 'Did the victim nearly die?'. Whether the offence was caused by negligence, recklessness or intention would not be relevant to a decision on the amount to be awarded.

Let us consider an award of compensation under this new criminal tariff and compare it with the civil tariffs now operating. Some parts of the award will be similar. There will still be a division into expenses paid out (special damages) and the more general symbolic sum for pain and suffering. But, under a criminal tariff, expenses incurred during participation in the criminal justice system would obviously be included. The present civil tariff considers only the actual consequences of the offence in calculating an amount for pain and suffering. There is, however, no particular reason why the actual values given to, say, a broken leg or a cut requiring a number of stitches, should have the monetary values they do at present. The criminal tariff for the general symbolic sum would take into account the consequences (with a greater weighting for mental effects), symbolic gravity and criminal nature of the offence, but these would probably not be additive, at least in a simple fashion, since they tend to be interrelated. It would not be necessary that the total award should be greater than the present civil award. There would, however, be a greater differentiation by type and seriousness of offence.

Let us take two examples. One would be an offence of high symbolic gravity but low consequences (for example, a knife blow which was deflected and merely scratched the skin). Here, the general part of the award would be higher under the criminal tariff than under a civil tariff using the same figures as to actual consequences, since the symbolic gravity would be high. The other example is potentially much more difficult. It is the opposite case, where the symbolic gravity is low but the consequences high (for example, the eggshell or thin skull case, in which a slight blow or push with no serious intention causes serious injury). If the total amount of money that could be given to all victims who apply under the criminal scale were to be the same as that available under the civil one, then the victim would receive much less under the criminal scale. If we wish compensation to operate as a welfare system (perhaps because we do not have a full welfare system for those disabled as a result of accidents or, indeed, any other cause), then this will be seen as a major stumbling block to the use of a criminal scale, though the victim would still, of course, have the possibility of recourse to the civil courts. If, however, compensation is to be a statement about the victim of crime, then it might be argued that such social welfare considerations are irrelevant – we cannot attempt to mitigate any general lack of welfare provision by giving it only to victims under a rubric of compensation.

An integrated system for victim compensation and assistance
The adoption of a retributive ideology and a criminal scale for victim compensation, both from State funds and from the offender, allows, for the first time, for a comprehensive and co-ordinated system for victim compensation and assistance. Here, all the relevant agencies could work together on the same basis, with the calculation of compensation being made by the criminal courts, together with those running the new statutory CICB. If compensation is being calculated on the same basis,

the prevention of double payment from state funds is a much simpler matter and could be co-ordinated by the agencies themselves, rather than by the victim.

It must not be forgotten that the need of victims for recognition in both real and symbolic terms, does not preclude their parallel wish for emotional support and help. The two only seem incompatible in organisational systems, not from the point of view of the recipient. Though many victims obtained all the support they needed from friends, relatives and workmates, they also expressed a desire for greater help and support both from the police and from a specialised victim support agency. This support should cover practical matters and information as well as emotional needs.

A co-ordinated and comprehensive system for victim assistance and compensation for victims of violent crime, constructed according to the experiences and wishes of the sample of victims in the present study, would have four parts. The first would be provision for immediate payment of expenses incurred and wages lost. It would also include payment for damaged clothing, spectacles and teeth and the cost of travel to hospitals, doctors etc. It would be an emergency service and so should be widely publicised. As we saw in Chapter 6, financial losses only affected a small proportion of victims and many were able to cope with these themselves. However, a few, with no such resources, suffered very severely. The requirement for immediacy has two implications. First, it will not be possible to conduct exhaustive investigations into whether the offence is a crime of violence (simple recording by the police will have to suffice) or into all the financial resources of the victim. Secondly, the process of application should be simple and speedy. This implies a locally-based distribution agency.

The second part would be a system for practical, information and emotional support for victims, perhaps organised between victim support schemes, the police and the courts. It would assist victims to claim emergency aid and to apply for compensation and would publicise services. It would also refer victims to more specialised agencies (such as psychiatric services, housing services, refuges etc.). It would attempt to co-ordinate services for victims, so that it is the agencies, not the victims, who have to iron out inconsistencies and incompatibilities. It might make use of past victims, to ensure the process of assistance remains victim-centred.

The third part of the system would be an increased use of compensation orders by the courts, amounting to a presumption that compensation should be *considered* in every case. The information required to assess the value of such orders should be routinely gathered during the investigation of the case by the police or prosecution (preferably using the form and leaflet system introduced in Scotland). If the court wishes to gather more evidence, or if there is a query about the effects cited, then the victim should be called to give evidence. Victims should always be notified of the making of such an order (in the context of informing them of the outcome of the case). They should then receive regular reports on the progress of payment of the order and on any enforcement action taken by the court. Failure to pay compensation must be treated at least as seriously as failure to pay fines. Throughout, the victim should be treated with care and consideration by those employed by the criminal justice system.

The fourth stage of the process would act as a back-up (admittedly a very substantial one) to the third. This would involve a body such as the CICB, set up on a statutory basis and making compensation a right to those deemed to be eligible. The basis of awards for both the third and fourth parts should be similar, preferably on a criminal tariff.

Implications of a victim-oriented system

If provisions for victims are to be located according to a criminal justice or retributive ideology, then it is necessary to explore the implications of introducing these provisions for the other parties in that system. Otherwise, one runs the danger of falling into the trap of naive victimagogy – of doing things thought to be beneficial to victims with no thought as to their consequences for victims or for any other participant.

The recommendations outlined above are drawn from the experiences of the sample of victims in our study. These are experiences with the present criminal justice system. If the system were to change, then so would the attitudes, experiences and expectations of victims. At the moment, similarities in attitudes between victims of different offences and victims in different countries are extraordinary. They tend to suggest similar roles for victims and a similar perception of victims in different countries and in different systems. If we change our criminal justice system to the more victim-oriented one suggested above, we may merely produce a system more rounded in its concerns but otherwise essentially similar to the present one. Or we may, in so doing, alter expectations and attitudes so that, by a gradual process, a different model appears.

We shall attempt to peer into the future and to discuss the implications of a victim-oriented system at two levels: the practical implications of the above proposals for the victim, the offender and the professional participants; and the theoretical implications for the model of the criminal justice system and the substantive criminal law. Though our study has been confined to victims of violent crime, these implications can be argued to pertain to victims of all offences.

Practical implications

Many of the suggested changes have no direct disadvantages for the offender. The provision of information, of better court facilities and the adoption of a more considerate attitude towards the difficulties of lay people caught up in the criminal justice system may indeed benefit both victims and offenders. These recommendations are very similar to those that have been made on behalf of offenders (see, for example, Shapland 1981). Helping victims does not have any automatic implication of being more unpleasant to offenders. Nor will the greater participation of victims necessarily cause any further problems for offenders, given that victims wished, in general, only for information and consultation, rather than for decision-making power over the case. Even a shift to compensation from offenders, rather than compensation from the State or other sources outside the criminal justice system, will not be to the disadvantage of offenders if it is kept within the current framework of sentencing, such that the offender's means and circumstances are taken into account. This would be the wish of victims, who, as we have seen, are neither punitive nor unrealistic about sentencing and compensation.

There would, however, be considerable implications for the working habits of the professional participants in the system. The suggestions above mark a major shift towards the greater participation of lay actors and, therefore, more consideration of the part they play and their needs by the professionals, whether these be the police, prosecutors, court staff or those involved with compensation. It will no longer be possible for decisions and the information surrounding those decisions to be kept as the sole province of the professionals. They will still, of course, have the ultimate decision-making power (otherwise, it would no longer be a criminal justice system, but a civil law-based mediation system). But the role of the police and prosecution will move towards having a greater service component. The way of working of all the professional participants will change to being more open and more reminiscent of a participatory rather than directional management style. Initially, this may be perceived as a threat to the autonomy of these participants and may even be presented as a threat to the nature of the criminal justice system itself. It will certainly be seen as involving more work (informing victims, consulting them, thinking about them). However, this view ignores the major and necessary role being played by victims in the present system and the problems encountered in detecting and investigating offences and in presenting cases at court when victims are not involved. Our present criminal justice system, though run by the professional participants, is based on the idea of offences committed by individual offenders against individual victims and on the necessity for oral testimony by victims and witnesses in court before there can be a conviction. We cannot ignore these lay participants and still retain our criminal justice system.

Paradoxically, then, greater participation by victims may appear to lead to more work, more difficulty and more effort for the professionals but may also result in easier detection, a higher standard of prosecution evidence and fewer cases thrown out at court. It may be more difficult initially, but it is also likely to be more rewarding.

Theoretical implications for the criminal law and criminal justice system
The greater involvement of victims does, however, have major implications for the way in which we think about the criminal justice system and the criminal law. It brings in another party, the victim, to join the present two-party system of the State and the offender. The State is represented in the criminal justice system by two kinds of participants – prosecutors and the judiciary. In speaking of the State as one party, we must not forget that these two participants may be in conflict on some matters in particular cases (for example, whether no evidence should be offered on a particular charge against a defendant).

We saw at the beginning of the chapter that the system has not always been restricted to two parties. Until the development of police forces in the last century, the victim had a definite role. There was even a right for the victim to appear and ask for compensation at the time of sentence, at least in serious cases. However, it is always very difficult to reintroduce another party into a system which, it will be argued, has worked very well since then and which has many advantages over a system dependent upon the wishes of the individual victim as prosecutor.

Without denying these advantages, we would argue that, in fact, the complete disappearance of the victim has posed major problems. The two-party system, because it has retained the necessary tradition of prosecuting an individual offender for a particular offence, has had also to retain some notion of a person against whom that offence was committed. This has been the idealised victim – a person unspecified in the substantive criminal law, but who must have contrasting characteristics to those of the offender. The idealised victim is, as we discussed in Chapter 5, absolutely innocent, passive as far as his conduct during the offence is concerned and has had no previous relationship with the offender which has any bearing on the reasons for the offence or on its commission. The conception of the offence is that of a sudden interaction between strangers, that of the victim as close as possible to the clichéd little old lady. These ideas do not stem merely from the adoption of a two-party formulation for the criminal justice system: they are embedded in the ways in which offences are defined in the substantive criminal law. The primacy of the offence *per se* and the non-appearance of descriptions of either the offender or the victim in most of the criminal law, whether in statute or common law, has led to the development of stereotypes of both offender and victim, which have opposite characteristics. It is interesting that most of the current statutory offences which do mention a particular type of victim concern victims who might be expected to be even more 'innocent' than the stereotype (such as sexual offences against children or mental patients).

Unfortunately, however, the stereotypes do not correspond to reality. Offences take place between real people who interact with each other according to social rules. Incidents do not often fall into neat slots in time and may well have a previous history which has relevance to the participants. The criminal justice system, because it has had to retain the offender as an acknowledged party to the system, has devised ways of coping with this problem as far as the offender is concerned. He is allowed to have different degrees of intention from the stereotype, some of which are a defence to some charges (such as being merely negligent, rather than reckless or intentional; or not intending permanently to deprive for a charge of theft). Conviction is an all-or-nothing process, but, in sentencing, the nature of the offence and the offender is able to be considered in much finer detail. Large numbers of different mitigating and aggravating factors are allowed, many of which distance the offence or the offender to a greater or lesser degree from the stereotyped offender and the stereotyped offence (Shapland 1981).

The two-party system of State and offender, however, is unable to deal adequately with a non-idealised victim. This is a major problem, since the tradition of retaining oral evidence means that it does have a real victim giving evidence in court. The consequent attempts at management of the 'real' victim or efforts to ignore the 'real' nature of his victimisation can tie the prosecution in knots and seriously impair the balance between prosecution and defence in adversarial systems (such as those in Britain) or the efficacy of an inquisitorial one. It also makes it very difficult to introduce a reparative element into sentencing.

We would argue that the readoption of a three-party criminal justice system (State, offender and victim) would restore much needed balance to the system and enable the adoption of measures to cope with real victims in a proper way. It would remain a criminal justice system, with decision-making power in the hands of the State. But it would bring ideas about offending back towards the reality of offending – offending as an interactive process between victim and offender. So, the prosecutor would retain the ultimate authority over prosecution and the judiciary that over the conduct of the case in court and over sentencing. The victim would be consulted by the prosecutor in respect of certain decisions on prosecution and would have a right, for example, to ensure that an application for compensation is presented to the judge. His powers would be similar in nature to those of the offender – to be an active participant, especially at certain stages of the process, but not to have a pre-eminent position. Of course, the above discussion relates to cases in which there is an identifiable victim who is an individual or organisation. Where this does not pertain, for example, in public order offences, then the proposed three-party system is effectively collapsed into two parties, with the State playing the roles of judge, prosecutor and victim.

Such a view would permit a real role for the victim in the criminal justice system, one that would be acknowledged by all participants. It would enable adoption of reparative measures towards the victim as a 'proper' element in penal philosophy. It would allow for the development of a 'criminal scale' of compensation. The courts, the prosecution, the victim and the offender could work together towards a more helpful definition of their respective roles in investigation, prosecution and sentencing. Victims would be respected as the important participants that they are, rather than the ignored and unacknowledged ones they seem to be today.

Summary of recommendations for change in the present system

Finally, it may be helpful to draw together the specific changes and improvements suggested in this and the previous chapters, in order to provide an overview of the ways in which a more victim-oriented criminal justice system would affect the different professional participants.

1. General

The study has shown that victims should have an accepted role within the system such that their contribution is acknowledged by the professional participants. This implies that victims need to be treated with care and respect by police officers, prosecutors, court officials and compensation agency personnel. It would be a major realignment of the system and would need to be promoted through training, supervision and policy documents and guidelines.

2. The provision of information to victims

At present, victims have insufficient knowledge both about the progress of their case through the system and about the part that they may be expected to play. They also require information about compensation and support services. To alleviate these difficulties:

(1) A booklet or series of pamphlets should be produced covering basic criminal justice system procedure, victim 'rights' and obligations, possibilities for compensation and details of victim services. It should be

available free from police stations, courts, victim support agencies and Citizens' Advice Bureaux.

(2) National and local co-ordinating committees should be set up, with representatives from all the professional and voluntary agencies who have dealings with victims, to review and improve services and to ensure that such co-ordination becomes the responsibility of the agencies rather than the individual victim.

(3) The police, as the first agency with whom victims come into contact, should ensure that victims receive information about compensation orders, the CICB and victim support services. A supply of leaflets and posters should be available at all police stations. Training for police officers should include the acquisition of knowledge about all these services.

(4) The police (or any future independent prosecution service) should inform victims when or if the offender is caught, whether he is on bail or in custody and whether he will be prosecuted. Victims should be informed of the outcome of the case and the full details of any sentence passed in writing (whether or not, in addition, any personal contact is made). If possible, they should also be told of the dates of any court appearances.

(5) To this end, a victim liaison officer should be appointed at each divisional or sub-divisional police station. His function would be to act as a referral source for victims unable to contact the officer in their case, to liaise with victim support agencies, to co-ordinate with other agencies and to ensure that other officers have the necessary information about the case to give to victims.

(6) Witness orders, sent out after committal to the Crown Court, should be made more intelligible and should include a telephone number to contact if the victim or witness requires or wishes to impart information about attending the Crown Court.

(7) The courts should notify victims formally of the making of any compensation order and, at intervals, of the progress of payments and of any enforcement action taken.

3. Investigation and prosecution

The major requirement during investigation and prosecution is for a more thoughtful attitude towards the needs and difficulties of victims. In particular:

(1) Controllers operating the 999 system need to have a greater appreciation of the ways in which callers will structure the information they are attempting to give. Computerised systems should be pro-grammed to aid this.

(2) Police officers attending the scene of a crime should be aware that

victims are under stress and need reassurance and support. Where possible, detailed investigative procedures, such as the taking of formal witness statements, should be left to a later time.

(3) Transport home should be provided for victims who attend hospital or the police station.

(4) Provision of care and treatment for victims attending hospital or other medical facilities should take priority over the collection of evidence for any possible prosecution. Where more convenient for the victim, the taking of routine samples for forensic analysis should be left until a later date.

(5) Appointments made by the police to see the victim should be kept, or the victim informed otherwise. Appointments (for example, to take photographs) should not be made at a time or place obviously inconvenient to the victim (such as the morning after an offence committed late the previous night).

(6) Any personal property of the victim taken for forensic tests should be returned as soon as possible. Consideration should be given to the possibility of using photographs, rather than requiring the property to be kept by the police pending a possible trial. Victims should be compensated for any damage done as a result of forensic tests or the retention of property by the police (for example, permanent staining by blood).

(7) Sexual assault victims should have the possibility that their statement be taken by a woman police officer. Such police officers will require special training to enable them to give the support needed by victims.

(8) No information which could identify the victim should be given to the press by the police or prosecutor prior to any court appearance unless the victim has specifically consented to this.

(9) Victims should be allowed to see a copy of their statement under the conditions set out in the relevant Home Office circular.

(10) Victims should not be pressurised to press charges against the offender. They should be consulted before any subsequent decision not to prosecute or to caution and, if possible, before charges are dropped at court. Before taking a decision not to prosecute on that charge or to caution, consideration should be given to any need by the victim for compensation.

(11) The prosecutor should, as a matter of courtesy, introduce himself to a victim who is present at court and attempt to answer any queries that he may have about court procedure.

(12) If the victim complains to the police about retaliation by the offender, the police should take all possible steps to deal with this and should certainly inform the victim of their actions.

4. At court

(1) Adequate facilities should be provided for victims at court. There should be a separate waiting area for prosecution witnesses and a place, other than the public gallery, for the victim to sit in court, should he wish to do so.

(2) Victim-witness information points should be set up at court to tell victims where to go and what they may be required to do. Ushers should ensure that victims are told when their case comes on and are brought into court, if they wish it, when no longer required as a witness.

(3) Victims need to be given a real role in the criminal justice system. Consideration needs to be given to the tendency in the law and in the criminal process to ignore the 'true' nature of victimisation.

5. Compensation and victim support services

There should be a co-ordinated system for victim compensation and support. To this end:

(1) The police and prosecution should undertake to obtain information from the victim about the effects of the offence on him, including full details of any financial losses or injuries suffered (preferably using the Scottish system) and to present this to the sentencer.

(2) Victims should have a right to apply in person for compensation at the time of sentence, should they wish to exercise it.

(3) There should be better guidance for sentencers as to the circumstances in which compensation orders can be made and as to quantum, particularly in personal injury cases.

(4) The number of victim support schemes should be expanded to cover the whole country. They perform a very valuable and appreciated service, in the realm of emotional support, in giving information and in referring victims to other agencies. It would be useful if they could expand their services to include help to victims in applying for compensation and in attending court.

(5) The application form for the CICB should be expanded to include details necessary to apply for the other forms of State aid, so that victims do not have to take part in several application processes in order to receive the same sum. Any benefits other than those from the CICB should be accomplished by transfers between the funds, as occurs at present with compensation orders. The application form and enquiry forms sent to medical practitioners should ask specifically about any mental effects.

(6) Administrative delays in the operation of the CICB should be kept to a minimum. The necessity of preventing fraudulent applications should not be given such a priority that exhaustive inquiries are made about very small sums relating to special damages.

(7) The CICB should be put on a statutory footing as a right for all eligible victims. Purely administrative minimum or maximum limits should not be a reason for refusing an award.

(8) CICB award offers should give a breakdown of special damages included. The full cost to the applicant of applying to the CICB, apart from legal expenses, should be included in any award. Legal aid should be available for advice on applications and for advice and, possibly, representation at hearings.

(9) Consideration should be given to the setting up of local or regional centres where applicants could discuss their case personally with CICB staff.

(10) Awards of compensation made by the courts and by the CICB should be co-ordinated, preferably using a criminal scale as regards quantum.

(11) Locally administered funds should be set up for immediate and emergency compensation for victims with urgent financial needs.

References

Advisory Council on the Penal System 1970, *Reparation by the offender*, London, HMSO.

Atiyah, P. S. 1979, 'Compensation orders and civil liability', *Criminal Law Review*, pp. 504–9.

Baril, M., Durand, S., Cousineau, M. and Gravel, S. 1984, *Victimes d'actes criminels: mais nous, les temoins . . .* , Department of Justice, Canada.

Bolton, W. W. 1971, *Conduct and etiquette at the bar*, 5th edn., London, Butterworths.

Bonta, J. L., Boyle, J., Sonnichsen, P. and Motiuk, L. L. 1982, *Restitution programming: victim satisfaction, community resource centres and recidivism*, Report to Ministry of Correctional Services, Ontario, Canada.

Bottomley, A. K. and Coleman, C. A. 1980, 'Police effectiveness and the public: the limitations of official crime rates', in R. V. G. Clarke and J. M. Hough (eds.), *The effectiveness of policing*, Farnborough, Gower.

Bottomley, A. K. and Coleman, C. A. 1981, *Understanding crime rates*, Farnborough, Gower.

Bottoms, A. E. 1983, 'Neglected features of contemporary penal systems', in D. Garland and P. Young, *The power to punish*, London, Heinemann Educational Books.

Brazier, R. 1977, 'Appellate attitudes towards compensation orders', *Criminal Law Review*, p. 710.

Brown, S. D. and Yantzi, M. 1980, *Needs assessment for victims and witnesses of crime*, Report prepared for the Mennonite Central Committee and Ministry of Correctional Services, Province of Ontario, Canada.

Burns, P. 1980, *Criminal injuries compensation*, Canada, Butterworths.

Burns-Howell, A. J. *et al.* 1982, *Policing strategy: organisational or victim needs?*, Police Staff College, Bramshill, unpublished manuscript.

Canadian Federal-Provincial Task Force 1983, *Justice for victims of crime: report*, Ottawa, Canadian Government Publishing Centre.

Caplan, G. 1976, 'Studying the police', address to the Executive Forum on Upgrading the Police, Washington, DC, 13 April, cited in P. K. Manning 1979, *Police work*, Cambridge, Mass., MIT Press.

Carlen, P. 1976, *Magistrates' justice*, London, Martin Robertson.

Carrow, D. 1980, *Crime victim compensation*, Program model, US Department of Justice, National Institute of Justice, Office of Development, Testing and Dissemination.

Chambers, G. and Millar, A. 1983, *Investigating sexual assault*, Edinburgh, HMSO.

Chambers, G. and Tombs, J. 1984, *The British crime survey Scotland*, Edinburgh, HMSO.

Chibnall, J. S. 1977, *Law and order news*, London, Tavistock Publications.

Christie, N. 1977, 'Conflicts as property', *British Journal of Criminology*, vol. 17, pp. 1–15.

CICB (pre-1.10.79) *Criminal Injuries Compensation Scheme A*, the Scheme and the Statement.

CICB (post-1.10.79) *Criminal Injuries Compensation Scheme B*, the Scheme and the Statement.

CICB 1972, *Eighth Report*, London, HMSO, Cmnd. 5127.

CICB 1976, *Twelfth Report*, London, HMSO, Cmnd. 6656.

CICB 1977, *Thirteenth Report*, London, HMSO, Cmnd. 7022.

CICB 1979, *Fifteenth Report*, London, HMSO, Cmnd. 7752.

CICB 1980, *Sixteenth Report*, London, HMSO, Cmnd. 8081.

CICB 1981, *Seventeenth Report*, London, HMSO, Cmnd. 8401.

Coleman, C. A. and Bottomley, A. K. 1976, 'Police conceptions of crime and "no crime" ', *Criminal Law Review*, pp. 344–60.

Council of Europe 1978, *Compensation of victims of crime*, Strasbourg, European Committee on Crime Problems.

Council of Europe 1983, *European convention on the compensation of victims of violent crimes*, Strasbourg, Council of Europe.

Cozijn, C. 1984, *Schadefonds geweldsmisdrijven*, The Hague, Ministerie van Justitie.

Criminal Statistics 1979, London, HMSO, Cmnd. 8098.

Criminal Statistics 1980, London, HMSO, Cmnd. 8376.

Ditton, J. and Duffy, J. 1982, *Bias in newspaper crime reports*, Background Paper no. 3, Glasgow, Department of Sociology, University of Glasgow.

Dix, M. C. and Layzell, A. D. 1983, *Road users and the police*, London, Croom Helm.

Doerner, W. G. and Lab, S. P. 1980, 'The impact of crime compensation upon victim attitudes towards the criminal justice system', *Victimology*, pp. 61–7.

Duff, P. 1981, 'The compensation order', *Scots Law Times* (News), pp. 285–91.

Duff, P. 1982, 'Compensation orders in the sheriff court', *Scots Law Times* (News).

Dümig, A. G. and van Dijk, J. J. M. 1974, 'Acties en reacties van geweldslachtoffers; enige uitkomsten van een victimologisch onderzoek', *Nederlands tijdschrift voor criminologie*, vol. 17, pp. 63–73.

Dunpark Committee 1978, *Reparation by the offender to the victim in Scotland*, Edinburgh, HMSO, Cmnd. 6802.

Durant, M., Thomas, M. and Willcock, H. 1972, *Crime, criminals and the law*, Office of Population Censuses and Surveys, Social Survey Division.

Ekblom, P. and Heal, K. 1982, *The police response to calls from the public*, Research and Planning Unit Paper 9, London, Home Office.

Elias, R. 1983, *Victims of the system*, New Brunswick, Transaction Books.

Ericson, R. V. 1981, *Making crime: a study of detective work*, Canada, Butterworth & Co.

Gandy, J. T. 1978, 'Attitudes towards the use of restitution', in J. Hudson and B. Galaway (eds.), *Offender restitution in theory and action*, Lexington, Massachusetts, Lexington Books.

Gandy, J. T. and Galaway, B. 1980, 'Restitution as a sanction for offenders: a public's view', in J. Hudson and B. Galaway (eds.), *Victims, offenders and alternative sanctions*, Lexington, Massachusetts, Lexington Books.

Garofalo, J. and Connelly, K. J. 1980, 'Dispute resolution centers', *Criminal Justice Abstracts*, pp. 416–611.

Genn, H. 1982, *Meeting legal needs? An evaluation of a scheme for personal injury victims*, ESRC Centre for Socio-Legal Studies, Oxford and Greater Manchester Legal Services Committee.

Genn, H. 1983a, 'Who claims compensation?', in D, Harris and others, *Compensation and support for illness and injury*, Oxford, OUP.

Genn, H. 1983b, 'Criminal injuries compensation', in D. Harris and others, *Compensation and support for illness and injury*, Oxford, OUP.

Glasgow Media Group 1976, *Bad news*, London, Routledge and Kegan Paul.

Greenwood, P. W. 1980, 'The Rand study of criminal investigation: the findings and its impact to date', in R. V. G. Clarke and J. M. Hough (eds.), *The effectiveness of policing*, Farnborough, Gower.

Harding, J. 1982, *Victims and offenders: needs and responsibilities*, NCVO Occasional Paper Two, London, Bedford Square Press.

Harland, A. T. 1978, 'Compensating the victims of crime', *Criminal Law Bulletin*, pp. 203–24.

Harland, A. T. 1981a, *Restitution to victims of personal and household crimes*, US Department of Justice, Bureau of Justice Statistics, Analytic Report VAD-9.

Harland, A. T. 1981b, *Monetary remedies for the victims of crime:*

assessing the role of the criminal courts, Working Paper 16, Criminal Justice Research Center, Albany, New York, USA.

Harland, A. T. 1983, 'One hundred years of restitution: a review and prospectus for research', *Victimology,* vol. 8, nos. 1–2.

Hodgson Committee 1984, *Profits of crime and their recovery,* London, Heinemann.

Holmstrom, L. L. and Burgess, A. W. 1978, *The victim of rape: institutional reactions,* Chichester, John Wiley.

Home Office 1961, *Compensation for victims of crimes of violence,* London, HMSO, Cmnd. 1406.

Home Office and Law Officers' Department 1983, *An independent prosecution service for England and Wales,* London, HMSO, Cmnd. 9074.

Home Office and Scottish Home and Health Department 1978, *Review of the criminal injuries compensation scheme: report of an interdepartmental working party,* London, HMSO.

Hough, M. and Mayhew, P. 1983, *The British crime survey: first report,* Home Office Research Study no. 76, London, HMSO.

Howley, J. 1982, *Victim-police interaction and its effects on public attitudes to the police,* M.Sc. thesis, Cranfield Institute of Technology.

Hudson, J. and Chesney, S. 1978, 'Research on restitution: a review and assessment', in B. Galaway and J. Hudson (eds.), *Offender restitution in theory and action,* Lexington, Massachusetts, Lexington Books.

Hudson, J. and Galaway, B. 1980, 'A review of the restitution and community-service sanctioning research', in *Victims, offenders and alternative sanctions,* Lexington, Massachusetts, Lexington Books.

Hulsman, L. H. C. 1977, 'Slachtoffers van delicten', *Delikt en delinkwent,* vol. 7, pp. 577–85.

Jaywardene, C. and Jaywardene, H. 1982, 'The victim and the criminal law', in H. Schneider (ed.), *The victim in international perspective,* Berlin, Walter de Gruyter.

Johnson, N. J. 1977, *Prosecutors and prosecution,* unpublished M.A. thesis, Brunel University.

Jones, S. 1983, 'The human factor and policing', *Home Office Research Bulletin,* no. 16, pp. 9–12.

Kelly, D. P. 1982, 'Victims' reactions to the criminal justice response', Paper delivered at 1982 Annual Meeting of the Law and Society Association, 6 June 1982, Toronto, Canada.

Knudten, R. D., Meade, A. C., Knudten, M. S. and Doerner, W. G. 1977, *Victims and witnesses: their experiences with crime and the criminal justice system,* Executive Summary, National Institute of Law Enforcement and Criminal Justice, LEAA, US Department of Justice.

LEAA 1977, *Criminal victimization surveys in Miami*, US Department of Justice.

Lenman, B. and Parker, G. 1980, 'The state, the community and the criminal law in early modern Europe', in V. Gatrell, B. Lenman and G. Parker (eds.), *Crime and the law*, London, Europa Publications.

Lynch, R. P. 1976, 'Improving the treatment of victims: some guides for action', in W. F. McDonald (ed.), *Criminal justice and the victim*, Beverly Hills, Sage.

McBarnet, D. J. 1976, *Victim in the witness-box – confronting the stereotype*, Paper presented at the Second International Symposium on Victimology, Boston.

McCabe, S. and Sutcliffe, F. 1978, *Defining crime*, Oxford, Basil Blackwell.

McConville, M. and Baldwin, J. 1981, *Courts, prosecution and conviction*, Oxford, OUP.

McDonald, W. F. 1976, 'Criminal justice and the victim: an introduction', in W. F. McDonald (ed.), *Criminal justice and the victim*, Beverly Hills, Sage.

Magistrates' Association 1978, 'Compensation for personal injury', *The Magistrate*, vol. 34, pp. 137–8.

Maguire, M. 1982, *Burglary in a dwelling*, London, Heinemann.

Maguire, M. 1984, 'Meeting the needs of burglary victims: questions for the police and the criminal justice system', in R. Clarke and T. Hope (eds.), *Coping with burglary: research perspectives on policy*, Boston, Kluwer-Nijhoff.

Manning, P. K. 1981, 'The technological conceit', Paper given to the Centre for Criminological Research, Oxford University, 3 December, 1981.

Mawby, R. 1979, *Policing the city*, Saxon House.

Mawby, R. I. and Brown, J. M., *Crime in the press*, unpublished manuscript.

Miers, D. 1978, *Responses to victimization*, Abingdon, Professional Books.

Miers, D. 1980, 'Victim compensation as a labelling process', *Victimology*, vol. 5, pp. 3–16.

Miers, D. 1983, 'Compensation to victims of crime', *Victimology*, vol. 8, nos. 1–2, pp. 204–12.

Ministère de la Justice 1982, *Guides des droits des victimes*, Saint-Amand, Gallimard.

Nagel, W. H. 1974, 'The notion of victimology in criminology', in I. Drapkin and E. Viano (eds.), *Victimology*, Lexington, Lexington Books.

National Association of Victim Support Schemes 1983, *Newsletter*, no. 15.

Newton, A. 1976, 'Aid to the victim', *Crime and Delinquency Literature*, pp. 368–90 and 508–28.

Parliamentary All-Party Penal Affairs Group 1984, *A new deal for victims*, London, HMSO.

Philips, D. 1977, *Crime and authority in Victorian England*, London, Croom Helm.

R. v. Broad 1978, 68 *Cr. App. R.* 281.

Riley, D. and Mayhew, P. 1980, *Crime prevention publicity: an assessment*, Home Office Research Study no. 63, London, HMSO.

Royal Commission on Criminal Procedure 1981, *The investigation and prosecution of criminal offences in England and Wales: the law and procedure*, London, HMSO.

Schafer, S. 1968, *The victim and his criminal; a study in functional responsibility*, New York, Random House.

Schneider, A. L. with Griffith, W. R., Sumi, D. H. and Burcart, J. M. 1978, *Portland forward records check of crime victims*, US Department of Justice.

Sebba, L. 1982, 'The victim's role in the penal process; a theoretical orientation', *American Journal of Comparative Law*, vol. 30, pp. 217–40.

Shapland, J. 1981, *Between conviction and sentence – the process of mitigation*, London, Routledge and Kegan Paul.

Shapland, J. 1983, *Social control and policing in rural and urban areas*, Interim Report to the Home Office, August 1983, Oxford, Centre for Criminological Research.

Shubert, A. 1981, 'Private initiative in law enforcement: Associations for the Prosecution of Felons, 1744–1856', in V. Bailey (ed.), *Policing and punishment in nineteenth century Britain*, London, Croom Helm.

Smandych, R. 1981, *Research note on the use and effectiveness of reparative sanctions*, Research and Evaluation Unit, Policy Planning Division, Ministry of Attorney General, British Columbia, Canada.

Smith, D. 1983, *Police and people in London*, London, Policy Studies Institute, nos. 618–21.

Softley, P. 1978a, *Compensation orders in magistrates' courts*, Home Office Research Study no. 43, London, HMSO.

Softley, P. 1978b, *Fines in magistrates' courts*, Home Office Research Study no. 46, London, HMSO.

Sparks, R., Genn, H. and Dodd, D. 1977, *Surveying victims*, London, John Wiley.

Steer, D. 1980, *Uncovering crime: the police role*, Royal Commission on Criminal Procedure, Research Study no. 7, London, HMSO.

Thorvaldson, S. A. 1980, 'Towards the definition of the reparative aim', in J. Hudson and B. Galaway (eds.), *Victims, offenders and alternative sanctions,* Lexington, Massachusetts, Lexington Books.

Thorvaldson, S. A. 1982, *Redress by offenders: the basic issues,* Paper given to Canadian Federal and British Columbia Conference on Reparative Sanctions, Vancouver, June 1982.

Thorvaldson, S. A. and Krasnick, M. R. 1980, 'On recovering compensation funds from offenders', *Victimology,* vol. 5, pp. 18–29.

Van Dijk, J. J. M. 1983a, 'Victimologie in theorie en praktijk; een kritische reflectie op de bestaande en nog te creëren voorzieningen voor slachtoffers van delicten', *Justitiële verkenningen,* no. 6, pp. 5–35.

van Dijk, J. J. M. 1983b, 'The use of guidelines by prosecutors in The Netherlands', in J. Shapland (ed.), *Decision making in the legal system,* Issues in Criminological and Legal Psychology, no. 5, Leicester, British Psychological Society.

van Dijk, J. and Vianen, A. 1978, *Criminal victimization in The Netherlands,* Ministry of Justice, Research and Documentation Centre.

Vennard, J. 1976, Justice and recompense for victims of crime', *New Society,* vol. 35, pp. 378–80.

Vennard, J. 1978, 'Compensation by the offender: the victim's perspective', *Victimology,* vol. 3.

Vennard, J. 1979, 'Magistrates' assessment of compensation for injury', *Criminal Law Review,* pp. 510–23.

von Hirsch, A. 1976, *Doing justice; the choice of punishment,* New York, Hill and Wang.

Walster, E., Berscheid, E. and Walster, G. W. 1976, 'New directions in equity research', *Advances in Experimental Social Psychology,* vol. 9, pp. 1–42.

Wasik, M. 1978, 'The place of compensation in the penal system', *Criminal Law Review,* pp. 599–611.

Index